T0305367

The Distributional Effects of Indirect Taxes

The Distributional Effects of Indirect Taxes

Models and Applications from New Zealand

John Creedy

Truby Williams Professor of Economics,
University of Melbourne, Australia

Cath Sleeman

Edward Elgar
Cheltenham, UK · Northampton, MA, USA

Published by
Edward Elgar Publishing Limited
Glensanda House
Montpellier Parade
Cheltenham
Glos GL50 1UA
UK

Edward Elgar Publishing, Inc.
136 West Street
Suite 202
Northampton
Massachusetts 01060
USA

A catalogue record for this book
is available from the British Library

Library of Congress Cataloguing in Publication Data

Creedy, John, 1949–
   The distributional effects of indirect taxes : models and applications
from New Zealand / John Creedy, Cath Sleeman.
      p. cm.
   Includes bibliographical references and index.
   1. Taxation–New Zealand. 2. Indirect taxation–New Zealand. I. Sleeman
Cath. II. Title.

   HJ5255.N45C74 2006
   336.2'94–dc22   2006013270

ISBN-13: 978 1 84720 042 6
ISBN-10: 1 84720 042 7

Printed and bound in Great Britain by MPG Books Ltd, Bodmin, Cornwall

Contents

III Environmental Taxes

IV Tax Revenue

V Some Measurement Issues

List of Figures

List of Tables

Acknowledgements

The first versions of chapters 4, 5, 6, and 9 were written while the authors were at the New Zealand Treasury. Work on chapter 3 was supported by a Treasury Post-Graduate Scholarship to Cath Sleeman. The first version of chapter 7 was written while Norman Gemmell was a Visiting Research Fellow at the New Zealand Treasury. However, the views, opinions, findings, and conclusions or recommendations expressed in this book are strictly those of the authors. They do not necessarily reflect the views of the New Zealand Treasury or the Reserve Bank of New Zealand. We benefited from significant help from our Treasury colleagues.

We should like to thank Ivan Tuckwell for providing the Household Expenditure Survey data in the form required for this analysis and Statistics New Zealand for permission to use the data. Louise Lennard provided the effective *ad valorem* tax-exclusive rates used. Matthew Schofield carried out the many budget share regressions. Matthew Bell provided the regression results for incomes in consecutive years. Iris Claus helped with the Input–Output data. We owe a special debt to Statistics New Zealand, in particular Jeremy Webb, for making available its monetary and physical estimates of fuel use by industry. Chapters 3–9, and Appendices A and B are based respectively on Creedy and Sleeman (2005c), Creedy (2004a), Creedy and Sleeman (2005b, 2005a), Creedy and Gemmell (2004), Creedy and Sleeman (2006, 2005d) and Creedy (1998c, 2004b). We are grateful for permission to use this material here.

We have also benefited from helpful comments on earlier drafts of particular chapters by David Black, John Gibson, Wayne Heerdegen, Seamus Hogan, Guyonne Kalb, Nathan McLellan, Martin Weale, Peter Wilson, Alan Woodfield and the many anonymous referees.

Part I

Introduction

Chapter 1

Introduction

The aim of this book is to present a number of empirical analyses relating to indirect taxation in New Zealand. The equity and efficiency effects of the existing tax system, and of a range of policy reforms, are examined in detail. Policy debates are inevitably influenced by value judgements, which are seldom made explicit either by governments or those engaging in public discussion. By concentrating on the empirical orders of magnitude, and by examining the implications of adopting alternative value judgements, it is hoped that the findings of this book can contribute towards rational policy debate on the subject, rather than relying on guesswork and rhetoric.

The emphasis of the following chapters is on measurement aspects and the reporting of quantitative estimates of the implications – particularly for the welfare effects on different types of household – of the price changes arising from the imposition of indirect taxes. This inevitably involves some technical discussion of economic concepts. The emphasis is on the details of measurement, rather than attempting a broad-brush or comprehensive discussion of the wide range of policy issues involved in tax policy. The absence of any treatment of certain aspects of indirect taxes should not be taken to imply that those features are judged to be unimportant: they simply cannot be examined by the limited range of analytical tools which provide the basis of the following analyses.

The indirect tax system in New Zealand is relatively simple. At the heart of the structure is a broad-based Goods and Services Tax (GST) imposed at a single *ad valorem* rate; that is, the tax on any commodity is a fixed proportion of the tax-exclusive price of the good or service. The simplicity of the GST and its broad base, which includes food, has often been praised by international commentators and contrasts with the use of (often arbitrary) exemptions introduced in other countries. In addition, there are excise taxes imposed on three broad commodity groups – alcohol, tobacco and petrol. These excises are somewhat less transparent than GST as they are expressed in terms of an amount of money per specified physical unit of the relevant good, rather than in value terms. In addition, GST is imposed on the excise-tax-inclusive price of the commodity, so that an increase in any excise tax automatically brings with it an increase in the GST raised per unit of the good.

It is therefore not surprising that recent policy debates have concerned the excise taxes. For example, in a major review of the tax system, carried out under the aegis of the New Zealand Treasury, McLeod *et al.* (2001) argued that excise taxes are inefficient at raising tax revenue and are inequitable, being regressive in nature. They argued (2001, p.41) that, 'the current excise and duty regime cannot readily be justified on conventional tax policy grounds. As a matter of tax principle the general revenue component of these taxes should be replaced by an increase in GST. At a minimum, the many anomalies in this area of the tax system should be subject to further review'. These views are expressed rather dogmatically and without reference to original empirical research, but the argument that 'further review' of the system is needed suggests at least that the present analysis is warranted. In recent years there has also been much debate regarding the potential effects of a carbon tax, and the role of particular excises as revenue-raising devices. An example of the latter is the use of a petrol tax increase to finance road building projects. These issues are also discussed in this book.

As mentioned above, the analysis in this book does not pretend to be comprehensive. Little emphasis is given to separate discussion of the Goods and Services Tax, which was examined in detail in Creedy (1997). The externality and merit good arguments which are widely used to justify special excise taxes – and which were dismissed without analysis by McLeod *et al.* – view such taxes in terms of correcting market failures. However, it is notoriously difficult to evaluate the quantitative orders of magnitude and thus the precise 'corrective', or Pigovian, taxes required by such arguments. The fact that they are not examined here should not be taken to imply that the authors accept the views of McLeod *et al.* (either with regard to the extent of externalities, or the value judgements involved in merit good arguments). They are omitted from the analysis on the grounds that it is of value to consider the equity and efficiency arguments separately: the results can form a useful component of a more comprehensive view.

In looking at the impact of taxes on various household types, and on inequality, the analyses presented in this book contrast with studies of indirect taxes that are based only on computations of tax paid, and expenditure net of taxes, using the assumption that expenditure patterns remain fixed when taxes, and hence prices, change. In practice, households are expected to substitute away from those goods whose prices increase by relatively more as a result of a tax change. Indeed, the reduction in consumption of some goods is regarded by many people as a primary aim of some indirect taxes. It therefore seems worthwhile, despite the use of strong assumptions about consumer demands, to model behavioural responses and, in so doing, to obtain more satisfactory measures of the effects of taxes on households. The following analyses report calculations of equivalent variations, which reflect the maximum amount a household would be prepared to pay to avoid the tax or a change in it. Furthermore, a central concept is that of the excess burden of taxation; this reflects the fact that the welfare loss arising from a tax exceeds the amount of the tax actually paid. The excess burden therefore measures the inefficiency caused by the distortion to consumers' expenditure patterns arising from a change in relative prices arising from taxes. Such excess burdens are intangible and, for example, are not necessarily reflected in lower levels of Gross Domestic Product; but they are nevertheless important. Rational policy analysis requires that such inefficiencies are compared with any redistributive (equity) or other effects arising from taxation. Tax revenue is used to finance government expenditure on a range of projects as well as paying for transfer payments, such as benefits to specified low-income households. Since the burden imposed on taxpayers exceeds the tax they pay, it is important to ensure that the perceived benefits arising from government expenditure are sufficient to outweigh the efficiency losses.

Several features of the following analyses are worth stressing at this point. First, the models used are 'partial equilibrium' in nature; that is, they examine the effects of hypothetical policy reforms involving indirect taxes, without allowing for any possible changes in, say, wage rates and income levels of households. Second, concentration is on indirect taxes, rather than the tax system as a whole. It can of course be argued that what utlimately matters is the combined effect of the complete tax structure, including direct taxes and transfer payments. However, given the complexities involved it is nevertheless useful to be able to isolate the effects of specific taxes and to 'take one thing at a time'. Indeed, policy discussions often focus on a single tax. However, one common misconception requires comment; this is the idea that the impact of a consumption tax on households should be measured in terms of the ratio of the consumption tax paid to gross income, rather than taking total household expenditure, the base of the tax, as the denominator. As the former ratio is usually observed in cross-sectional studies to fall as income rises (as households with high incomes typically save relatively more than those with low incomes), it is often argued that a general consumption tax is necessarily regressive. It is argued here that if it is desired to consider a consumption tax in isolation in a cross-sectional context, the distributional impact is best measured in terms of total household expenditure, rather than gross income. This issue is discussed in more detail in Appendix A.[1]

1.1 Outline of the Book

The remaining chapter in Part I of this book, chapter 2, is largely descriptive. It discusses the structure of indirect taxes in New Zealand and explains how a set of effective *ad valorem* tax rates can be produced. A set of rates is produced, and reference to these is made at several points in later chapters. Chapter 2 also describes the dataset used for modelling the effects on a wide range of household types of changes in the indirect tax structure.

Part II concentrates on excise taxes. Chapter 3 examines the welfare effects of current taxes, and simulates a range of reforms to the system which have been proposed by a number of commentators. Efficiency effects are examined in terms of excess burdens, while equity effects are examined by considering the welfare losses of households at different levels of total weekly expenditure, and by looking at changes in inequality measures. Chapter 4 concentrates on the potential effects of an increase in the excise tax on petrol. This has been proposed in recent years, not for its environmental effects but as a revenue raising device to finance road building projects. Part II of the book makes extensive use of a simulation model designed to examine the welfare effects of price changes.

Part III turns to environmental taxes. In particular, chapter 5 examines the use of a carbon tax designed to reduce carbon dioxide emissions. This involves a further model to examine the likely effects on consumer prices

---

[1]The existence of savings means that in principle it is desirable to consider a multi-period or lifetime framework, although this aspect is usually ignored. In such a framework, the influence of differential saving patterns on tax progressivity arises only if the income arising from savings is taxable. In the absence of an interest-income tax, savings only affect the time stream of tax and consumption. It is the tax treatment of investment income that has lifetime distributional implications, so it is misleading to suggest that differential saving propensities cause the consumption tax to be regressive.

of the imposition of a carbon tax. Chapter 6 then considers the minimum disruption changes to outputs, consistent with meeting a target reduction in carbon dioxide emissions subject to various constraints, including growth and employment.

Part IV is concerned with indirect taxes and tax revenue growth in New Zealand. Chapter 7 examines the 'built-in flexibility' of taxes – the extent to which the total tax revenue increases when individual and aggregate income levels increase, when no adjustments to tax rates occur. As indirect taxes arise from expenditures which are clearly influenced by the structure of income taxation, it is necessary to consider the interaction between the two tax systems. This chapter uses a model designed to produce estimates of tax revenue elasticities using a minimim amount of data, and at a fairly high level of aggregation.

Part V covers a number of measurement topics. Chapter 8 is concerned with the measurement of tax progressivity. In particular, measures based on tax revenue (requiring information only on budget shares) are compared with those based on equivalent variations: it is shown that the former can be misleading. The extra work involved in modelling households' demands, necessary to produce the welfare measures of Parts II and III, is warranted despite the need to make strong assumptions. Finally, in chapter 9 the use of alternative income units and income concepts in measuring inequality and tax progressivity are discussed and compared.

Finally, a set of appendices provide further details of modelling approaches and data.

Chapter 2

New Zealand Taxes and Data

This chapter provides details of the effective indirect tax rates in New Zealand, which are used as the basis for a number of the empirical analyses reported in later chapters. The tax structure is described in section 2.1. The nature of the commodity groups used, as some consolidation is inevitable in studies of this kind, is influenced substantially by the household data used and the need to obtain estimates of the relationship between total household expenditure and the proportion of expenditure on particular commodity groups. The data are described in section 2.2.

2.1 The Structure of Indirect Taxes in NZ

The indirect tax structure is relatively simple in New Zealand, and comprises a broad-based Goods and Services Tax (GST) using a single rate, plus excise taxes on three broad commodity groups: alcohol, tobacco and petrol. The annual revenue raised by excise taxes is approximately $1.6 billion.

In defining tax rates a distinction is made between the tax-exclusive and tax-inclusive rates. The tax-exclusive tax rate is defined as the ratio of tax paid to the producer price of the good, the net amount received by the producer after forwarding the required indirect tax to the authorities. The tax-inclusive tax rate is defined as the ratio of tax paid to the consumer

price of the good. For the empirical analyses in this book, it is necessary
to express all indirect taxes in terms of a tax-exclusive *ad valorem* tax rate.
This is straightforward for the majority of commodity groups, which attract
only GST of 12.5 per cent. However, the translation between tax rates and
effective *ad valorem* rates is more complex for the three commodity groups
subject to excise taxes, as they are expressed in commodity units rather
than values, and GST is then imposed on the excise-tax-inclusive price of
the commodity.

The relationships can be expressed formally as follows. Let E denote the
per unit excise tax, g the GST rate and P^0 the tax-exclusive, or producer,
price of the good. The total tax paid, T, on a unit of the commodity is given
by:

$$
\begin{aligned}
T &= \left(P^0 + E\right)g + E \\
  &= P^0 g + E\left(1 + g\right)
\end{aligned}
\tag{2.1}
$$

It is required to obtain an expression for the effective tax-exclusive *ad valorem*
tax rate, $t = T/P^0$. In partial equilibrium tax studies of this kind, the most
common assumption made is that the full amount of the tax is passed forward
to consumers, while recognising that this is in fact an extreme case. Empirical
evidence relating to the extent of shifting is scarce. There is a substantial
theoretical literature which, starting from the view that an excise tax shifts
firms' costs, examines the role of market structure, in particular conjectural
variations; a review is given by Baker and Brechling (1992).[1] Using UK
data, they could not reject the hypothesis that excises on beer, spirits and
petrol were fully shifted. Their finding that price rises overcompensated for
higher excises imposed on wine, while the opposite was found for tobacco,
was attributed to the high degree of concentration in those markets. To the

---

[1] A different argument, based on quality substitution effects, was used by Barzel (1976)
and Johnson (1978) to argue that the price may increase by more than the increase in a
unit tax. However, this interpretation was criticised by Sumner and Ward (1981).

extent that incomplete shifting takes place for tobacco, eliminating the excise would provide a windfall gain to those companies, complicating redistributive effects.

In the case of full shifting, the tax-inclusive price of the good, P^1, is:

$$
\begin{aligned}
P^1 &= P^0 + P^0 g + E(1+g) \\
&= (P^0 + E)(1+g)
\end{aligned} \tag{2.2}
$$

Hence:

$$
P^0 = \frac{P^1}{(1+g)} - E \tag{2.3}
$$

The effective tax-exclusive *ad valorem* tax rate, $t = T/P^0$, is therefore:

$$
t = g + \frac{E}{P^0}(1+g) \tag{2.4}
$$

For example, in 2001 the petrol excise tax, E, was \$0.343 per litre, and the proportional GST rate, g, was 0.125. Using a consumer price of petrol of $P^1 = \$1.08$ per litre, from equation (2.3) the tax-exclusive price, P^0, was \$0.617. Hence, from equation (2.4) the effective tax-exclusive *ad valorem* tax rate on petrol, t, was equal to 75 cents in the dollar.

The analysis uses Household Economic Survey (HES) data, described further in the following section. However, it is not possible, mainly because of estimation difficulties, to use all the separate and highly detailed HES commodity categories. Instead, these were consolidated into 22 groups. Where several HES categories are combined into a single commodity group, computation of the effective rate also required the production of a weighted average of the individual components. Table 2.1 shows the commodity groups used and the effective *ad valorem* tax-exclusive percentage rates at 2001, the last year for which HES data were available to the authors. The rates shown in Table 2.1 were produced following the procedure described above and are taken from Young (2002).

The group described as 'Petrol' actually combines petrol with diesel, CNG and LPG. Hence the appropriate tax rate for this combination requires a

Table 2.1: Commodity Groups and Tax Rates

No.	Tax Rate	Commodity Group	HES Categories
1	12.5	Food	00-08
2	12.5	Food outside home	10
3	0	Rent	11
4	12.5	Pay to Local Authorities	13
5	12.5	House maintenance	15-17
6	12.5	Domestic fuel and power	18-30
7	12.5	Household equipment	31-32
8	12.5	Furnishings	33-36
9	12.5	Household services	37-38
10	12.5	Adult clothing	39-40,42-45,47-48
11	12.5	Children's clothing	41,46
12	12.5	Public transport in NZ	49
13	0	Overseas travel	50
14	7.05445	Vehicle purchase	51-53
15	71.776	Petrol etc	54-59
16	12.5	Vehicle supplies, parts etc	60-69
17	239.845	Cigarettes and tobacco	70-73
18	46.8191	Alcohol	74-85
19	12.5	Medical, cosmetic etc	86-88
20	12.5	Services	94-101
21	6.25	Recreational vehicles	58
22	12.5	Other expenditure	89-91,102

weighted average of petrol and other fuel taxes. The year 2001 rate used for this group is 0.718, which is correspondingly lower than the effective rate of 0.75 on petrol discussed above.

Two commodity groups do not attract indirect tax. Overseas Travel (Group 1) is zero rated, while Rent (Group 2) is exempt from GST. Recreational Vehicles (Group 3) and Vehicle Purchases (Group 4) do attract GST; however, for both groups, the HES includes expenditures on second-hand vehicles, which are exempt. The effective rate is therefore correspondingly lower. The majority of commodity groups attract the standard GST rate of 12.5 per cent.

Table 2.1 clearly indicates the high effective rates on petrol, cigarettes and tobacco and alcohol. The excise rates are clearly substantial, with the effective *ad valorem* tax rate on tobacco of 240 per cent. These high rates are typically rationalised on merit good and externality grounds; the various arguments are discussed further below, when examining their detailed effects on New Zealand households: for a case study of alcohol, see Barker (2002).

2.2 The Household Economic Survey

This section describes the data used and the aggregation into household groups. A special dataset was constructed using household expenditure data from the Household Economic Survey (HES) for the five years 1995, 1996, 1997, 1998 and 2001. Unfortunately, surveys have been conducted only triannually since 1998. The values were adjusted to 2001 prices using the consumer price index (CPI). Over this period there were very few changes in indirect taxes. The surveys were then pooled to form one large dataset, in order to estimate (for each commodity group) the relationship between the household budget shares and total household expenditure, for a range of household types. The budget share relationships are described in more detail in chapter 3 and Appendix C.

Table 2.2 shows the household types used. For the first two types, the age refers to that of the 'head' of the household. In each case households are further divided into smoking (S) and non-smoking (NS) households; a positive weekly expenditure on tobacco (group 17 in Table 2.1) was sufficient for the household to be designated as a smoking household. The division into smoking and non-smoking households, for examination of all commodity groups, was found to improve the goodness of fit of most of the budget share relationships substantially. Table 2.2 also gives the arithmetic mean total household expenditure for each household type.

Table 2.2: Household Categories

No.	Household type	Number of households		Mean total expenditure	
		S	NS	S	NS
1	65+ single	161	1282	267	274
2	65+ couple	224	1191	498	540
3	Single: no children	384	1098	406	437
4	Single: 1 child	148	239	400	403
5	Single: 2 children	148	181	428	438
6	Single: 3 children	59	75	468	475
7	Single: 4+ children	33	39	501	539
8	Couple: no children	966	2036	690	766
9	Couple: 1 child	381	643	668	763
10	Couple: 2 children	435	916	707	896
11	Couple: 3 children	207	458	805	844
12	Couple: 4+ children	98	195	673	822
13	3 adults: no children	319	456	975	992
14	3 adults: 1 child	122	157	898	1038
15	3 adults: 2+ children	117	34	826	920
16	4+ adults: no children	179	192	1311	1282
17	4+ adults: 1 child	65	60	1110	1129
18	4+ adults: 2+ children	47	47	1070	925

These data were used to estimate the relationship between total household expenditure, y, and the proportion of expenditure, or the budget share, devoted to each commodity group, for each household type. If w_i is the budget share of the ith good, a flexible specification that has been found to provide a good fit is (omitting subscripts):[2]

$$w = \delta_1 + \delta_2 \log y + \frac{\delta_3}{y} \tag{2.5}$$

This form has the convenient property that, if parameters are estimated using ordinary least squares, the adding-up condition, $\sum_{i=1}^{n} w_i = 1$, holds for predicted shares, at all total expenditure levels, y. As there are 22 commodity groups and 18 household types, for smoking and non-smoking households, a total of 792 (22 times 18 times 2) budget share regressions were performed. Hence these cannot be reported here.

At any given level of y, the expenditure elasticity (for a required commodity group and household type) can be expressed as:

$$e = 1 + \frac{dw}{dy} \frac{y}{w} \tag{2.6}$$

Using 2.5, this elasticity is given by:

$$e = 1 + \frac{(y/\delta_3) \delta_2 - 1}{(y/\delta_3) (\delta_1 + \delta_2 \log y) + 1} \tag{2.7}$$

so that $e = 0$ for $y = 0$, and converges to 1 as $y \to \infty$, though of course it may exceed unity over certain ranges of y.

2.3 Conclusions

This chapter has described the structure of indirect taxation in New Zealand, concentrating on the effective *ad valorem* rates which are needed for the empirical analyses reported in this book. The general form of budget share relationship, which also plays a large role in the modelling used here, was also presented.

---

[2]For further discussion of this form, see Deaton and Muellbauer (1980). One small difficulty with its use is that ordinary least squares estimators do not guarantee that predicted budget shares are always non-negative. In the few cases where this arises – for very low y – the w are replaced by zero, and others are adjusted to ensure additivity.

Part II

Excise Taxes and Welfare

Chapter 3

Excise Taxation, Equity and Efficiency

The indirect tax system in New Zealand, as described in the previous chapter, consists of a broad-based Goods and Services Tax (GST) imposed at a single rate, plus excise taxes on three broad commodity groups: alcohol, tobacco and petrol. In a major review of the tax system, carried out under the aegis of the New Zealand Treasury, McCleod *et al.* (2001) argued that excise taxes are inefficient at raising tax revenue and are inequitable, being regressive in nature. They argued that, 'the current excise and duty regime cannot readily be justified on conventional tax policy grounds. As a matter of tax principle the general revenue component of these taxes should be replaced by an increase in GST. At a minimum, the many anomalies in this area of the tax system should be subject to further review' (2001, p.41).

In suggesting that the excise taxes cannot be justified on conventional grounds, McLeod *et al.* (2001) rapidly dismissed externality and merit good arguments. They viewed excises merely as revenue-raisers. In taking this position they were not alone, although no references were made to supporting literature. Similar views dismissive of standard arguments can be found in, for example, Shughart (ed.) (1997), McGee (1998) and Holcombe (2003). For a broad discussion of environmental excises, see Barthold (1994) and on excises generally, see Cnossen (2005). For a treatment concentrating on

17

revenue-raising aspects of an excise tax, see Bahl *et al.* (2003). Despite the widespread acceptance of externality and merit good arguments, there is indeed very little information about the orders of magnitude required of such 'corrective' taxes.[1]

The view of McLeod *et al.* that excises are regressive was based simply on the assertion that the relevant commodity groups typically form a relatively larger proportion of the budgets of low-income households. Their discussion did not include empirical evidence to support their assertions regarding either efficiency or equity. The present chapter therefore explores the welfare and redistributive effects of the price effects of excise taxes and the changes that would be expected to result from the revenue-neutral removal of excise taxes in New Zealand, as recommended by the *Review*. The aim is to focus solely on the effects that the higher prices, attributed to excise taxes, have on consumers. Accordingly, no judgements are made regarding the externality and merit good arguments rejected by McLeod *et al.* Instead, this chapter evaluates the *Review's* assessments on its authors' own terms; that is, it suspends disbelief regarding other aspects. The restrictive nature of this task should be borne in mind, though hopefully this analysis can make a contribution to the wider debate on the role of excise taxes. As suggested in Chapter 1, the absence of any treatement of wider aspects should not be taken as implying a view that they are unimportant. Rather, the empirical methods devised here are not applicable to these aspects, and it is believed that a partial analysis can contribute a component of a broader evaluation.

The analysis proceeds as follows. The welfare effects of excise taxes are considered to arise from the higher prices imposed on consumers, so it is necessary to evaluate the likely price changes that result from any tax reform. The previous chapter has shown how the GST and excise taxes interact to influence final prices, and reports calculations of effective rates for a range of

---

[1] A case study discussing the practical problems of measuring external costs of alcohol consumption is provided by Barker (2002).

commodity groups. The evaluation of efficiency and equity effects of excise taxes is substantially more involved than simply examining (as suggested by McLeod *et al.*) the budget shares which households devote to these goods.[2] Instead, the chapter undertakes the computation of welfare changes and excess burdens, measured here in terms of Hicksian equivalent variations, for a variety of demographic groups over a range of total expenditure levels. The equivalent variation is chosen as it simplifies the computation of efficiency measures: the excess burden based on the compensating variation would require the evaluation of the tax changes after allowing for compensation. Furthermore, the ratio of the equivalent variation to total expenditure can be conveniently interpreted as the proportional change in money metric utility, where the latter is based on pre-reform prices. A brief discussion of the welfare measures and modelling approach is given in section 3.1. More detailed descriptions of these welfare changes are given in Appendix B, and technical details of the modelling approach are given in Appendix C.

Section 3.2 examines the welfare effects of the current indirect tax structure, where the price changes are those resulting from the imposition of the taxes. Two hypothetical reforms are then considered in section 3.3. In the first, the excise taxes currently levied on alcohol and tobacco are removed, but the petrol excise tax is retained. In the second reform, the excise taxes on all three commodity groups are removed. The distinction was made as the equity effects of the two reforms, considered in section 3.4, were found to differ. Different types of argument typically relate to these groups. Discussion of the petrol excise tax usually revolves around environmental considerations relating to the over-use of scarce resources and pollution issues. Alcohol and tobacco excise taxes are usually justified on demerit good and externality grounds. An important qualification is that the approach is partial equilibrium in nature: any changes to factor prices, and hence incomes, resulting

---

[2]For example, an analysis of tobacco taxation in the US, highlighting the role of elasticity variations with income, is detailed in Colman and Remler (2004).

from a tax policy change are ignored.

For each reform, the standard GST rate that would be required to achieve revenue neutrality is obtained. In computing this rate, allowance is made for the changes in consumption which arise from the tax and relative price changes. Welfare measures are reported for representative total expenditure levels within a large number of demographic groups.

Section 3.4 turns to measures of inequality and reports overall summary indications of the direction and extent of the redistributive effects of the reforms. The sensitivity of the results to adult equivalence scales and the degree of inequality aversion are also considered.

3.1   The Modelling Approach

This section describes the computation of the welfare measures for each demographic group and total expenditure level. Only the main results are stated, as their derivations are available elsewhere; for example, see Powell (1974) and Creedy (1998a,b). The basis of the approach is the use of the linear expenditure system to model households' behaviour, though considerable heterogeneity is allowed. Total expenditure, though not its composition, of each household is assumed to remain fixed when prices of goods and services change.

The direct utility function for the linear expenditure system is:

$$U = \prod_{i=1}^{n} (x_i - \gamma_i)^{\beta_i} \tag{3.1}$$

with $0 \leq \beta_i \leq 1$ and $\sum_{i=1}^{n} \beta_i = 1$. Here, x_i and γ_i are respectively the total and the committed consumption of good i. If p_i is the price of good i, and y is total household expenditure, the budget constraint is $\sum_{i=1}^{n} p_i x_i = y$. In the present context, the parameters of the utility function differ according to both household type and total expenditure, as discussed further below.

The equivalent variation, EV, is the difference between total expenditure, y, which remains unchanged by assumption, and the expenditure that would be needed to place the household at the new level of utility at the old (pre-change) prices. More formally, this can be defined in terms of the expenditure function as $EV = E(p_1, U_1) - E(p_0, U_1)$, where $E(p, U)$ is the minimum expenditure required to reach utility level U at prices p. Defining the terms A and B respectively as $\sum_{i=1}^{n} p_i \gamma_i$ and $\prod_{i=1}^{n} (p_i/\beta_i)^{\beta_i}$, the indirect utility function, $V(p, y)$, is:

$$V = (y - A)/B \tag{3.2}$$

The expenditure function is found by inverting (3.2) and substituting E for y to get:

$$E(p, U) = A + BU \tag{3.3}$$

Suppose that the vector of prices changes from p_0 to p_1. Substituting for E using (3.3) and assuming that total expenditure remains constant at y, gives:

$$EV = y - (A_0 + B_0 U_1) \tag{3.4}$$

Substituting for U_1, using equation (3.2), into (3.4) gives:

$$EV = y - A_0 \left[1 + \frac{B_0}{B_1} \left(\frac{y}{A_0} - \frac{A_1}{A_0} \right) \right] \tag{3.5}$$

The term A_1/A_0 is a Laspeyres type of price index, using γ_is as weights. The term B_1/B_0 simplifies to $\prod_{i=1}^{n} (p_{1i}/p_{0i})^{\beta_i}$, which is a weighted geometric mean of price relatives. The corresponding result for the compensating variation follows by substituting into $CV = E(p_1, U_0) - E(p_0, U_0)$.

A convenient feature of the present approach is that the expression for the equivalent variation requires only the percentage changes in prices to be specified. The relevant terms can be expressed in terms of the $\dot{p}$s. Since $p_{1i} = p_{0i}(1 + \dot{p}_i)$, and defining $s_i = p_{0i}\gamma_i / \sum_i p_{0i}\gamma_i$, it can be shown that $A_1/A_0 = 1 + \sum_i s_i \dot{p}_i$ and $B_1/B_0 = \prod_i (1 + \dot{p}_i)^{\beta_i}$. Suppose that all prices change by the same proportion. If all prices change in the same proportion, $\dot{p}_i = \dot{p}$ for all i, and $B_1/B_0 = A_1/A_0 = 1 + \dot{p}$.

3.2   Welfare Effects of Existing Indirect Taxes

This section examines the welfare effects of New Zealand's current indirect tax system. Hence, the starting point was considered to be an economy with no indirect taxes. The current schedule, as shown in chapter 2 above, was then imposed and the resulting welfare changes from the price rises were analysed. This analysis was actually accomplished by moving in the opposite direction; that is, from current prices and associated consumption patterns, a set of proportional price *reductions* were imposed, equal to the current set of tax rates. The required equivalent variations arising from the existing tax structure were therefore obtained as the negative of the compensating variations produced by the set of price reductions.

The first step in the analysis is that effective tax rates must be translated into proportionate price changes. In general, suppose that the tax-exclusive *ad valorem* tax rate imposed on good i is denoted t_i. This is equivalent to a tax-inclusive rate of $t_i/(1 + t_i)$. The revenue, R_i, from this indirect tax is equal to expenditure multiplied by the tax-inclusive rate. If t_i is increased by a proportion, $\dot{t}_i$, the resulting proportionate increase in the price of the ith good, $\dot{p}_i$, is given by:

$$\dot{p}_i = \dot{t}_i \left(\frac{t_i}{1 + t_i} \right) \tag{3.6}$$

In the case where the effects of the existing tax structure are required, the 'initial' tax rate is obviously zero, so the proportional price change is simply the actual effective tax-exclusive rate, as reported earlier in chapter 2.

The results presented below are based on the use of the Linear Expenditure System (LES), where expressions for welfare changes are readily obtained. However, the parameters of the LES utility function are allowed to vary across households; they depend on total household expenditure and the demographic structure of the household. The basic analytics of the method are set out in Appendix C, following the general method introduced by Creedy (1998a, b). Broadly, it involves obtaining, from the budget share patterns for each demographic group, the variation in total expenditure elasticities, as total expenditure varies, for each of the commodity groups. These are combined with a Frisch parameter (the value of the elasticity of the marginal utility of 'income') to obtain own-price elasticities, using Frisch's (1959) result for additive demand systems. From these elasticities the LES parameters can be computed for each group and any desired total expenditure level. As there are 22 commodity groups and 18 demographic groups for both non-smoking and smoking households, a total of 792 budget share relationships were produced. As described in chapter 2 and in more detail in Appendix C, the specification of the budget share relationship is one in which the budget share is a function of both the reciprocal of total household expenditure and its logarithm. This is a highly flexible functional form which allows for the considerable variation observed in practice.

In addition to equivalent variations, EV, it is useful to examine the welfare costs of the indirect tax system. Welfare cost, WC, provides a measure of efficiency loss and is defined as the excess burden per dollar of tax raised, or:

$$WC = \frac{EV - Tax}{Tax} \tag{3.7}$$

Further, the ratio of equivalent variation to total expenditure, EV/m, can be used to examine the proportionate change in the money metric measure of utility when pre-change prices are used as the reference set of prices. Therefore, the relationship between the ratio, EV/m, and m within each household group can be used to gauge the disproportionality of the welfare impact from imposing the current indirect tax system. The system is described as progressive when EV/m rises with m, and regressive when it falls with m. Hence, for each household group, measures of welfare change were computed for a range of total expenditure levels.

It is not possible to report the detailed results here, in view of the large number and size of tables involved, but the general patterns can be summarised as follows. The existing tax system was found to be regressive for multi-adult smoking households. However, among single adult smoking households, the system is progressive. Furthermore, the rate at which EV/m rises with total expenditure increases with the number of children in the household.

Among the non-smoking households the effect of the current system was found to be ambiguous in terms of the behaviour of EV/m. The tax system is generally regressive over lower levels of total expenditure, but becomes increasingly progressive over higher levels, particularly among single adult households and those with multiple children. Hence, when examining separate demographic groups, there is no strong evidence of a regressive effect of indirect taxes: a more detailed analysis thus requires overall summary measures of inequality, as given in section 3.4 below.

In order to give a representative indication of the likely welfare costs faced by each household group, and allow between-group comparisons to be made more easily, summary welfare measures were computed for each household group, based on its arithmetic mean total expenditure level, $\bar{m}$. These results are reported in Tables 3.1 and 3.2 for smoking and non-smoking households respectively. The column headed '*Tax*' describes the weekly amount of indirect tax paid by each household group at arithmetic mean expenditure level, $\bar{m}$.

The equivalent variation, as a ratio of $\bar{m}$, varies among demographic groups, ranging between approximately 8 to 16 per cent. The ratio is in fact similar for most household groups, yet is notably smaller for single adult household groups with children and higher for pensioner households (Groups 1 and 2) who smoke. The ratio $EV/\bar{m}$ is higher among smoking households in comparison with non-smoking households, with large differences in some

Table 3.1: Effects of Existing Taxes at Mean Total Expenditure Levels: Smoking Households

No.	Household Group	Smoking Households			
		$\bar{m}$	*Tax*	$EV/\bar{m}$	*WC*
1	65+ Single	267	42.23	0.1709	0.0805
2	65+ Couple	498	78.68	0.1656	0.0483
3	Single Adult & No Children	406	60.14	0.1567	0.0582
4	Single Adult & 1 Child	400	44.58	0.1165	0.0455
5	Single Adult & 2 Children	428	48.44	0.1195	0.0562
6	Single Adult & 3 Children	468	47.29	0.1096	0.0848
7	Single Adult & 4+ Children	501	51.82	0.1086	0.0498
8	Adult Couple & No Children	690	100.57	0.1509	0.0356
9	Adult Couple & 1 Child	668	92.52	0.1448	0.0452
10	Adult Couple & 2 Children	707	94.33	0.1361	0.0197
11	Adult Couple & 3 Children	805	106.71	0.1355	0.0223
12	Adult Couple & 4+ Children	673	92.90	0.1432	0.0375
13	3 Adults & No Children	975	139.50	0.1468	0.0262
14	3 Adults & 1 Child	898	127.99	0.1464	0.0270
15	3 Adults & 2+ Children	826	116.38	0.1496	0.0620
16	4+ Adults & No Children	1311	173.93	0.1349	0.0167
17	4+ Adults & 1 Child	1110	168.93	0.1574	0.0345
18	4+ Adults & 2+ Children	1070	145.72	0.1412	0.0371

Table 3.2: Effects of Existing Taxes at Mean Total Expenditure Levels: Non-smoking Households

No.	Household Group	Non-Smoking Households			
		$\bar{m}$	Tax	$EV/\bar{m}$	WC
1	65+ Single	274	29.49	0.1092	0.0142
2	65+ Couple	540	62.73	0.1181	0.0171
3	Single Adult & No Children	437	46.94	0.1092	0.0166
4	Single Adult & 1 Child	403	37.12	0.0938	0.0189
5	Single Adult & 2 Children	438	38.37	0.0896	0.0232
6	Single Adult & 3 Children	475	42.62	0.0914	0.0188
7	Single Adult & 4+ Children	539	45.17	0.0853	0.0177
8	Adult Couple & No Children	766	86.46	0.1145	0.0142
9	Adult Couple & 1 Child	763	85.17	0.1131	0.0128
10	Adult Couple & 2 Children	896	102.44	0.1157	0.0118
11	Adult Couple & 3 Children	844	96.12	0.1149	0.0091
12	Adult Couple & 4+ Children	822	90.84	0.1141	0.0326
13	3 Adults & No Children	992	114.24	0.1169	0.0154
14	3 Adults & 1 Child	1038	121.04	0.1182	0.0132
15	3 Adults & 2+ Children	920	102.96	0.1162	0.0381
16	4+ Adults & No Children	1282	147.83	0.1172	0.0162
17	4+ Adults & 1 Child	1129	130.73	0.1207	0.0428
18	4+ Adults & 2+ Children	925	105.96	0.1158	0.0109

cases, in particular between smoking and non-smoking pensioners.

For the majority of household groups, the welfare costs per dollar of tax raised, at mean total expenditure, are small, suggesting that the indirect tax system as a whole is relatively efficient at raising revenue. This is not surprising in view of the fact that indirect taxes are relatively flat, with the main exception of the excise taxes. These welfare cost values are substantially lower than figures generally suggested for income tax revenue, for example, where there is an increasing marginal rate structure. However, as shown in Figures 3.1 and 3.2, smoking household groups do incur relatively higher welfare costs on average than their non-smoking counterparts. For every dollar of indirect tax paid, the efficiency losses incurred by smoking household

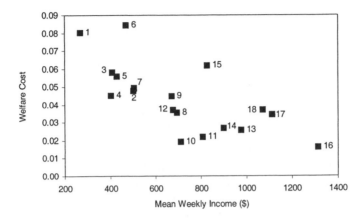

Figure 3.1: Welfare Costs of Current System (Smoking Households)

groups (at their respective average total expenditures) range between about 2 and 8 cents, while for non-smoking households, these losses range between only about 1 and 4 cents.

Furthermore, there is a negative correlation between the welfare costs incurred by smoking household groups and their mean total expenditure levels. Accordingly, pensioners and single adult household groups, who have the lowest mean total expenditure levels, incur the largest welfare costs. This correlation reflects the effects of the excise tax on tobacco, towards which poorer household groups devote larger fractions of their total weekly budget. This correlation is not observed among the non-smoking household groups, as seen in Figure 3.2.

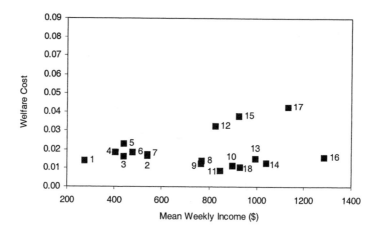

Figure 3.2: Welfare Costs of Current System (Non-smoking Households)

3.3   Revenue-Neutral Tax Reforms

This section examines the welfare and redistributive effects of the revenue-neutral removal of excise taxes in New Zealand; this is the policy reform recommended by the 2001 *Tax Review*. Two reforms are considered, both of which involve the removal of the alcohol and tobacco excise taxes, which McLeod *et al.* (2001) regarded as highly regressive. The petrol excise tax is retained in the first reform but removed in the second. The first subsection provides the schedule of adjusted GST rates which are required to achieve revenue neutrality for each reform. The marginal welfare implications for each household group are analysed in the second subsection.

3.3.1   Revenue Neutrality

For each reform the standard GST rate was raised to ensure that the total amount of indirect tax paid by households remained constant, allowing for the changes in demands following the relative price changes. This involved the use of an iterative search procedure. It was found that to support the revenue-neutral removal of the alcohol and tobacco excise taxes, the standard GST rate would need to rise from 12.5 to 14.4 per cent. The corresponding rates on Recreational Vehicles and Vehicle Purchases increase to 8.1 and 8.9 per cent respectively, while by assumption the effective rate of petrol tax was fixed at 71.8 per cent. The excise tax on petrol was considered to be lowered sufficiently to counter the rise in the standard GST rate to ensure the effective *ad valorem* tax rate on petrol remained constant. When in addition, the petrol excise tax is removed, the required GST rate rises to 15.9 per cent, with the rates on commodity groups 3 and 4 increasing to 9.7 and 10.5 per cent respectively. This is similar to the value suggested by McLeod *et al.* (2001).

3.3.2 Welfare Results

The measures of welfare change arising only from the price changes associated with each reform were computed for a range of total expenditure levels for each household type. When examining tax reforms, the appropriate efficiency concept is the marginal excess burden, MEB, defined as:

$$MEB = EV - \Delta T \qquad (3.8)$$

where ΔT is the change in the amount of indirect tax paid. The closely related measure of marginal welfare cost, MWC, is obtained by scaling the marginal excess burden by the absolute value of the change in tax paid, ΔT:

$$MWC = \frac{MEB}{|\Delta T|} \qquad (3.9)$$

In cases where households pay less tax as a result of a reform and are better off, the equivalent variation is negative and the efficiency gain, the MEB, is that remaining after (hypothetically) returning the tax 'rebate'. As the marginal welfare cost measures the gain per dollar of (reduced) revenue, the

marginal excess burden must be divided by the absolute tax change. Thus a
negative value for MWC denotes an efficiency gain.

Again, examination of the variation in welfare changes, as total expenditure varies within each household group, involves too many tables for pre-
sentation here, though the results can be summarised briefly. In terms of
the equity effects of the reforms, it was found that with the alcohol and
tobacco excise taxes removed, the ratio of EV/m increased with total expenditure within all smoking household groups. This suggests that the reform
is progressive within smoking household types. In contrast, the reform produced profiles of the ratio that were non-monotonic for the majority of non-
smoking households, for whom the ratio of EV/m showed no systematic rise
or fall with total expenditure. The additional removal of the petrol excise tax
caused no substantial changes in the progressivity of the reform for smoking
households. However, for non-smoking households, the removal prompted
substantial increases in EV/m with total expenditure within each group.
This led the reform to appear progressive for the majority of non-smoking
household groups. These results concentrate purely on changes, related to
total expenditure, *within* each of the household groups. Further analysis of
overall equity and efficiency effects is provided in section 3.4.

The remainder of the present section concentrates on comparisons *between*
the demographic groups. As before, welfare measures were computed at each
household group's arithmetic mean total expenditure level, $\bar{m}$. The use of
the mean expenditure levels provides representative indications of the welfare
changes faced by each household type. Tables 3.3 and 3.4 report the results
for the first reform, and 3.5 and 3.6 report the summary results for the second
reform.

For both reforms, all smoking household types experience reductions in
the amount of weekly indirect tax paid, with the largest reductions obtained
by households with three or more adults. The smallest reductions are gained
by household groups with single adults. Although all non-smoking house-

Table 3.3: Welfare Changes: Removal of Alcohol and Tobacco Excise Taxes

No.	Household Group	Smoking Households			
		$\bar{m}$	ΔT	$EV/\bar{m}$	MWC
1	65+ Single	267	-12.02	-0.0673	-0.4950
2	65+ Couple	498	-15.99	-0.0445	-0.3859
3	Single Adult & No Children	406	-15.32	-0.0519	-0.3760
4	Single Adult & 1 Child	400	-6.47	-0.0203	-0.2566
5	Single Adult & 2 Children	428	-6.74	-0.0216	-0.3694
6	Single Adult & 3 Children	468	-5.38	-0.0190	-0.6561
7	Single Adult & 4+ Children	501	-2.65	-0.0096	-0.8226
8	Adult Couple & No Children	690	-17.88	-0.0339	-0.3082
9	Adult Couple & 1 Child	668	-14.91	-0.0310	-0.3870
10	Adult Couple & 2 Children	707	-11.05	-0.0217	-0.3910
11	Adult Couple & 3 Children	805	-9.94	-0.0163	-0.3189
12	Adult Couple & 4+ Children	673	-10.87	-0.0227	-0.4039
13	3 Adults & No Children	975	-18.97	-0.0250	-0.2826
14	3 Adults & 1 Child	898	-16.89	-0.0246	-0.3073
15	3 Adults & 2+ Children	826	-13.57	-0.0236	-0.4363
16	4+ Adults & No Children	1311	-19.37	-0.0177	-0.1982
17	4+ Adults & 1 Child	1110	-23.87	-0.0254	-0.1789
18	4+ Adults & 2+ Children	1070	-16.99	-0.0222	-0.3949

Table 3.4: Welfare Changes: Removal of Alcohol and Tobacco Excise Taxes

No.	Household Group	Non-Smoking Households			
		$\overline{m}$	ΔT	$EV/\overline{m}$	MWC
1	65+ Single	274	2.91	0.0116	0.0928
2	65+ Couple	540	4.76	0.0095	0.0735
3	Single Adult & No Children	437	3.41	0.0083	0.0587
4	Single Adult & 1 Child	403	3.48	0.0093	0.0718
5	Single Adult & 2 Children	438	3.80	0.0095	0.0921
6	Single Adult & 3 Children	475	4.46	0.0103	0.0987
7	Single Adult & 4+ Children	539	4.35	0.0088	0.0943
8	Adult Couple & No Children	766	5.43	0.0074	0.0460
9	Adult Couple & 1 Child	763	6.94	0.0098	0.0749
10	Adult Couple & 2 Children	896	8.57	0.0103	0.0817
11	Adult Couple & 3 Children	844	8.45	0.0109	0.0899
12	Adult Couple & 4+ Children	822	9.59	0.0131	0.1251
13	3 Adults & No Children	992	7.10	0.0074	0.0352
14	3 Adults & 1 Child	1038	9.62	0.0101	0.0852
15	3 Adults & 2+ Children	920	9.30	0.0113	0.1161
16	4+ Adults & No Children	1282	8.55	0.0068	0.0199
17	4+ Adults & 1 Child	1129	10.61	0.0103	0.1008
18	4+ Adults & 2+ Children	925	9.64	0.0116	0.1089

Table 3.5: Welfare Changes: Removal of All Excise Taxes

| No. | Household Group | Smoking Households | | | |
		$\bar{m}$	ΔT	$EV/\bar{m}$	MWC
1	65+ Single	267	-11.04	-0.0640	-0.5480
2	65+ Couple	498	-16.47	-0.0471	-0.4250
3	Single Adult & No Children	406	-16.02	-0.0556	-0.4101
4	Single Adult & 1 Child	400	-7.44	-0.0244	-0.3132
5	Single Adult & 2 Children	428	-7.97	-0.0265	-0.4228
6	Single Adult & 3 Children	468	-5.56	-0.0210	-0.7644
7	Single Adult & 4+ Children	501	-2.27	-0.0110	-1.4361
8	Adult Couple & No Children	690	-19.74	-0.0381	-0.3303
9	Adult Couple & 1 Child	668	-17.24	-0.0366	-0.4182
10	Adult Couple & 2 Children	707	-12.54	-0.0252	-0.4211
11	Adult Couple & 3 Children	805	-11.51	-0.0192	-0.3440
12	Adult Couple & 4+ Children	673	-14.35	-0.0301	-0.4105
13	3 Adults & No Children	975	-22.12	-0.0297	-0.3092
14	3 Adults & 1 Child	898	-19.23	-0.0285	-0.3323
15	3 Adults & 2+ Children	826	-18.47	-0.0325	-0.4543
16	4+ Adults & No Children	1311	-24.84	-0.0229	-0.2093
17	4+ Adults & 1 Child	1110	-33.18	-0.0363	-0.2140
18	4+ Adults & 2+ Children	1070	-22.62	-0.0296	-0.4010

Table 3.6: Welfare Changes: Removal of All Excise Taxes

No.	Household Group	Non-Smoking Households			
		$\bar{m}$	ΔT	$EV/\bar{m}$	MWC
1	65+ Single	274	3.95	0.0151	0.0456
2	65+ Couple	540	4.91	0.0088	-0.0285
3	Single Adult & No Children	437	2.86	0.0060	-0.0874
4	Single Adult & 1 Child	403	2.82	0.0066	-0.0532
5	Single Adult & 2 Children	438	3.65	0.0081	-0.0219
6	Single Adult & 3 Children	475	4.76	0.0100	-0.0063
7	Single Adult & 4+ Children	539	2.75	0.0053	0.0473
8	Adult Couple & No Children	766	4.58	0.0055	-0.0852
9	Adult Couple & 1 Child	763	6.50	0.0083	-0.0231
10	Adult Couple & 2 Children	896	8.85	0.0101	0.0260
11	Adult Couple & 3 Children	844	8.76	0.0108	0.0445
12	Adult Couple & 4+ Children	822	9.76	0.0129	0.0861
13	3 Adults & No Children	992	4.58	0.0038	-0.1659
14	3 Adults & 1 Child	1038	7.59	0.0073	0.0040
15	3 Adults & 2+ Children	920	7.83	0.0085	-0.0051
16	4+ Adults & No Children	1282	5.37	0.0031	-0.2551
17	4+ Adults & 1 Child	1129	6.99	0.0057	-0.0858
18	4+ Adults & 2+ Children	925	5.58	0.0056	-0.0627

hold groups incur increases in tax paid, these are generally small in size. The absolute differences in tax for the smoking and non-smoking households are explained by the fact that there are many more of the latter groups of household. The revenue-neutral removal of the alcohol and tobacco excise taxes generates increases in tax paid for non-smoking households that rise with the number of adults in the household. However, the removal of all excise taxes leads household groups with three or more adults to experience smaller increases in tax paid relative to other groups.

Figures 3.3 and 3.4 plot the indirect tax paid under the current schedule of indirect taxes (Tables 3.1 and 3.2) against the changes in tax paid which result from the revenue-neutral removal of the alcohol and tobacco excise taxes for smoking and non-smoking household groups respectively. Among smoking household groups, those currently paying the largest amounts of indirect tax stand to experience the greatest reductions in tax paid. However, as Figure 3.4 shows, these reductions are funded primarily by the non-smoking household groups which already pay the largest amounts of indirect tax under the current schedule.

The welfare gains experienced by smoking household groups were similar for both reforms and lay primarily between 2 and 6 per cent of the groups' mean weekly expenditure level. Household groups containing one and two adults with no children enjoyed the largest welfare gains as a fraction of their mean total expenditure. The welfare losses which were incurred by all non-smoking household groups were trivial in size, typically forming less than 1 per cent.

Tables 3.3 to 3.6 also provide the marginal welfare costs of both reforms. Excise taxes create efficiency losses by distorting the prices of the affected commodities relative to other commodity prices. The elimination of all excise taxes reduces these distortions, which lead the majority of household groups to experience marginal welfare benefits. However, both reforms also entail raising the rate of GST to achieve revenue neutrality. As the rate of GST

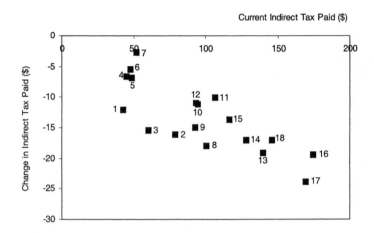

Figure 3.3: Current Tax and Changes in Tax (Smoking Households)

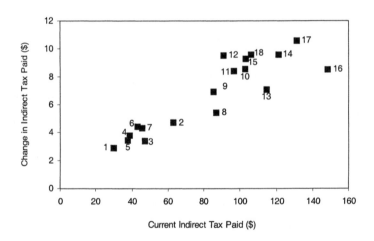

Figure 3.4: Current Tax and Changes in Tax (Non-smoking Households)

rises, the commodities groups Rent and Overseas Travel remain, respectively, exempt and zero rated. Hence, the reforms enlarge the distortions between the prices of these commodities relative to those which attract GST. This counters the efficiency gains which stem from the removal of the excise taxes and leads some non-smoking household groups to incur marginal welfare costs or efficiency losses. This is particularly true of the first reform, in which the petrol excise tax is retained.

For both reforms, all smoking household groups experience substantial marginal welfare benefits. For every dollar reduction in tax paid, the revenue-neutral removal of all excise taxes leads smoking household groups to experience efficiency gains ranging between about 20 and 50 cents. However, for single adult households with three or more children these are much higher, despite the fact that they devote the smallest budget shares to alcohol, tobacco and petrol. This counterintuitive result may be explained by the resulting small reduction in tax paid by these household groups, so that the denominator is close to zero (the MWC expression has a singularity when there is no change in tax paid). For both reforms, the efficiency gains of smoking household groups typically rise with the number of children, while at the same time the reductions in tax paid fall.

The revenue-neutral removal of the alcohol and tobacco excise taxes leads all non-smoking household groups to incur marginal welfare costs. However, these costs are small. Furthermore, the removal of the petrol excise tax leads two thirds of all non-smoking household groups to acquire small gains in efficiency. Thus, these household groups experience increases in efficiency despite paying more tax. In contrast to smoking household groups, non-smoking household groups with no children incur the smallest marginal welfare costs and largest marginal welfare benefits from the first and second reforms respectively. Non-smoking household groups with multiple children fared worst, sustaining the largest efficiency losses. No significant correlations were found between the budget shares which non-smoking household groups devote to the excise commodities and either the groups' changes in tax paid or their marginal welfare costs. The marginal changes in welfare are more varied across the smoking household groups than the non-smoking household groups.

3.4   Indirect Taxes and Inequality

It was found in the previous section that the analysis of ratios of equivalent variations to total expenditure does not generally give an unambiguous indication of the progressivity or otherwise of excise tax reforms within each demographic group. The ratio EV/m gives only a local measure of progressivity. This section therefore considers the equity effects of the excise tax reforms by examining overall measures of inequality, both within demographic groups and over all households combined. It is important to be able to provide an overall measure of progressivity using all households, allowing for all within-group and between-group changes, as this most closely captures the broad statement made in the *Tax Review*.

Several issues are raised when considering inequality measures. First, when producing overall measures, and in examining demographic groups containing households with differing compositions, it is necessary to use some kind of adult equivalence scale. Second, a decision must be made regarding the 'income' measure itself; in measuring inequality in the present context, it is not appropriate simply to use a measure of total expenditure net of indirect taxes. Such a measure would not accurately reflect welfare changes. Third, a measure of inequality must be chosen. These issues are considered in section 3.5, and in further detail in chapter 5. Results are reported in section 3.6 below, which also contains a range of sensitivity analyses.

3.5 Money Metric Measures and Equivalence Scales

The analysis here uses a money metric measure of each household's utility to measure wellbeing. For distributional analyses of tax reforms, it is necessary to have a money metric measure of each household's utility. A suitable money metric is defined as the value of total expenditure, m_e, which, at some reference set of prices, p_r, would give the same utility as the actual total expenditure.[3] A feature of this metric is that it ensures that alternative situations are evaluated using a common set of reference prices. It is, importantly, invariant with respect to monotonic transformations of utility. Using the expenditure function gives:

$$m_e = E\left(p_r, V\left(p, m\right)\right) \tag{3.10}$$

For the linear expenditure system, this is found to be:

$$m_e = \sum_{i=1}^{n} p_{ri}\gamma_i + \left\{\prod_{i=1}^{n}\left(\frac{p_{ri}}{p_i}\right)^{\beta_i}\right\}\left\{m - \sum_{i=1}^{n} p_i\gamma_i\right\} \tag{3.11}$$

The effect on welfare can be measured in terms of a change in m_e from m_{e0} to m_{e1}, where, as before, the indices 0 and 1 refer to pre- and post-change values respectively. If pre-change prices are used as reference prices, so that $p_{ri} = p_{0i}$ for all i, m_{e1} is simply the value of actual total expenditure after the change less the value of the equivalent variation; that is, $m_{e1} = m - EV$. Hence the proportionate change, $(m - m_{e1})/m$, is conveniently the ratio of EV to m. This provides a rationale for the earlier discussion of local progressivity in terms of the variation in this ratio with total expenditure.

Measures of inequality are designed for populations that are demographically homogeneous. However, populations comprise households which have

---

[3]In terms of the indirect utility function, y_e is defined by $V\left(p_r, y_e\right) = V\left(p, y\right)$. This metric was called 'equivalent income' by King (1983), but this term can lead to confusion when used in conjunction with adult equivalent scales. It was used by Fortin and Truchon (1993) with the LES and an early brief discussion of this money metric, also using the LES, was provided by Roberts (1980).

a variety of different demographic structures. Achieving the required homogeneity to compute the inequality measures involves creating, as Ebert (1997, p.235) aptly put it, 'an (artificial) income distribution for a fictitious population'. The artificial income distribution is created by scaling the money metric measure of utility by an adult equivalence scale, h. The resulting distribution, $z = m_e/h$, provides a measure of 'wellbeing' that is comparable across all individuals in a population.[4] The present analysis uses the two-parameter equivalence scale, which takes the form:

$$h = (n_a + \theta n_c)^\alpha \qquad (3.12)$$

where n_a and n_c are the number of adults and children in the household respectively. The parameter measures the size of children relative to adults, and the term α reflects economies of scale in consumption. On the use of this form, see Jenkins and Cowell (1994, p. 894). The results reported here use the values $\theta = 0.65$ and $\alpha = 0.75$. These values are roughly 'mid-range' values of a large number of scales examined in chapter 9, where these issues are discussed in more detail. However, sensitivity results are also reported below.

The fictitious population is created by selecting a unit of analysis for which the inequality measures are calculated. Possible units include the household, the equivalent adult and the individual. The present analysis uses the individual as the unit. The inequality measure reported is the Atkinson measure of inequality.[5] This is based on the social welfare function, W, defined as:

$$W = \frac{1}{\sum\limits_{i=1}^{N} n_i} \sum_{i=1}^{N} n_i V(z_i) \qquad (3.13)$$

---

[4] For within-group inequality, the equivalence scale chosen only affects the calculations for household groups: 7, 12 and 15-18, which do not contain a homogeneous number of adults and children.

[5] A range of extended Gini measures was also computed, but gave similar results.

where n_i is the number of individuals in the ith household ($i = 1, \ldots, N$) and $V(z)$ is increasing and concave. Most commonly, it takes the form:

$$V(z) = \frac{z^{1-\varepsilon}}{1 - \varepsilon} \tag{3.14}$$

for $\varepsilon \neq 1$, and $V(z) = \log z$ when $\varepsilon = 1$. The parameter ε reflects the policymaker's aversion to inequality. It is a measure of relative inequality aversion which, as the degree of concavity of $x^{1-\varepsilon}/(1 - \varepsilon)$, reflects the judge's view of the 'wastefulness' of inequality. The value of ε is often linked to a judge's tolerance of the loss involved (using a 'leaky bucket') in making a transfer from a richer to a poorer individual. For individuals i and j, with $x_j > x_i$, then $\left.\frac{dx_i}{dx_j}\right|_W = -\left(\frac{x_j}{x_i}\right)^{\varepsilon}$. Hence, if j has twice the income of i, a value of $\varepsilon = 1$ means that the judge is prepared to take \$1 from j and transfer only 50 cents to i, losing the remaining 50 cents. For survey results on attitudes to inequality, producing values of ε substantially below 1, see Amiel *et al.* (1999).

The following section reports results for ε of 1.2, which represents substantial aversion to inequality, though sensitivity analyses are also discussed. The equally distributed equivalent, $\tilde{z}$, is the money metric which, if received by every individual, would give the same level of social welfare, W, as the actual distribution. The Atkinson measure of inequality is the proportional difference between the arithmetic mean, $\bar{z}$, and the equally distributed equivalent, $\tilde{z}$, and is thus:

$$A(\varepsilon) = \frac{\bar{z} - \tilde{z}}{\bar{z}} \tag{3.15}$$

Pre-reform and post-reform measures of inequality are generated for each household group and for all households combined. The percentage difference between the pre-reform and post-reform measures provides an indication of the redistributive effect of the tax reforms.

3.6   Tax Reforms and Inequality

Tables 3.7 and 3.8 report the pre-reform and post-reform values of the Atkinson inequality measure for the first reform, for smoking and non-smoking households respectively. Tables 3.9 and 3.10 report the pre-reform and post-reform values of inequality for the second reform. For both reforms, all smoking household groups experience reductions in inequality. For the revenue-neutral removal of all excise taxes, these reductions range from 0.1 to 8.6 per cent. Smoking household groups with two or more adults have greater reductions in inequality from the second as opposed to the first reform. These household groups were found to devote the largest budget shares to petrol. In contrast, smoking household groups with one adult, which devote smaller budget shares to petrol, generally experience larger reductions in inequality from the revenue-neutral removal of just the alcohol and tobacco excise taxes.

Among the non-smoking household groups, the removal of the alcohol and tobacco excise taxes causes the majority to incur a slight increase in inequality. However, the additional removal of the petrol excise tax leads to all but one non-smoking household group experiencing a reduction in inequality. As with the welfare results, the percentage changes in inequality for the smoking household groups exhibit greater variation than those for the non-smoking household groups.

An important question concerns the overall or aggregative effect of the policy reforms. After allowing for differences in household size, and using a money metric utility measure of 'wellbeing' for each individual, would the revenue-neutral elimination of excise taxes increase or reduce inequality? The overall comparisons are provided on the final row of each table. When alcohol and tobacco excise taxes are removed, overall inequality is found to fall from 0.1739 to 0.1724, which is less than 1 per cent. When, in addition, the petrol excise is removed, overall inequality falls to 0.1710, a percentage decrease of just over 1.5 per cent. Hence, the tax reforms reduce inequality, but these

Table 3.7: Inequality: Removal of Alcohol and Tobacco Excise Taxes

No.	Household Group	Atkinson Inequality Measure ($\varepsilon = 1.2$) Smoking Households		
		Pre:	Post:	% change:
1	65+ Single	0.1567	0.1502	-4.1481
2	65+ Couple	0.1044	0.1001	-4.1188
3	Single Adult & No Children	0.1804	0.1728	-4.2129
4	Single Adult & 1 Child	0.0876	0.0849	-3.0822
5	Single Adult & 2 Children	0.1027	0.1001	-2.5316
6	Single Adult & 3 Children	0.1140	0.1131	-0.7895
7	Single Adult & 4+ Children	0.0722	0.0708	-1.9391
8	Adult Couple & No Children	0.1285	0.1230	-4.2802
9	Adult Couple & 1 Child	0.1237	0.1189	-3.8804
10	Adult Couple & 2 Children	0.1072	0.1039	-3.0784
11	Adult Couple & 3 Children	0.1656	0.1592	-3.8647
12	Adult Couple & 4+ Children	0.1236	0.1206	-2.4272
13	3 Adults & No Children	0.1354	0.1305	-3.6189
14	3 Adults & 1 Child	0.1284	0.1231	-4.1277
15	3 Adults & 2+ Children	0.1269	0.1226	-3.3885
16	4+ Adults & No Children	0.1120	0.1085	-3.1250
17	4+ Adults & 1 Child	0.1120	0.1047	-6.5179
18	4+ Adults & 2+ Children	0.1675	0.1619	-3.3433
	Overall	0.1739	0.1724	-0.8626

Table 3.8: Inequality: Removal of Alcohol and Tobacco Excise Taxes

No.	Household Group	Atkinson Inequality Measure ($\varepsilon = 1.2$) Non-Smoking Households		
		Pre:	Post:	% change
1	65+ Single	0.1695	0.1700	0.2950
2	65+ Couple	0.1733	0.1736	0.1731
3	Single Adult & No Children	0.1928	0.1929	0.0519
4	Single Adult & 1 Child	0.1310	0.1313	0.2290
5	Single Adult & 2 Children	0.1318	0.1315	-0.2276
6	Single Adult & 3 Children	0.1270	0.1267	-0.2362
7	Single Adult & 4+ Children	0.1162	0.1158	-0.3442
8	Adult Couple & No Children	0.1670	0.1671	0.0599
9	Adult Couple & 1 Child	0.1658	0.1659	0.0603
10	Adult Couple & 2 Children	0.1749	0.1749	0.0000
11	Adult Couple & 3 Children	0.1463	0.1462	-0.0684
12	Adult Couple & 4+ Children	0.1411	0.1409	-0.1417
13	3 Adults & No Children	0.1387	0.1392	0.3605
14	3 Adults & 1 Child	0.1387	0.1385	-0.1442
15	3 Adults & 2+ Children	0.1474	0.1473	-0.0678
16	4+ Adults & No Children	0.1122	0.1127	0.4456
17	4+ Adults & 1 Child	0.2092	0.2098	0.2868
18	4+ Adults & 2+ Children	0.1748	0.1743	-0.2860
	Overall	0.1739	0.1724	-0.8626

Table 3.9: Inequality: Removal of All Excise Taxes

No.	Household Group	Atkinson Inequality Measure ($\varepsilon = 1.2$) Smoking Households		
		Pre:	Post:	% change
1	65+ Single	0.1567	0.1510	-3.6375
2	65+ Couple	0.1044	0.1001	-4.1188
3	Single Adult & No Children	0.1804	0.1731	-4.0466
4	Single Adult & 1 Child	0.0876	0.0847	-3.3105
5	Single Adult & 2 Children	0.1027	0.1005	-2.1422
6	Single Adult & 3 Children	0.1140	0.1137	-0.2632
7	Single Adult & 4+ Children	0.0722	0.0721	-0.1385
8	Adult Couple & No Children	0.1285	0.1217	-5.2918
9	Adult Couple & 1 Child	0.1237	0.1184	-4.2846
10	Adult Couple & 2 Children	0.1072	0.1027	-4.1978
11	Adult Couple & 3 Children	0.1656	0.1562	-5.6763
12	Adult Couple & 4+ Children	0.1236	0.1197	-3.1553
13	3 Adults & No Children	0.1354	0.1287	-4.9483
14	3 Adults & 1 Child	0.1284	0.1210	-5.7632
15	3 Adults & 2+ Children	0.1269	0.1217	-4.0977
16	4+ Adults & No Children	0.1120	0.1063	-5.0893
17	4+ Adults & 1 Child	0.1120	0.1024	-8.5714
18	4+ Adults & 2+ Children	0.1675	0.1600	-4.4776
	Overall	0.1739	0.1710	-1.6676

Table 3.10: Inequality: Removal of All Excise Taxes

No.	Household Group	Atkinson Inequality Measure ($\varepsilon = 1.2$) Non-Smoking Households		
		Pre:	Post:	% change:
1	65+ Single	0.1695	0.1701	0.3540
2	65+ Couple	0.1733	0.1728	-0.2885
3	Single Adult & No Children	0.1928	0.1914	-0.7261
4	Single Adult & 1 Child	0.1310	0.1298	-0.9160
5	Single Adult & 2 Children	0.1318	0.1316	-0.1517
6	Single Adult & 3 Children	0.1270	0.1265	-0.3937
7	Single Adult & 4+ Children	0.1162	0.1140	-1.8933
8	Adult Couple & No Children	0.1670	0.1652	-1.0778
9	Adult Couple & 1 Child	0.1658	0.1640	-1.0856
10	Adult Couple & 2 Children	0.1749	0.1725	-1.3722
11	Adult Couple & 3 Children	0.1463	0.1442	-1.4354
12	Adult Couple & 4+ Children	0.1411	0.1392	-1.3466
13	3 Adults & No Children	0.1387	0.1373	-1.0094
14	3 Adults & 1 Child	0.1387	0.1360	-1.9466
15	3 Adults & 2+ Children	0.1474	0.1461	-0.8820
16	4+ Adults & No Children	0.1122	0.1113	-0.8021
17	4+ Adults & 1 Child	0.2092	0.2084	-0.3824
18	4+ Adults & 2+ Children	0.1748	0.1717	-1.7735
	Overall	0.1739	0.1710	-1.6676

overall reductions in inequality are small. The small extent of the reductions is explained by the fact that they are dominated by the non-smoking household types, within which there are some of the smallest reductions, and in some cases increases, in inequality from the reforms. Although most stress is usually placed on the regressive role of alcohol and tobacco taxes, it is of interest that the overall reduction in inequality approximately doubles when the petrol excise tax is also removed.

Although a small overall reduction in inequality has been found, the question arises of whether there is a substantial effect on efficiency. This can be examined using the abbreviated form of the social welfare function, in equation (3.13) above, on which the Atkinson inequality measure is based. The abbreviated form, where welfare is expressed in terms of the mean and inequality of money metric utility, rather than all individual values as in (3.13), is given by $W = \bar{z}(1 - A(\varepsilon))$. Social welfare is thus interpreted as the arithmetic mean value, $\bar{z}$, less the 'welfare cost of inequality', $\bar{z}A(\varepsilon)$. For both tax reforms examined, social welfare was found to increase, within each demographic group, for the smoking households (by about 2-5 per cent). However, it decreased for all non-smoking households by about 1 per cent. Over all households combined, social welfare was found to increase by only 0.26 per cent for the first reform (removal of tobacco and alcohol excise taxes) and by 0.50 per cent for the second reform (where the petrol excise is also removed). While the overall equity effects are found to be small, the overall efficiency effects are even smaller.

These results relate to a single choice of inequality aversion parameter and set of adult equivalence scales, both of which involve fundamental value judgements. For this reason it is necessary to consider the sensitivity of the results to changes in these parameters; this is the subject of the following subsection.

3.6.1   Sensitivity Analyses

This subsection analyses the sensitivity of the Atkinson measure of inequality to the parameters of the equivalence scale, θ and α, along with the degree of inequality aversion. The sensitivity analysis is based on the percentage reduction in the overall measure of inequality that results from the revenue-neutral removal of all three excise taxes. Figure 3.5 shows the sensitivity of the reductions in overall inequality to the weight attached to children, θ, while the economies of scale parameter, α, is held fixed at 0.75. Conversely, Figure 3.6 shows the sensitivity to the economies of scale parameter, α, holding θ fixed at 0.65. In both figures, inequality measures are given for three levels of aversion to inequality, $\varepsilon = 0.2$, 0.6 and 1.2. The lower value of 0.2 corresponds to that found among economics students by Amiel *et al.* (1999) using surveys. The higher value represents substantial aversion, in terms of the tolerance of a 'leaky bucket' in making transfers from rich to poor. For example, in taking \$1 from one person and transferring it to someone with half the income, an aversion coefficient of 2 implies that a leak of 75 cents is tolerated.

All values of the parameters continued to produce reductions in the overall level of Atkinson inequality. However, the magnitudes of these reductions varied greatly. Figure 3.5 shows that the percentage reduction in overall inequality falls as the weight attached to children increases. In contrast, Figure 3.6 shows that the relationship between the percentage reduction in inequality and the economies of scale parameter is a relatively flat U-shape. Increases from the $\alpha = 0.75$ used earlier lead to smaller percentage reductions in inequality, while reductions in α, below about 0.4, also lead to smaller reductions in inequality.

Both figures show that the pattern of inequality reductions is similar for different degrees of inequality aversion, though the absolute levels change. A lower aversion to inequality is associated with a larger percentage reduction

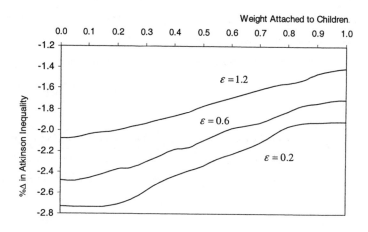

Figure 3.5: Sensitivity of Inequality to Weight Attached to Children

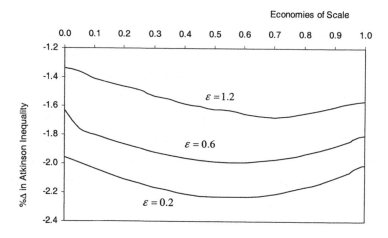

Figure 3.6: Sensitivity of Inequality to Economies of Scale

in inequality. A reason for this finding is that a lower aversion increases the sensitivity of the Atkinson inequality measure to changes in the upper ranges of the distribution, and it has been seen that the largest effects of the policy changes examined have been on larger, higher-income, households.

3.7   Conclusions

McLeod *et al.* (2001) recommended the revenue-neutral removal of excise taxes in New Zealand. The authors of the *Tax Review* were dismissive of standard externality and merit good arguments for excise taxes, and argued that their abolition would reduce inequality and increase the efficiency of the tax system by reducing excess burdens. They suggested that excises are 'highly regressive' (2001, p. 38). No detailed empirical analyses were reported in the *Tax Review*, but references were made to the budget share variations for the relevant goods.

Serious analysis of this issue requires more than an examination of budget shares. This chapter has therefore analysed the welfare and redistributive effects arising from consumer price changes produced by the removal of excise taxes in New Zealand. Welfare changes were measured using equivalent variations and efficiency effects were measured in terms of excess burdens. All measures were computed for thirty-six demographic groups and for all households combined (after adjustments using adult equivalence scales). The welfare effects were computed using results for the Linear Expenditure System and data pooled from several Household Economic Surveys. By enabling parameters to vary with total household expenditure levels, this approach allowed for considerable preference heterogeneity.

New Zealand's current system of indirect taxes was found to be relatively efficient at raising tax revenue, having generally low marginal welfare costs per dollar of revenue raised. However, smoking household groups incur larger welfare costs on average than their non-smoking counterparts, reflecting the high effective tax rate on tobacco. The standard GST rate required to support the revenue-neutral removal of the alcohol and tobacco excise taxes was found to be 14.4 per cent. If in addition the petrol excise tax is removed, the required GST rate rises to 15.9 per cent. The direction and magnitude of the welfare and redistributive effects of the reforms were found to vary substantially among household groups. Smoking households experienced relatively larger efficiency gains and greater reductions in inequality than non-smoking households. The increases in the standard GST rate required to achieve revenue neutrality enlarged the distortions between the prices of the commodity groups which attract GST relative to the two commodity groups which do not attract GST. These countered the efficiency gains generated by the removal of the excise taxes and led some non-smoking household groups to incur efficiency losses from the reforms. For both reforms, the large reductions in tax paid that were acquired by smoking household groups were found to be primarily funded by those non-smoking household groups who already pay the largest amounts of indirect tax under the current schedule.

This chapter has found efficiency, measured by marginal welfare gains, for such a reform to be of the order of approximately 40 cents per dollar of (reduced) tax revenue for smoking households, and only 5 cents per dollar of (extra) tax revenue for non-smoking households. Comparable estimates for other taxes are not available, and it would be interesting to compare these welfare effects, particularly for smoking households, with those arising from income taxation. In terms of equity, the overall reduction in inequality (of money metric utility per adult equivalent) resulting from the proposed reform was found to be around the range of 1.5 to 2.5 per cent, depending on the degree of inequality aversion and the parameters used in the adult equivalence scale. Overall measures of social welfare over all households, allowing for the combined effect of equity and efficiency, were found to increase by only one half of one per cent when all excises are removed. The results therefore offer little support for the McLeod *et al.* (2001) argument that excises are highly regressive and inefficient.

Any policy decision in this context must of course balance these findings against perceived advantages, including environmental and health considerations. Policy views must inevitably depend on value judgements, but it is hoped that the findings of this chapter can contribute towards rational debate on the subject, rather than relying on guesswork.

Chapter 4

A Petrol Tax Increase

In the previous chapter, a separate policy reform was considered in which alcohol and tobacco excise taxes were removed in a revenue-neutral manner, while retaining a constant effective tax on petrol. A reason for looking at this type of reform is that the arguments relating to the imposition of excise taxes for petrol are rather different from those for alcohol and tobacco. The petrol excise tax is typically regarded as being imposed to attempt to correct a pollution externality arising from the use of a scarce resource. However, the petrol excise is clearly also used simply as a revenue-raising tax. Indeed, an increase in the petrol excise tax has been proposed in New Zealand in order to help finance major road building schemes. This chapter therefore concentrates on an examination of the potential welfare and redistributive effects of an increase in the petrol excise tax in New Zealand.

The modelling approach follows that described in the previous chapter. Equivalent variations and excess burdens are obtained for a variety of household types at a range of total expenditure levels. Households are divided into a number of categories according to their composition. Also, overall summary measures of the distributional effects are reported using a money metric utility measure. Changes in indirect taxes give rise to changes in prices, assuming tax shifting to consumers so, as before, the core of the modelling involves a method of examining the welfare effects of price changes.

Household demand responses to price changes are modelled using the Linear Expenditure System (LES), with the modification that parameters are allowed to vary by total expenditure level and household characteristics. The demands are assumed to vary in a partial equilibrium context. Thus, possible changes in production (associated with the changing structure of demands) and factor prices, along with the distribution of income, are ignored.

Section 4.1 briefly describes the relationship between tax rates and price changes, discussed earlier in chapter 2. This is complicated in the present context by the fact that the Goods and Services Tax (GST) is imposed on the excise-inclusive price, and the excise is a unit tax rather than an *ad valorem* tax. The measurement of welfare changes and the way in which household demands are modelled were described in the previous chapter. The approach is used in section 4.2 to examine the potential implications of a tax reform involving an increase in the petrol excise tax.

4.1   Indirect Taxes and Price Changes

To simulate the effects of an increase in the excise tax, it is required to calculate the tax-exclusive price and the effective *ad valorem* tax rate on petrol, given information about the consumer price (which is tax inclusive) of petrol per litre, along with the excise per litre and the GST rate. This is partly complicated by the fact that the excise tax is a unit tax and GST is imposed on the excise. Hence an increase in the excise automatically increases the absolute amount of GST raised per litre of petrol.

Let P_0 and P_1 denote the tax-exclusive and tax-inclusive price of petrol per litre. The petrol excise per litre is E, and the GST (tax-exclusive *ad valorem*) rate is g. The tax paid per litre, T, is given by:

$$
\begin{aligned}
T &= E + (P_0 + E)\,g \\
  &= E\,(1 + g) + P_0 g
\end{aligned}
\tag{4.1}
$$

Hence the relationship between P_1 and P_0, assuming that the tax is passed
to consumers, is:

$$P_1 = P_0 + E(1+g) + P_0 g \qquad (4.2)$$

Hence:

$$P_0 = \frac{P_1}{1+g} - E \qquad (4.3)$$

The effective *ad valorem* rate, t, is therefore given by T/P_0, or:

$$t = g + (1+g)\frac{E}{P_0} \qquad (4.4)$$

For example, in 2001 the petrol excise was $0.343 per litre, and the pro-
portional GST rate was 0.125. Suppose the consumer price of petrol was
$1.08. Hence from (4.3) the tax-exclusive price was $0.617. From (4.4) the
effective *ad valorem* tax rate on petrol was 0.75. An increase in the excise
of 5 cents per litre, to $0.393, produces an effective tax rate of 0.842; an
increase of 10 cents produces a rate of 0.933; and an increase of 15 cents
gives an effective rate of 1.024.

It was necessary to group the Household Expenditure Survey (HES) categories 54 to 59, as explained in chapter 2. This combines petrol with diesel,
CNG and LPG. Hence the appropriate tax rate for this combination requires
a weighted average of petrol and other fuel taxes. The basic (year 2001)
rate used for this group is thus 0.71776, which is correspondingly lower than
the effective rate of 0.75 on petrol. For an increase of 5 cents in the excise,
the new effective rate for this commodity group becomes 0.787, and for an
increase of 15 cents the effective rate becomes 0.952. The results reported
below are obtained using these values.

Changes in effective rates must then be translated into proportionate
price change. In general, suppose that the tax-exclusive *ad valorem* tax rate
imposed on good i is denoted t_i, which is equivalent to a tax-inclusive rate
of $t_i/(1+t_i)$. The revenue, R_i, from the indirect tax on the ith good is
simply expenditure multiplied by the tax-inclusive rate. If t_i increases at the

proportional rate $\dot{t}_i$, the resulting proportionate increase in the price of the ith good, $\dot{p}_i$, is given by:

$$\dot{p}_i = \dot{t}_i \left(\frac{t_i}{1 + t_i} \right) \qquad (4.5)$$

The price changes can then be fed into the expressions for the welfare changes, as discussed briefly in the previous chapter and in detail in Appendix C.

4.2   Simulation Results

This section reports the main results of simulations of the potential effects of an increase in the petrol excise tax in New Zealand. Two cases are considered, of 5 and 15 cent increases. Subsection 4.2.1 reports the welfare changes for a range of total expenditure levels and household types. Finally, subsection 4.2.2 examines the overall effects on inequality.

4.2.1   Welfare Changes

The welfare change obtained for each household is the equivalent variation, EV. This is the difference between total expenditure, m, which remains unchanged by assumption, and the expenditure that would be needed to place the household at the new level of utility at the old (pre-change) prices. Since the pre-change prices are lower, and households are worse off as a result of the increase, the equivalent variation must be positive.

Tables 4.1 to 4.4 summarise the welfare changes resulting from the two hypothetical excise tax changes, for the various household types. The first two tables refer to households with positive expenditure on tobacco, while the second two tables are for non-smoking households. For each household type, the welfare changes are given for three different levels of total household expenditure per week. The respective average expenditure levels are shown in Table 2.2, in chapter 2.

The equivalent variation is given along with its ratio to total expenditure. The variation in EV/m with m gives an initial idea of whether the tax change is progressive or regressive: a progressive change is associated with an increase in EV/m with m. It can be seen that for many household types, the change is very slightly progressive. In some cases it appears to be slightly regressive, while in some cases the change in EV/m is not monotonic.[1] The welfare losses are typically a small percentage of total expenditure, but are relatively higher for smoking households and for multi-adult households.

It is important to consider the marginal excess burdens arising from the tax change, equal to the excess of the change in welfare over the extra tax raised, since this indicates the degree to which inefficiencies arise from the distortionary effect of the tax change. The columns headed Δt give the increase in tax paid per week. The marginal excess burdens arising from the policy change can therefore be obtained by subtracting Δt from EV, for each household type and total expenditure level. A related concept is that of the marginal welfare cost of the tax increase, equal to the ratio of the marginal excess burden to the change in tax revenue. The tables show that the marginal welfare cost, the excess burden per dollar of extra tax revenue, varies substantially among the household types and total expenditure levels. However, for most cases the variation lies between about 35 cents and 55 cents per dollar of additional revenue. It is widely recognised that excess burdens are approximately proportional to the square of the tax rate, and the present simulations involve non-marginal increases to an effective tax rate that is already very high, second only to that imposed on alcohol.

The excess burdens and marginal welfare costs found here are substantially higher than those reported by Davies (2003). However, Davies computed an approximation, the consumers' surplus triangle, to the welfare change, based on an own-price elasticity for the aggregate market demand curve. However, excess burdens obtained using this approach are known to be unreliable approximations. Furthermore, where an approximation is used,

---

[1]The following subsection examines this issue in more detail.

the appropriate demand curve is not the Marshallian curve but the Hicksian (or compensated) demand curve.[2]

4.2.2   Inequality Measures

In the previous subsection it was suggested that the variation in EV/m as m increases gives an indication of whether the tax change is progressive or regressive. However, this indication is incomplete because it does not reflect information about the distribution of changes, involving the numbers of households at the various total expenditure levels. Furthermore, it only allows comparisons among households in the same demographic group. The present subsection, as in the analysis of inequality in the previous chapter, examines the inequality of individual money metric utilities, where each individual in a household is given that household's value of $z = m_e/h$, where h is the adult equivalent size. Equivalence scales are again based on the following function:

$$h = (n_a + \theta n_c)^\gamma \tag{4.6}$$

where n_a and n_c respectively are the number of adults and children in the household. The parameter θ measures the 'size' of children relative to adults, and the term γ reflects economies of scale in consumption. The following results were obtained using values of $\theta = 0.3$ and $\gamma = 0.7$.

The inequality measure reported is again the Atkinson measure, A, where inequality is the proportional difference between the equally-distributed-equivalent, $\tilde{z}$, and the arithmetic mean, $\bar{z}$. Hence, $\tilde{z}$ is the money measure per equivalent adult which, if received by every person, produces the same social welfare as the actual distribution, and:

$$A = 1 - \frac{\tilde{z}}{\bar{z}} \tag{4.7}$$

---

[2]It seems that an income term was not included in the demand study from which Davies took his elasticity, so 'exact' measures cannot be computed by appropriate integration of the demand curve.

Table 4.1: Welfare Changes for Smoking Households: Types 1-9

HH Type	m	5 Cents			15 Cents		
		EV	EV/m	Δt	EV	EV/m	Δt
65+ single	300	0.25	0.0008	0.16	0.81	0.0027	0.53
	600	0.65	0.0011	0.42	2.12	0.0035	1.35
	1000	1.45	0.0015	0.87	4.73	0.0047	2.77
65+ couple	300	0.46	0.0015	0.32	1.50	0.005	1.06
	600	0.9	0.0015	0.66	2.98	0.005	2.16
	1000	1.48	0.0015	1.05	4.90	0.0049	3.45
Single: no children	300	0.42	0.0014	0.29	1.39	0.0046	0.95
	600	0.90	0.0015	0.63	2.97	0.0049	2.06
	1000	1.58	0.0016	1.09	5.21	0.0052	3.55
Single: 1 child	300	0.41	0.0014	0.29	1.36	0.0045	0.95
	600	0.80	0.0013	0.6	2.64	0.0044	1.96
	1000	1.28	0.0013	0.9	4.23	0.0042	2.97
Single: 2 children	300	0.42	0.0014	0.29	1.37	0.0046	0.94
	600	0.89	0.0015	0.63	2.95	0.0049	2.06
	1000	1.63	0.0016	1.08	5.36	0.0054	3.5
Single: 3 children	300	0.28	0.0009	0.16	0.91	0.003	0.52
	600	0.69	0.0011	0.48	2.26	0.0038	1.55
	1000	1.29	0.0013	0.84	4.25	0.0042	2.74
Single: 4+ children	300	-	-	-	-	-	-
	600	0.75	0.0013	0.43	2.42	0.004	1.33
	1000	1.83	0.0018	1.12	5.95	0.0059	3.56
Couple: no children	300	0.61	0.002	0.43	2.00	0.0067	1.41
	600	1.08	0.0018	0.83	3.58	0.006	2.74
	1000	1.44	0.0014	1.18	4.81	0.0048	3.93
Couple: 1 child	300	0.56	0.0019	0.41	1.86	0.0062	1.33
	600	1.07	0.0018	0.78	3.53	0.0059	2.57
	1000	1.71	0.0017	1.24	5.65	0.0056	4.08

Table 4.2: Welfare Changes for Smoking Households: Types 10-18

HH Type	m	5 Cents			15 Cents		
		EV	EV/m	Δt	EV	EV/m	Δt
Couple: 2 children	300	0.57	0.0019	0.38	1.88	0.0063	1.23
	600	1.01	0.0017	0.78	3.37	0.0056	2.57
	1000	1.41	0.0014	1.13	4.71	0.0047	3.78
Couple: 3 children	300	0.78	0.0026	0.56	2.58	0.0086	1.86
	600	1.13	0.0019	0.90	3.78	0.0063	3.00
	1000	1.44	0.0014	1.19	4.82	0.0048	3.97
Couple: 4+ children	300	0.56	0.0019	0.34	1.83	0.0061	1.08
	600	1.26	0.0021	0.94	4.17	0.0069	3.10
	1000	1.71	0.0017	1.42	5.74	0.0057	4.73
3 adults: no children	300	0.57	0.0019	0.34	1.84	0.0061	1.06
	600	1.25	0.0021	0.91	4.12	0.0069	3.00
	1000	1.81	0.0018	1.44	6.04	0.006	4.78
3 adults: 1 child	300	0.88	0.0029	0.68	2.94	0.0098	2.25
	600	1.28	0.0021	1.01	4.26	0.0071	3.35
	1000	1.68	0.0017	1.35	5.61	0.0056	4.48
3 adults: 2+ children	300	-	-	-	-	-	-
	600	1.29	0.0022	0.83	4.22	0.007	2.66
	1000	2.11	0.0021	1.62	7.02	0.007	5.37
4+ adults: no children	300	0.47	0.0016	0.46	1.53	0.0051	1.47
	600	1.60	0.0027	1.20	5.28	0.0088	3.95
	1000	2.22	0.0022	1.79	7.39	0.0074	5.95
4+ adults: 1 child	300	0.81	0.0027	0.49	2.64	0.0088	1.56
	600	1.81	0.0030	1.32	5.96	0.0099	4.32
	1000	2.68	0.0027	2.09	8.92	0.0089	6.91
4+ adults: 2+ children	300	1.05	0.0035	0.83	3.5	0.0117	2.77
	600	1.51	0.0025	1.19	5.02	0.0084	3.93
	1000	2.09	0.0021	1.61	6.94	0.0069	5.32

Table 4.3: Welfare Changes for Non-smoking Households: Types 1-9

HH Type	m	5 Cents			15 Cents		
		EV	EV/m	Δt	EV	EV/m	Δt
65+ single	300	0.26	0.0009	0.19	0.87	0.0029	0.64
	600	0.52	0.0009	0.38	1.73	0.0029	1.24
	1000	0.92	0.0009	0.63	3.02	0.003	2.05
65+ couple	300	0.45	0.0015	0.34	1.49	0.005	1.11
	600	0.83	0.0014	0.65	2.75	0.0046	2.14
	1000	1.11	0.0011	0.92	3.70	0.0037	3.06
Single: no children	300	0.50	0.0017	0.38	1.66	0.0055	1.26
	600	0.79	0.0013	0.64	2.64	0.0044	2.14
	1000	0.96	0.001	0.82	3.22	0.0032	2.77
Single: 1 child	300	0.46	0.0015	0.36	1.52	0.0051	1.19
	600	0.71	0.0012	0.56	2.37	0.0039	1.84
	1000	1.01	0.001	0.74	3.37	0.0034	2.46
Single: 2 children	300	0.40	0.0013	0.35	1.36	0.0045	1.17
	600	0.71	0.0012	0.48	2.33	0.0039	1.54
	1000	1.79	0.0018	0.93	5.8	0.0058	2.96
Single: 3 children	300	0.34	0.0011	0.26	1.12	0.0037	0.85
	600	0.66	0.0011	0.46	2.18	0.0036	1.48
	1000	1.37	0.0014	0.83	4.49	0.0045	2.68
Single: 4+ children	300	0.53	0.0018	0.41	1.76	0.0059	1.35
	600	0.78	0.0013	0.7	2.64	0.0044	2.35
	1000	0.67	0.0007	0.6	2.25	0.0023	2.04
Couple: no children	300	0.60	0.002	0.45	1.97	0.0066	1.48
	600	1.04	0.0017	0.82	3.45	0.0057	2.72
	1000	1.33	0.0013	1.12	4.46	0.0045	3.75
Couple: 1 child	300	0.64	0.0021	0.5	2.13	0.0071	1.66
	600	0.99	0.0016	0.78	3.30	0.0055	2.6
	1000	1.33	0.0013	1.06	4.44	0.0044	3.53

Table 4.4: Welfare Changes for Non-smoking Households: Types 10-18

HH Type	m	5 Cents			15 Cents		
		EV	EV/m	Δt	EV	EV/m	Δt
Couple: 2 children	300	0.68	0.0023	0.52	2.25	0.0075	1.72
	600	1.04	0.0017	0.83	3.47	0.0058	2.76
	1000	1.34	0.0013	1.11	4.48	0.0045	3.69
Couple: 3 children	300	0.60	0.0020	0.47	2.00	0.0067	1.54
	600	1.01	0.0017	0.81	3.37	0.0056	2.68
	1000	1.26	0.0013	1.07	4.23	0.0042	3.59
Couple: 4+ children	300	0.56	0.0019	0.39	1.84	0.0061	1.28
	600	0.98	0.0016	0.77	3.25	0.0054	2.54
	1000	1.28	0.0013	1.05	4.29	0.0043	3.52
3 adults: no children	300	0.62	0.0021	0.43	2.04	0.0068	1.39
	600	1.28	0.0021	0.98	4.24	0.0071	3.22
	1000	1.75	0.0017	1.44	5.85	0.0058	4.80
3 adults: 1 child	300	0.87	0.0029	0.63	2.88	0.0096	2.08
	600	1.38	0.0023	1.09	4.6	0.0077	3.62
	1000	1.77	0.0018	1.48	5.95	0.0059	4.94
3 adults: 2+ children	300	0.35	0.0012	0.17	1.12	0.0037	0.52
	600	1.05	0.0018	0.75	3.46	0.0058	2.46
	1000	1.62	0.0016	1.26	5.39	0.0054	4.16
4+ adults: no children	300	0.42	0.0014	0.28	1.36	0.0045	0.86
	600	1.25	0.0021	0.90	4.12	0.0069	2.94
	1000	1.91	0.0019	1.48	6.35	0.0064	4.90
4+ adults: 1 child	300	0.54	0.0018	0.33	1.76	0.0059	1.04
	600	1.29	0.0022	0.94	4.26	0.0071	3.07
	1000	1.97	0.002	1.51	6.56	0.0066	4.98
4+ adults: 2+ children	300	0.97	0.0032	0.75	3.22	0.0107	2.47
	600	1.46	0.0024	1.16	4.87	0.0081	3.86
	1000	1.93	0.0019	1.56	6.46	0.0065	5.18

Table 4.5 lists the pre- and post-increase inequality measures for each household type, for the higher excise increase of 15 cents for a relative inequality aversion coefficient of 1.2. This indicates a substantial degree of aversion. Within many of the demographic groups, the choice of adult equivalence scales does not affect the inequality comparison because those groups contain homogeneous households. But for categories 7, 13 and 15-18, the adult equivalent household size can vary.

The final row of the table provides an overall indication of the redistributive effect of the tax change; this shows a very small increase from 0.1622 to 0.1627. This overall change also reflects the relative numbers of households in the various demographic groups, as well as the distribution of total expenditure among households. When a lower degree of inequality aversion is used, the overall increase is trivial, being from 0.0297 to 0.0298. A wide range of inequality measures, included extended Gini measures for varying inequality aversion, was computed, and in all cases the changes were very small. The comparisons were also not affected by the choice of equivalence scale in this case, though the absolute size changes (except of course for single adult households).

When the inequality of individual values of m_e/h is considered, the overall effect is to increase inequality slightly. Furthermore, inequality increases slightly within most of the demographic groups, the exceptions being 1, 3 and 6-7 inclusive for the smoking households and groups 1 and 6 for the non-smoking households. However, these changes in inequality are negligible, typically involving either the third or fourth decimal place, and are most unlikely to be statistically significant.

4.3 Conclusions

This chapter has examined the potential implications for New Zealand households of a hypothetical increase in the petrol excise tax. Two cases were

Table 4.5: Inequality Measures for Excise Increase of 15 Cents

No.	Household Type	Smoking Pre-	Smoking Post-	Non-smoking Pre-	Non-smoking Post-
1	65+ single	.1553	.1551	.1692	.1692
2	65+ couple	.1012	.1012	.1728	.1731
3	Single: no children	.1804	.1802	.1928	.1933
4	Single: 1 child	.0876	.0876	.1310	.1314
5	Single: 2 children	.1027	.1026	.1318	.1318
6	Single: 3 children	.1140	.1137	.1270	.1269
7	Single: 4+ children	.0696	.0690	.1126	.1131
8	Couple: no children	.1285	.1290	.1670	.1677
9	Couple: 1 child	.1236	.1238	.1657	.1664
10	Couple: 2 children	.1072	.1076	.1749	.1757
11	Couple: 3 children	.1656	.1666	.1463	.1470
12	Couple: 4+ children	.1207	.1210	.1381	.1386
13	3 adults: no children	.1354	.1360	.1387	.1394
14	3 adults: 1 child	.1284	.1291	.1387	.1396
15	3 adults: 2+ children	.1173	.1174	.1409	.1412
16	4+ adults: no children	.1114	.1121	.1121	.1125
17	4+ adults: 1 child	.1120	.1127	.2092	.2095
18	4+ adults: 2+ children	.1683	.1689	.1738	.1748
	All Individuals	Pre-: 0.1622		Post-: 0.1627	

considered, of increases of 5 cents and 15 cents per litre. Changes in indirect taxes lead to changes in prices, so the core of the model is a method of examining the welfare effects of price changes. Household demand responses to price changes were modelled using the Linear Expenditure System, with the modification that parameters vary by total expenditure level and household characteristics. Pooled Household Economic Survey data were used to divide households into 18 demographic categories, and commodity groups were consolidated into 22 groups. In addition, households were distinguished according to whether their tobacco consumption was positive.

The welfare effects of the excise tax increase were found to vary considerably among demographic groups, reflecting the different variations in budget shares with total expenditure. Importantly, the marginal excess burdens also varied substantially, though most cases ranged between about 35 and 55 cents per dollar of extra revenue. Public expenditure financed from such a tax increase would therefore need to establish significant external benefits.

Inequality comparisons, based on money metric utility per adult equivalent, were also made based on the distribution of individual values. The majority of household types, along with the overall comparison, showed very small – indeed negligible – increases in inequality. The results suggest that the most important consideration from such a selective tax increase arises from the marginal welfare costs generated.

Part III

Environmental Taxes

Chapter 5

Effects of a Carbon Tax

A carbon tax, designed to reduce carbon dioxide emissions, operates by providing an incentive for consumers and firms to substitute away from those goods which have the highest carbon intensities. The prices of the more carbon intensive goods increase proportionately more than those with lower intensities. These intensities in turn depend on the fossil fuels used in the production of each good and the nature of inter-industry transactions. Such a tax is obviously designed to correct a market failure – the absence of a market for carbon dioxide – but it can also have unintended consequences. These include the fact that the price changes induced by the tax may give rise to excess burdens. In addition, there may be adverse impacts on the distribution of welfare. Inequality may increase if the price changes are higher for those goods which form a larger share of the budgets of relatively low-income households. If the welfare of low-income households is more severely affected than the welfare of high-income households, then information about those distributional effects can be used to design compensating changes to the direct tax and transfer system. More widely discussed positive effects are associated with the use of carbon tax revenue to reduce other distorting taxes, such as income taxation. On these aspects, see for example Carraro *et al.* (1996), McKitrick (1997) and Smith (1998).

The aim of this chapter is to investigate the likely orders of magnitude of the welfare and distributional effects of the price changes arising from a carbon tax in New Zealand. The government was initially committed to such a tax as part of its policy package on climate change and it was planned to begin in April 2007. As explained by Cullen and Hodgson (2005), the carbon tax was designed to meet New Zealand's greenhouse gas reduction target under the Kyoto Protocol.[1] The proposed charge would approximate international emissions prices, capped at NZ$25 per tonne of carbon dioxide. This decision was subsequently reversed in late 2005. Despite the widespread discussion, there were no studies of the detailed implications for prices and their welfare effects on different households. Since the debate on environmental taxes is certain to continue, it is useful to consider a carbon tax here.

The majority of carbon tax studies have concentrated on emissions reductions using general equilibrium or macroeconomic models which allow very little disaggregation of the household sector. The approach used here is based on the pioneering work of Proops et al. (1993) and Symons et al. (1994), but uses the demand system and welfare measurement used in earlier chapters of this book.[2] Other studies concentrating on microeconomic aspects include Nichele and Robin (1995) for France, Labandeira and Labeaga (1999) for Spain and Brannlund and Nordstrom (2004) for Sweden. In order to allow for substantial population heterogeneity, the model is necessarily partial equilibrium in nature, in that it makes no allowance for factor price changes that may arise from demand and output changes. It also concentrates on consumer demands, making extensive use of cross-sectional household expenditure data. Hence possible changes to inter-industry transactions, reflected in changes in coefficients of the input–output matrix, and producer substitutions between fuels, are ignored here.[3]

---

[1] For extensive discussion, see Ministry for Environment (2005). The New Zealand context is complicated by the fact that a substantial proportion of emissions come from the agricultural sector.

[2] The method was developed by Creedy and Cornwell (1996, 1997) to examine carbon taxation in Australia.

[3] Allowance for such effects in the context of Australia are modelled by Creedy and

The analysis proceeds as follows. First, it is necessary to provide a link between a carbon tax, expressed in terms of tonnes of carbon dioxide, and the price changes of commodities. This link depends on the carbon dioxide intensities of each good. Second, given the price changes, it is necessary to evaluate the effect on the welfare of households; this stage requires the use of a demand model. This chapter applies the model, used elsewhere in this book, involving the Linear Expenditure System, where the parameters are allowed to vary among household types and total expenditure levels. Third, the overall evaluation of the carbon tax requires the calculation of inequality measures, involving an allowance for differences in household composition.

Section 5.1 sets out the basic framework of analysis. The expression for the carbon dioxide intensities of commodities is derived. These intensities together with a carbon tax rate are then used to calculate the effective carbon tax rates on commodities and subseqent price changes, expressions for which are provided in section 5.1. Section 5.2 applies the framework to produce the price changes arising from a carbon tax of NZ\$25 in New Zealand. It describes the main data sources and reports the effective *ad valorem* tax rates. Section 5.3 analyses the welfare effects arising from the carbon tax. It begins by describing the treatment of household demands and then examines welfare changes, measured in terms of equivalent variations, for a range of household types and levels of total weekly expenditure. These welfare measures give an indication of the disproportionality of the impact at different total expenditure levels, for the household types. Overall measures of inequality are reported in section 5.4, for each household type and for all households combined. These use the individual as the basic unit of analysis and make use of adult equivalence scales in measuring each individual's level of wellbeing.

Martin (2000).

5.1   A Carbon Tax and Price Changes

The first stage of the analysis is to apply a carbon tax and examine its effects on consumer prices. This section derives the expressions used to calculate such price changes. A carbon tax is specified as a number of dollars per tonne of carbon generated by the production of each good. It is therefore necessary to translate from a tax specified in terms of physical amounts of carbon into an equivalent tax imposed per dollar of expenditure by final consumers of each good. This is achieved through the carbon intensity of each good.

As with other studies of carbon taxes, the tax examined is considered to be imposed on carbon dioxide intensity, rather than carbon intensity. However, carbon content and carbon dioxide emissions are directly proportional by molecular weight, and the equivalent tax on carbon content can be obtained by multiplying the carbon dioxide tax by 44/12. Hence a tax is specified in terms of tonnes of carbon dioxide and consumer prices rise in proportion to their carbon dioxide intensity.

This intensity, defined by c_i, measures the tonnes of carbon dioxide emissions per dollar of final consumption of the output from industry i. Therefore, a carbon dioxide tax of α which is placed on carbon dioxide emissions is equivalent to an *ad valorem* tax-exclusive rate on the ith commodity group of τ_i, where:[4]

$$\tau_i = \alpha c_i \tag{5.1}$$

As the carbon intensity is expressed in terms of each dollar's worth of the output that contributes to final demands, the total amount of carbon dioxide arising from all industries, E, is given by:

$$E = \sum_{i=1}^{n} c_i y_i = c'y \tag{5.2}$$

---

[4]The tax-exclusive tax rate is simply the ratio of tax paid to the tax-exclusive price of the good. Conversely, the tax-inclusive tax rate is the ratio of tax paid to the tax-inclusive price of the good.

where y_i is the value of final demand for industry i for $i = 1, ..., n$. The terms c and y denote corresponding column vectors and the prime indicates transposition.

The carbon dioxide intensities depend in a direct way on the types and amounts of fossil fuels used by each industry, and the emissions per unit of those fossil fuels. However, the problem is complicated by the need to consider the total output of each industry, rather than merely the amount of that output which is consumed, that is the final demand. This problem is examined in the first subsection below. Having obtained the equivalent tax rates, the next stage is to obtain an expression for the overall tax rate imposed on each unit of the good consumed. This is discussed in the second subsection.

5.1.1 Carbon Intensities

Consider increasing the final consumption, in value terms, of a good by one dollar. The problem is to evaluate how much carbon dioxide this would involve. This increase in the final demand by one dollar involves a larger increase in the gross, or total output, of the good – as well as requiring increases in the outputs of other goods. This is because intermediate goods, including the particular good of interest, are needed in the production process. The extent to which there is an increase in carbon dioxide depends also on the intermediate requirements of all goods which are themselves intermediate requirements for the particular good. Indeed, the sequence of intermediate requirements continues until it 'works itself out'; that is, the additional amounts needed become negligible. This is in fact a standard multiplier process. It can be set out formally as follows.

An industry's gross output derives from both final demand and intermediate output, which serves as imput to other industries. Let x_{ij} denote the value of output flowing from industry i to industry j, and let y_i denote the

value of final demand by consumers for the output of industry i. The value
of an industry's gross output, x_i, may therefore be expressed as the sum of
the intermediate and final demands:

$$x_i = \sum_j x_{ij} + y_i \qquad (5.3)$$

The direct requirement coefficient, a_{ij}, measures the value of output from industry i directly required to produce one dollar's worth of output in industry
j. Hence:

$$a_{ij} = \frac{x_{ij}}{x_i} \qquad (5.4)$$

Using this to write $x_{ij} = a_{ij}x_i$ and substituting the resulting expression into
equation (6.1) gives gross output as:

$$x_i = \sum_j a_{ij}x_i + y_i \qquad (5.5)$$

Let x and y denote the n-element vectors of x_i and y_i respectively. Further, let A denote the n by n matrix of the direct requirement coefficients,
a_{ij}. These definitions enable the system of n equations described in (5.5) to
be expressed in matrix notation as:

$$x = Ax + y \qquad (5.6)$$

Continuous substitution of x on the right hand side of equation (5.6) produces
the following geometric sequence:

$$
\begin{aligned}
x &= A[Ax + y] + y \\
&= A[A[Ax + y] + y] + y \\
&= [I + A + A^2 + A^3 + ... + A^\infty x] y \qquad (5.7)
\end{aligned}
$$

If the condition $\lim_{n \to \infty} = 0$ is satisfied, the system is productive and the non-
negative solution is

$$x = (1 - A)^{-1} y \qquad (5.8)$$

where $(1 - A)^{-1}$ is the matrix multiplier. This is given from the solution to the geometric matrix series $I + A + A^2 + \ldots = (1 - A)^{-1}$, which must be non-negative given that all the elements of A are either zero or positive.

Let F denote the n by k matrix of energy requirements, in PJs, per unit of gross output, for n industries across k fossil fuel types. Let e denote the k-element vector of CO_2 emissions (tonnes of carbon dioxide) per unit of energy (PJ) associated with each of the k fossil fuels.

Multiplying the transpose of the e vector by the transpose of the F matrix gives the following row vector which contains the carbon dioxide emissions per unit of gross output from each industry:

$$e'F' = [e_1 \ldots e_k] \begin{bmatrix} f_{11} & \cdots & f_{n1} \\ \cdot & \cdot & \cdot \\ f_{1k} & \cdots & f_{nk} \end{bmatrix} \qquad (5.9)$$

Total carbon dioxide emissions, E, can then be obtained by post-multiplying the above row vector by the column vector of gross output, x:

$$\begin{aligned} E &= e'F'x \\ &= \left[e'F' (1 - A)^{-1} \right] y \end{aligned} \qquad (5.10)$$

The term in square brackets gives the row vector, c', of carbon dioxide intensities:

$$c' = e'F' (1 - A)^{-1} \qquad (5.11)$$

This expression is used together with a selected carbon tax rate to calculate the effective carbon tax rates given above. The expression in equation (5.11) is a simplified form of that obtained by Proops $et\ al.$ (1993) and Symons $et\ al.$ (1994). The present analysis abstracts from carbon dioxide emissions arising directly from the consumption of goods and services, which are small compared with those arising from production.

5.1.2   Effective Tax Rates

The carbon tax is imposed in addition to pre-existing indirect taxes. Hence
it is necessary to obtain an expression for the post-carbon-tax equivalent
indirect tax rates. Let p_0 denote the tax-exclusive price of commodity i;
here the subscript has been dropped for convenience. Prior to the imposition
of the carbon tax, the existing *ad valorem* tax rate is t and therefore the
tax-inclusive price of commodity i, p_1, is defined by:

$$p_1 = p_0 \left(1 + t \right) \tag{5.12}$$

The carbon (dioxide) tax is effectively a tax on final consumption at the rate,
τ, which is the resulting proportional increase in the price of the good. Hence
the new tax-inclusive price of commodity i, p_2, is given by:

$$
\begin{aligned}
p_2 &= p_1 \left(1 + \tau \right) \\
&= p_0 \left(1 + t \right) \left(1 + \tau \right)
\end{aligned}
\tag{5.13}
$$

The overall effective *ad valorem* tax rate on commodity i, t^*, may therefore
be calculated from the expression:

$$
\begin{aligned}
t^* &= \left(1 + t \right) \left(1 + \tau \right) - 1 \tag{5.14} \\
&= t + \tau \left(1 + t \right) \tag{5.15}
\end{aligned}
$$

In the following analysis the effects of shifting from t to t^* are examined.
The term τ, as the effective carbon tax on consumption, measures the proportional price increase for each good.

5.2   A Carbon Tax in New Zealand

This section outlines the New Zealand data used to determine the carbon
dioxide intensity of each industry and reports the effective tax rates and
price changes arising from a \$25 carbon dioxide tax rate. The values of final
demands are measured in thousands of dollars. Hence a carbon tax of \$25
per tonne of carbon dioxide translates into a value of α of 0.025.

5.2.1 Fuel Use and Carbon Content

Inter-industry flows in value terms were obtained from the 'Inter Industry Study of 1996' from New Zealand's *System of National Accounts* for a 49 industry group classification (IGC). This is the most recent year for which the data are available. The flows were divided by each industry's gross output to produce the direct requirement coefficients of the A matrix. By subtracting each industry's intermediate output from gross output, the *National Accounts* were also used to compile the 49-element vector of final demands.

The F matrix was constructed from New Zealand's *Energy Flow Accounts,* which provide the energy use arising from fossil fuels, expressed in physical terms (PJs), for the year ended March 1996 based on the Energy Account Industry Classification (EAIC). Hence it was necessary to translate between the Energy Account Industry Classification (EAIC) and the 49 Industry Group Classification (IGC) used for the present analysis. This provided 9 fossil fuels for analysis. Dividing these figures by each industry's gross output provided the required elements of the matrix. For details of the translations and data on fossil fuel use, see Appendix G.

Data from several sources were used to compile the 9-element vector of carbon dioxide emissions. Table 5.1 outlines the carbon dioxide emission factors for each of the 9 fossil fuels analysed: these are taken from Baines (1993) and Ministry of Economic Development (2003). The resulting values of e, F and A were used to calculate the 49-element vector, c, of carbon dioxide intensities, using the expression $c' = e'F'(1 - A)^{-1}$ derived above.

Not surprisingly, petroleum and industrial chemical manufacturing, which demands the greatest quantity of fuel across all industries, recorded by far the highest carbon content of 3.64 tonnes of carbon dioxide per dollar of gross output. Rubber, plastic and other chemical product manufacturing, and basic metal manufacturing, which respectively demand the largest quantities of natural gas and coal, also recorded high carbon contents of 1.83 and 1.40

Table 5.1: Carbon Dioxide Emissions Factors: Tonnes per PJ

Fuel	CO_2 Emission
Coal	90,010
Lignite	95,200
Crude Petroleum	65,100
Natural Gas	52,600
LPG	60,400
Petrol	66,600
Diesel	68,700
Fuel Oil	73,700
Aviation Fuels and Kero	68,700

tonnes of carbon dioxide per dollar of gross output. The only other industry whose carbon content exceeded 1 was electricity generation and supply, with 1.21.

5.2.2   Taxes and Prices

The existing indirect taxes were discussed in chapter . They must be expressed in terms of a tax-exclusive *ad valorem* tax rate. While this is straightforward for most commodity groups, for which only the Goods and Services Tax applies, the translation is more complex where an excise tax is also imposed, as these are typically based on units of the commodity rather than values. In modelling demands, only 22 commodity groups could be distinguished. Chapter 2 showed the groups used and the effective *ad valorem* tax-exclusive rates, t, expressed as percentages.

Table 5.2 shows the effective carbon tax rates for the 22 commodity groups, τ, and the new effective *ad valorem* tax rates, t^*, expressed as percentages, that result from a carbon tax of \$25. Petrol faces by far the greatest price increase. For the majority of household types, low-income earners spend a proportionately greater amount of their budget on petrol than high-income earners. Similarly, domestic fuel and power, and food both face substantial price rises as a result of the carbon tax, and also form relatively higher pro-

Table 5.2: Effective Carbon Tax and Effective Ad Valorem Tax Rates

No.	Commodity group	100τ	$100t$
1	Overseas Travel	2.16	2.16
2	Rent	0.40	0.40
3	Recreational Vehicles	0.56	6.85
4	Vehicle Purchases	0.56	7.65
5	Food	1.28	13.94
6	Food Outside Home	1.17	13.82
7	Pay to Local Authorities	0.43	12.99
8	House Maintenance	0.52	13.09
9	Domestic Fuel and Power	2.75	15.59
10	Household Equipment	0.90	13.52
11	Furnishings	0.71	13.30
12	Household Services	4.59	17.66
13	Adult's Clothing	0.63	13.21
14	Children's Clothing	0.63	13.21
15	Public Transport in NZ	1.40	14.08
16	Vehicle Supplies, Parts, etc	0.56	13.13
17	Medical, Cosmetic etc	0.37	12.92
18	Services	0.32	12.86
19	Other Expenditure	0.85	13.46
20	Alcohol	0.69	47.83
21	Petrol	7.60	84.83
22	Cigarettes and Tobacco	0.77	242.45

portions of the budgets of lower-income earners. These findings suggest that the carbon tax may have a proportionately greater impact on those households with relatively lower levels of total expenditure. However, the effect of a carbon tax is not unambiguous. The price of food consumed outside the home also rises substantially, and in this case higher-income earners spend a proportionately larger amount of their budgets on this good. Overseas travel incurs the fourth largest price increase, and its budget share increases with total expenditure.[5]

5.3 Welfare Changes for Households

This section reports the effects of a carbon tax on the welfare of different household types at different levels of total weekly expenditure. The welfare changes are obtained using the same simulation model as that used in Part II. In this model, the demand responses refer to the 22 commodity group classification, as described in chapter 2. However, the price changes arising from the carbon tax are given for a 49 industry group classification. The calculated price changes cannot therefore be directly used to evaluate the demand responses and welfare changes, and a translation between the two classifications must be used; this translation is given in Appendix G.

Tables 5.3 and 5.4 summarise the welfare changes that arise from the carbon tax. For the first two household groups, 65+ refers to the age of the head of the household. The analysis was conducted for a range of total weekly household expenditure levels, though for convenience only three values are shown in the tables for each of the eighteen household groups. The equivalent variation, EV, is given together with its ratio to total expenditure, EV/m. These results show that the welfare loss is generally around 1.4 per cent

---

[5]The question arises of how overseas travel should be treated. There are grounds for continuing to treat the effective tax on this commodity group as zero. However, sensitivity analyses showed that the results are not significantly affected by setting this price change to zero.

of total expenditure. The relationship between EV/m and m provides an indication of the disproportionality of the welfare impact of the carbon tax within each household type. A rising profile may be described as progressive. For nine non-smoking household groups and six smoking household groups, the ratio EV/m decreases with m. This suggests that the carbon tax may be slightly more regressive among non-smoking households. However, for the majority of household types, the carbon tax proves to be neither strictly regressive nor progressive. The column adjacent to EV/m gives the increase in tax paid per week, ΔT.

The marginal excess burden of the carbon tax, MEB, is the difference between the equivalent variation and the increase in tax paid, $MEB = EV - \Delta T$. It provides a measure of the efficiency loss arising from the carbon tax. Households, both smoking and non-smoking, with low to moderate expenditure levels incur similar excess burdens independent of type. However, among those households (smoking and non-smoking) with high levels of weekly expenditure, three groups incur significantly higher marginal excess burdens. The excess burdens incurred by households with one child rise with expenditure at a greater rate than the burdens incurred by households with no children. Single adult, relative to multi-adult households with higher total expenditure levels, are similarly more adversely affected by the carbon tax. This result holds regardless of the number of children in the household. When total expenditure levels exceed \$600 per week, the marginal excess burdens incurred by couples where the head of the household is aged over 65 are substantially greater than those incurred by couples where both are aged under 65.

Tables 5.5 and 5.6 report the welfare changes at arithmetic mean weekly total expenditure levels for each household type. The welfare loss is about 1.3 per cent, while the marginal welfare cost, defined as $MWC = MEB/\Delta T$, varies between approximately 15 and 18 cents for smoking households and 13 and 15 cents for non-smoking households per dollar of additional tax revenue.

Table 5.3: Welfare and Tax Changes: Carbon Tax of 25 Dollars

			Smoking Households		
No.	Household Group	m	EV	EV / m	ΔT
1	65+ Single	300	3.76	0.0125	3.17
		600	6.91	0.0115	5.86
		1000	11.63	0.0116	9.17
2	65+ Couple	300	4.29	0.0143	3.57
		600	7.89	0.0132	6.73
		1000	12.94	0.0129	10.67
3	Single Adult	300	3.89	0.0130	3.24
	& No Children	600	7.42	0.0124	6.22
		1000	12.12	0.0121	9.93
4	Single Adult	300	3.89	0.0130	3.37
	& 1 Child	600	6.94	0.0116	5.99
		1000	12.39	0.0124	9.67
5	Single Adult	300	3.92	0.0131	3.36
	& 2 Children	600	7.41	0.0124	6.25
		1000	13.10	0.0131	10.26
6	Single Adult	300	3.93	0.0131	3.33
	& 3 Children	600	6.97	0.0116	5.93
		1000	11.63	0.0116	9.03
7	Single Adult	300	2.90	0.0097	2.86
	& 4+ Children	600	7.33	0.0122	6.03
		1000	12.35	0.0124	9.83
8	Adult Couple	300	4.42	0.0147	3.64
	& No Children	600	7.91	0.0132	6.77
		1000	12.00	0.0120	10.59
9	Adult Couple	300	4.33	0.0144	3.60
	& 1 Child	600	7.99	0.0133	6.74
		1000	12.81	0.0128	10.73
10	Adult Couple	300	4.51	0.0150	3.58
	& 2 Children	600	7.83	0.0131	6.74
		1000	12.34	0.0123	10.64
11	Adult Couple	300	5.10	0.0170	4.01
	& 3 Children	600	8.31	0.0138	7.17
		1000	12.21	0.0122	10.68
12	Adult Couple	300	4.59	0.0153	3.66
	& 4+ Children	600	8.52	0.0142	7.18
		1000	12.76	0.0128	11.08
13	3 Adults	300	4.11	0.0137	3.19
	& No Children	600	8.10	0.0135	6.78
		1000	12.66	0.0127	10.94
14	3 Adults	300	5.16	0.0172	4.24
	& 1 Child	600	8.53	0.0142	7.29
		1000	12.63	0.0126	10.93
15	3 Adults	300	3.66	0.0122	2.72
	& 2+ Children	600	8.43	0.0140	6.64
		1000	13.71	0.0137	11.50
16	4+ Adults	300	4.11	0.0137	4.08
	& No Children	600	8.95	0.0149	7.51
		1000	13.13	0.0131	11.38
17	4+ Adults	300	4.79	0.0160	3.66
	& 1 Child	600	9.40	0.0157	7.71
		1000	14.89	0.0149	12.57
18	4+ Adults	300	5.16	0.0172	4.25
	& 2+ Children	600	8.96	0.0149	7.64
		1000	13.79	0.0138	11.78

Table 5.4: Welfare and Tax Changes: Carbon Tax of 25 Dollars

No.	Household Group	m	EV	EV / m	ΔT
			Non-Smoking Households		
1	65+ Single	300	3.94	0.013	3.48
		600	7.19	0.012	6.38
		1000	11.89	0.012	10.01
2	65+ Couple	300	4.27	0.014	3.78
		600	7.88	0.013	6.96
		1000	12.23	0.012	10.93
3	Single Adult	300	4.11	0.014	3.57
	& No Children	600	7.19	0.012	6.36
		1000	10.80	0.011	9.48
4	Single Adult	300	4.07	0.014	3.58
	& 1 Child	600	7.14	0.012	6.16
		1000	12.15	0.012	9.25
5	Single Adult	300	3.99	0.013	3.59
	& 2 Children	600	7.36	0.012	6.28
		1000	14.99	0.015	10.79
6	Single Adult	300	3.74	0.013	3.28
	& 3 Children	600	7.39	0.012	6.32
		1000	14.46	0.015	11.15
7	Single Adult	300	4.06	0.014	3.59
	& 4+ Children	600	7.07	0.012	6.40
		1000	10.85	0.011	9.38
8	Adult Couple	300	4.44	0.015	3.90
	& No Children	600	8.16	0.014	7.14
		1000	12.21	0.012	10.93
9	Adult Couple	300	4.64	0.016	4.02
	& 1 Child	600	8.19	0.014	7.14
		1000	12.38	0.012	10.75
10	Adult Couple	300	4.69	0.016	4.00
	& 2 Children	600	8.18	0.014	7.12
		1000	12.34	0.012	10.89
11	Adult Couple	300	4.63	0.015	4.07
	& 3 Children	600	8.16	0.014	7.12
		1000	12.22	0.012	10.83
12	Adult Couple	300	4.61	0.015	3.88
	& 4+ Children	600	8.01	0.013	6.96
		1000	12.46	0.013	10.64
13	3 Adults	300	4.49	0.015	3.78
	& No Children	600	8.53	0.014	7.33
		1000	12.98	0.013	11.50
14	3 Adults	300	5.32	0.018	4.35
	& 1 Child	600	8.92	0.015	7.69
		1000	13.05	0.013	11.49
15	3 Adults	300	4.32	0.014	3.56
	& 2+ Children	600	8.42	0.014	7.17
		1000	13.26	0.013	11.31
16	4+ Adults	300	4.51	0.015	3.93
	& No Children	600	8.70	0.015	7.33
		1000	13.15	0.013	11.34
17	4+ Adults	300	4.92	0.016	4.08
	& 1 Child	600	8.83	0.015	7.47
		1000	13.50	0.014	11.42
18	4+ Adults	300	5.91	0.020	4.99
	& 2+ Children	600	9.44	0.016	8.17
		1000	13.72	0.014	11.87

Table 5.5: Welfare and Tax Changes at Mean Weekly Expenditure: Smokers

No.	Household Group	Smoking Households			
		$\bar{m}$	EV	$EV/\bar{m}$	ΔT
1	65+ Single	267	3.14	0.0128	2.86
2	65+ Couple	498	6.71	0.0135	5.67
3	Single Adult & No Children	406	5.15	0.0127	4.32
4	Single Adult and 1 Child	400	4.89	0.0122	4.23
5	Single Adult & 2 Children	428	5.38	0.0126	4.58
6	Single Adult & 3 Children	468	5.66	0.0121	4.83
7	Single Adult & 4+ Children	501	6.11	0.0122	5.02
8	Adult Couple & No Children	690	8.87	0.0129	7.66
9	Adult Couple & 1 Child	668	8.78	0.0131	7.43
10	Adult Couple & 2 Children	707	8.96	0.0127	7.83
11	Adult Couple & 3 Children	805	10.39	0.0129	9.04
12	Adult Couple & 4+ Children	673	9.34	0.0139	7.95
13	3 Adults and No Children	975	12.40	0.0127	10.69
14	3 Adults & 1 Child	898	11.61	0.0129	10.03
15	3 Adults & 2+ Children	826	11.50	0.0139	9.42
16	4+ Adults & No Children	1311	16.12	0.0123	14.25
17	4+ Adults & 1 Child	1110	16.36	0.0147	13.83
18	4+ Adults & 2+ Children	1070	14.60	0.0136	12.47

Table 5.6: Welfare and Tax Changes at Mean Weekly Expenditure: Non-smokers

| No. | Household Group | Non-Smoking Households | | | |
		$\bar{m}$	EV	$EV/\bar{m}$	ΔT
1	65+ Single	274	3.65	0.0133	3.22
2	65+ Couple	540	7.21	0.0133	6.34
3	Single Adult & No Children	437	5.58	0.0128	4.91
4	Single Adult and 1 Child	403	5.12	0.0127	4.50
5	Single Adult & 2 Children	438	5.41	0.0123	4.73
6	Single Adult & 3 Children	475	5.76	0.0121	4.97
7	Single Adult & 4+ Children	539	6.49	0.0120	5.86
8	Adult Couple & No Children	766	9.92	0.0130	8.77
9	Adult Couple & 1 Child	763	9.92	0.0130	8.67
10	Adult Couple & 2 Children	896	11.29	0.0128	10.10
11	Adult Couple & 3 Children	844	10.66	0.0126	9.42
12	Adult Couple & 4+ Children	822	10.51	0.0128	9.05
13	3 Adults and No Children	992	12.90	0.0130	11.42
14	3 Adults & 1 Child	1038	13.41	0.0129	11.83
15	3 Adults & 2+ Children	920	12.35	0.0134	10.52
16	4+ Adults & No Children	1282	16.03	0.0125	13.96
17	4+ Adults & 1 Child	1129	14.96	0.0133	12.62
18	4+ Adults & 2+ Children	925	12.90	0.0140	11.21

These are lower values than are generally thought to apply to income taxes
and for more selective commodity taxes (for example increases in the excise
on petrol, as found in the previous chapter).

5.4   Changes in Inequality

The relationship between EV/m and m was used in the previous section to
provide an indication of the disproportionality of the impact of the carbon
tax. However, this does not reflect information concerning the distribution
of changes, involving the numbers of households at the various total expenditure levels. Furthermore, this measure only allows comparisons between
households in the same demographic group. This section derives a measure
of the redistributive effect of the carbon tax which as a summary measure
permits comparisons across different demographic groups.

The approach follows that used in Part II of this book. The redistributive
effect of the tax change can be examined using the distribution of money
metric utility, m_e, before and after the imposition of the carbon tax. A
suitable money metric is defined as the value of total expenditure which, at
some reference set of prices, would give the same utility as the actual total
expenditure. The effect on welfare can be measured in terms of a change in m_e
from m_{e0} to m_{e1}, where, as before, the indices 0 and 1 refer to pre- and post-
change values respectively. As suggested above, if pre-change prices are used
as reference prices, so that for all households m_{e1} is simply the value of actual
total expenditure after the change less the value of the equivalent variation;
that is, $m_{e1} = m - EV$. Hence the proportionate change, $(m - m_{e1})/m$, is
conveniently the ratio of EV to m.

The inequality measures reported here refer to the inequality of individual
money metric utilities. Each individual in a household is given that household's value of 'wellbeing', $z = m_e/h$, where adult equivalent size is defined
using the two-parameter form discussed in Part II (and in Part V).

Table 5.7: Inequality Measures for Smokers

No.	Household Type	Inequality Measures for Smoking Households		
		Pre-	Post-	%Δ
1	65+ Single	0.1567	0.1572	0.3191
2	65+ Couple	0.1044	0.1047	0.2874
3	Single Adult & No Children	0.1804	0.1806	0.1109
4	Single Adult & 1 Child	0.0876	0.0879	0.3425
5	Single Adult & 2 Children	0.1027	0.1029	0.1947
6	Single Adult & 3 Children	0.1140	0.1142	0.1754
7	Single Adult & 4+ Children	0.0722	0.0721	-0.1385
8	Adult Couple & No Children	0.1285	0.1290	0.3891
9	Adult Couple & 1 Child	0.1237	0.1239	0.1617
10	Adult Couple & 2 Children	0.1072	0.1076	0.3731
11	Adult Couple & 3 Children	0.1656	0.1666	0.6039
12	Adult Couple & 4+ Children	0.1236	0.1241	0.4045
13	3 Adults & No Children	0.1354	0.1359	0.3693
14	3 Adults & 1 Child	0.1284	0.1291	0.5452
15	3 Adults & 2+ children	0.1269	0.1270	0.0788
16	4+ Adults & No Children	0.1120	0.1126	0.5357
17	4+ Adults & 1 Child	0.1120	0.1124	0.3571
18	4+ Adults & 2+ Children	0.1675	0.1680	0.2985
	All Individuals	Pre: 0.1739	Post: 0.1745	%Δ:0.3450

Table 5.8: Inequality Measures for Non-smokers

No.	Household Type	Inequality Measures for Non-Smoking Households		
		Pre-	Post-	%Δ
1	65+ Single	0.1695	0.1701	0.3540
2	65+ Couple	0.1733	0.1739	0.3462
3	Single Adult & No Children	0.1928	0.1936	0.4149
4	Single Adult & 1 Child	0.1310	0.1315	0.3817
5	Single Adult & 2 Children	0.1318	0.1317	-0.0759
6	Single Adult & 3 Children	0.1270	0.1267	-0.2362
7	Single Adult & 4+ Children	0.1162	0.1166	0.3442
8	Adult Couple & No Children	0.1670	0.1677	0.4192
9	Adult Couple & 1 Child	0.1658	0.1665	0.4222
10	Adult Couple & 2 Children	0.1749	0.1757	0.4574
11	Adult Couple & 3 Children	0.1463	0.1470	0.4785
12	Adult Couple & 4+ Children	0.1411	0.1416	0.3544
13	3 Adults & No Children	0.1387	0.1393	0.4326
14	3 Adults & 1 Child	0.1387	0.1396	0.6489
15	3 Adults & 2+ children	0.1474	0.1479	0.3392
16	4+ Adults & No Children	0.1122	0.1127	0.4456
17	4+ Adults & 1 Child	0.2092	0.2100	0.3824
18	4+ Adults & 2+ Children	0.1748	0.1759	0.6293
	All Individuals	Pre: 0.1739	Post: 0.1745	%Δ:0.3450

Tables 5.7 and 5.8 provide the pre- and post-carbon-tax Atkinson measure of inequality for each of the 18 household groups, for smoking and non-smoking households respectively. Although a range of values of ε were used, the results are reported for the relative inequality aversion coefficient of 1.2, which represents substantial aversion to inequality. Despite this, the percentage increases in inequality were small. Indeed some falls in inequality were recorded. The overall redistributive effect of the tax was an increase in inequality of 0.345 per cent. This effect reflects the relative numbers of households in the various demographic groups, as well as the distribution of total expenditure among households.

5.5 Conclusions

This chapter analysed the potential effects on consumer prices in New Zealand arising from the imposition of a carbon tax rate of \$25 per tonne of carbon dioxide. The resulting effects of the price changes on the welfare of a range of household types and total expenditure levels were examined. Finally, the effects on a summary measure of inequality, within each demographic group and over all groups combined, were reported. The price changes were computed using information about inter-industry transactions and the welfare effects were examined using data from pooled Household Economic Surveys. The Linear Expenditure System was used to model the demand responses of consumers, from which the welfare and inequality effects were calculated.

Households with relatively low total expenditure levels were found to spend a proportionately greater amount of their income on carbon-intensive commodities such as petrol and domestic fuel and power. Despite this, the distributional effect of the carbon tax was not unambiguous, in view of the substantial price increases for several commodity groups on which households with relatively higher total expenditure spend proportionately more.

The ambiguity of the distributional effect of the carbon tax was confirmed by the welfare measures which show that for the majority of household types, the relative burden of the carbon tax (the equivalent variation divided by total expenditure) does not vary monotonically with total expenditure; over some ranges it is regressive while for other ranges of total expenditure it was found to be progressive.

The marginal excess burdens arising from the carbon tax were generally small. Even for very high inequality aversion, the carbon tax was found to give rise to a very small redistributive effect. The marginal welfare cost, reflecting the efficiency of the carbon tax, was found to be around 15 cents per dollar of additional tax revenue. These relatively small burdens and distributional effects can therefore be compensated by revenue recycling.

Chapter 6

Minimum Disruption Changes

The aim of this chapter is to examine the nature of the least disruptive changes in the New Zealand economy that are necessary to achieve a target annual rate of reduction in emissions. A reduction in carbon dioxide emissions arising from the production of goods and services can come from three main sources. These involve changes to the structure of final demands, changes to the fuel mix and its efficiency in production, and changes to the structure of inter-industry trading. The extent of the disruption to any variable, say the output of an industry, is measured by its proportional change. The chapter concentrates on changes in final consumer demands and changes in the quantities and mixture of fossil fuels used by industries. A situation in which the target reduction in emissions is achieved by reducing all final demands would imply an increase in aggregate unemployment and a negative growth rate of GDP. For this reason, and in the case of final demand changes, the effects of imposing constraints on GDP and employment growth are examined. These constraints imply that the final demands of some industries need to increase, while other industries decline. These changes are examined using constrained minimisation techniques within an input–output framework, following the methods developed by Proops *et al.* (1993).

The constrained minimisation method does not consider a specified means of reducing emissions, such as a carbon tax. Unlike the previous chapter, it is therefore not directly concerned with determining the economic costs associated with curbing carbon dioxide emissions. Instead the method attempts to find the minimum set of structural changes required in different industries of the economy that would achieve a target level of emissions reduction while maintaining predetermined levels of variables such as GDP growth and employment. In doing so, the method can determine the severity of the required changes.

Section 6.1 presents the input–output approach to modelling carbon dioxide emissions, and the method of allowing for the constrained minimisation of disruptions. The minimum disruption approach is applied to New Zealand in section 6.2, using the data described in the previous chapter. Minimum disruption results for final demands and fuel use are examined. Section 6.3 turns to the question of how minimum disruption changes might in practice be achieved using policy instruments. The relationship between the desired changes and those achieved by a differential carbon tax are considered.

6.1 An Input–Output Approach

This section presents the framework of analysis used to compute minimum disruption changes. The first subsection derives an expression for total carbon dioxide emissions: this was also presented in the previous chapter but is repeated here for convenience. The second subsection derives the minimum disruption changes to final demands necessary to achieve a required rate of reduction in total carbon dioxide emissions, subject to growth and employment constraints. The final subsection examines the changes in the fuel-use coefficients required to achieve a target carbon dioxide emissions reduction.

6.1.1 Total Carbon Dioxide Emissions

Total carbon dioxide emissions were derived in detail in the previous chapter, and are therefore stated more succinctly here. The first stage is to express an industry's gross output in terms of its final demand and intermediate requirements. Let x_{ij} denote the value of output flowing from industry i to industry j, and let y_i denote the value of final demand by consumers for the output of industry i. The value of an industry's gross output, x_i, may therefore be expressed as the sum of the intermediate and final demands:

$$x_i = \sum_j x_{ij} + y_i \qquad (6.1)$$

The direct requirement coefficient, a_{ij}, measures the value of output from industry i directly required to produce \$1 worth of output in industry j. Hence $a_{ij} = x_{ij}/x_i$. Using this to write $x_{ij} = a_{ij}x_i$ and substituting the resulting expression into equation (6.1) gives gross output in matrix terms as:

$$x = Ax + y \qquad (6.2)$$

where x and y denote the n-element vectors of x_i and y_i respectively. Further, let A denote the n by n matrix of the direct requirement coefficients, a_{ij}. Solving equation (6.2), assuming that the system is productive, gives:

$$x = (1 - A)^{-1} y \qquad (6.3)$$

Let F denote the n by k matrix of energy requirements, in PJs, per unit of gross output, for n industries across k fossil fuel types. Let e denote the k-element vector of CO_2 emissions (tonnes of carbon dioxide) per unit of energy (PJ) associated with each of the k fossil fuels. Multiplying the transpose of the e vector by the transpose of the F matrix gives $e'F'$, which contains the carbon dioxide emissions per unit of gross output from each industry. Total carbon dioxide emissions, E, can then be obtained by post-multiplying the row vector by the column vector of gross output, x:

$$\begin{aligned} E &= e'F'x \\ &= \left[e'F' \left(1 - A \right)^{-1} \right] y \qquad (6.4) \end{aligned}$$

The term in square brackets gives the row vector, c', of carbon dioxide intensities:

$$c' = e'F'(1-A)^{-1} \tag{6.5}$$

These results are used in the following subsection to derive expressions for the necessary structural changes to achieve a specified reduction in emissions. Proops *et al.* (1993, pp.11-12) identified three main areas where a change in economic structure might give rise to reductions in carbon dioxide emissions. First, there are changes to final demands, y. Second, there are changes to the efficiency of fuel use, F. Third, changes to the structure of inter-industry trading, A, can be made.

The objective is to minimise the disruption to industries with regard to one of these variables while achieving a specified reduction in emissions. Disruption to any variable, z_i say, in industry i is measured in terms of the proportional change in that variable, $\dot{z}_i$. In specifying an objective function, Proops *et al.* (1993, p.228) adopted a quadratic cost function, but it is useful to consider the more general form given by:

$$D = \frac{1}{\theta}\sum_{i=1}^{n}\dot{z}_i^{\theta} \tag{6.6}$$

For the quadratic case, $\theta = 2$, and the term $1/\theta$ is simply a scaling factor which drops out in differentiation. This objective function assumes that there is an equal social cost associated with a 1 percentage point change in a certain variable, irrespective of the industry. It might be argued that there should be some weighting attached to the different sectors, according to each sector's proportional contribution to the total level of an appropriate variable, such as aggregate employment. However, the method imposes constraints on such variables, so that further weighting is not necessary. Indeed, it can be shown that such further weighting is not possible if the weighting mechanism desired uses the same variable as that already accounted for in the constraint.

6.1.2 Disruptions to Final Demands

Carbon Dioxide Emissions Reduction Target

Consider first the problem of minimising the disruption to final demand. To impose no more than a constraint on the amount of emissions reduction is obviously not a case that should be considered seriously. In particular, the required final demand changes would all be negative. However, this case serves to introduce the basic approach adopted.[1]

Total emissions, when written in algebraic as opposed to matrix form, are equal to $E = \sum_{i=1}^{n} c_i y_i$, so that the proportional change in emissions is:

$$\frac{dE}{E} = \sum_{i=1}^{n} \left(\frac{c_i y_i}{\sum\limits_{i=1}^{n} c_i y_i} \right) \frac{dy_i}{y_i} \tag{6.7}$$

If $R = dE/E$ is the required proportional change in total carbon dioxide emissions, the constraint can be written as:

$$R = \sum_i w_i \dot{y}_i \tag{6.8}$$

where w_i is i's share of emissions, and denotes the proportional change in final demand for industry i. The Lagrangean for this problem is given by:

$$L = \frac{1}{\theta} \sum_{i=1}^{n} \dot{y}_i^{\theta} + \lambda \left[R - \sum_{i=1}^{n} w_i \dot{y}_i \right] \tag{6.9}$$

Differentiation gives the set of first-order conditions:

$$\dot{y}_i = (\lambda w_i)^{1/(\theta-1)} \tag{6.10}$$

Multiplying this equation by w_i, adding over all industries, and solving for λ gives:

$$\lambda = \left[\frac{R}{\sum_i w_i^{\theta/(\theta-1)}} \right]^{(\theta-1)} \tag{6.11}$$

---

[1] Allowing for these factors handles the problem of weighting discussed above, as doing so implicitly attaches weights according to each industry's contribution to the total level of the constraint variable in question.

Substituting this result into the first-order condition gives the solution for the required proportional reduction in output of:

$$\dot{y}_i = R \left[\frac{w_i^{1/(\theta-1)}}{\sum_i w_i^{\theta/(\theta-1)}} \right] \qquad (6.12)$$

This result shows that the larger is θ, the smaller is the dispersion in the required rates of change. Therefore, increasing the power ultimately leads towards an equalisation of the proportional changes. Furthermore, when additional constraints are imposed, the first-order conditions cannot be solved explicitly. For this reason, the quadratic form is retained in this study, and the substitution of $\theta = 2$ gives the result, as in Proops *et al.* (1993, p.144), that:

$$\dot{y}_i = R \left[\frac{w_i}{\sum_i w_i^2} \right] \qquad (6.13)$$

Carbon Dioxide Emissions and GDP Growth Targets

Suppose it is required to impose a constraint on GDP growth in addition to the constraint on the level of carbon dioxide emissions reduction. The rate of growth in GDP, G, can be written as:

$$G = \sum_{i=1}^{n} w_i^Y \dot{y}_i \qquad (6.14)$$

The desired rate of growth is expressed as a weighted sum of the changes in final demands, with each weight being the proportion of that industry's contribution to total GDP, that is:

$$w_i^Y = \frac{y_i}{\sum\limits_{i=1}^{n} y_i} \qquad (6.15)$$

The Lagrangean for this problem is:

$$L = \frac{1}{2} \sum_{i=1}^{n} \dot{y}_i^2 + \lambda \left[R - \sum_{i=1}^{n} w_i \dot{y}_i \right] + \mu \left[G - \sum_{i=1}^{n} w_i^Y \dot{y}_i \right] \qquad (6.16)$$

Differentiating with respect to each of the $\dot{y}_i$ gives rise to the first-order conditions:

$$\frac{\partial L}{\partial \dot{y}_i} = \dot{y}_i - \lambda w_i - \mu w_i^Y = 0 \tag{6.17}$$

along with the two constraints relating to R and G. Using $\dot{y}_i = \lambda w_i + \mu w_i^Y$ from the first-order conditions and substituting into the constraints gives the resulting two simultaneous equations:

$$\begin{bmatrix} R \\ G \end{bmatrix} = \begin{bmatrix} \sum_i w_i^2 & \sum_i w_i w_i^Y \\ \sum_i w_i w_i^Y & \sum_i \left(w_i^Y \right)^2 \end{bmatrix} \begin{bmatrix} \lambda \\ \mu \end{bmatrix} \tag{6.18}$$

If the determinant of the matrix on the right hand side of this equation is written as $\triangle = \sum w_i^2 \sum \left(w_i^Y \right)^2 - (\sum w_i w_i^Y)^2$, the solutions for the Lagrange multipliers λ and μ are:

$$\lambda = \frac{1}{\triangle} \left[R \sum_{i=1}^n \left(w_i^Y \right)^2 - G \sum_{i=1}^n w_i w_i^Y \right] \tag{6.19}$$

and:

$$\mu = \frac{1}{\triangle} \left[-R \sum w_i w_i^Y + G \sum w_i^2 \right] \tag{6.20}$$

Finally, the resulting multipliers can be substituted into the first-order conditions to solve for the $\dot{y}_i$s; see also Proops *et al.* (1993, pp.234-5).[2]

Carbon Dioxide, GDP and Employment Growth Targets

An additional constraint concerns the rate of growth in employment, M. This is expressed as:

$$M = \sum_i w_i^m \dot{y}_i \tag{6.21}$$

where the weights w_i^m are the levels of employment in each industry as a proportion of total employment. Minimising the disruption to final demands subject to all three constraints simultaneously, involves the Lagrangean:

---

[2] If weights equal to the proportional contribution of each industry to total GDP are attached to $\dot{y}_i^2$, the Lagrangean multipliers are not identified. That is, the constraints on the carbon dioxide emission target and the rate of growth of GDP, R and G, become equal to the sums of the Lagrangean multipliers, thus illustrating how additional weighting is not appropriate.

$$L = \frac{1}{2} \sum_{i=1}^{n} \dot{y}_i^2 + \lambda \left[R - \sum_{i=1}^{n} w_i \dot{y}_i \right] + \mu \left[G - \sum_{i=1}^{n} w_i^Y \dot{y}_i \right] + \gamma \left[M - \sum_{i=1}^{n} w_i^m \dot{y}_i \right]$$

(6.22)

In this case there are three Lagrangean multipliers, so that a set of three linear equations can be solved using matrix methods. The procedure is a simple extension of that described above although it involves the inverse of a 3 by 3 matrix: see also Proops *et al.* (1993, pp.238-9).

6.1.3   Disruptions to Fuel-Use Coefficients

As an alternative to reducing outputs, carbon dioxide emissions can also be reduced by the amount of fuel used in production. Thus instead of simply minimising changes to the vector of final demands, consider minimising changes in fuel-use coefficient subject to a carbon dioxide emissions-reduction target. The direct fuel-use coefficients are embodied in the matrix, F. The objective is to minimise:

$$D = \frac{1}{2} \sum_{i=1}^{n} \sum_{j=1}^{K} \dot{f}_{ij}^2$$

(6.23)

where $\dot{f}_{ij}$ represents the proportional change in the production fuel requirement per unit of total demand of fuel j in industry i. The change is minimised subject to the constraint that a target proportional reduction, R_F, in carbon dioxide emissions, attributable to changes in the production fuel-use coefficients, is achieved. Given that total emissions are $E = \sum_{i=1}^{n} \sum_{j=1}^{K} f_{ij} e_j x_i$, differentiation gives:

$$\frac{dE}{E} = \sum_{i=1}^{n} \sum_{j=1}^{K} \frac{f_{ij} e_j x_i}{E} \frac{df_{ij}}{f_{ij}}$$

(6.24)

The target reduction in carbon dioxide emissions can then be expressed as:

$$R_F = \sum_{i=1}^{n} \sum_{j=1}^{k} w_{ij} \dot{f}_{ij}$$

(6.25)

Hence R_F is a weighted row and column sum of the production fuel-use coefficients, with each weight given by $w_{ij} = f_{ij}e_j x_i/E$, which is the proportional contribution to emissions of fuel j in industry i. The Lagrangean is therefore:

$$L = \frac{1}{2} \sum_{i=1}^{n} \sum_{j=1}^{k} \dot{f}_{ij}^2 + \lambda \left[R_F - \sum_{i=1}^{n} \sum_{j=1}^{k} w_{ij} \dot{f}_{ij} \right] \tag{6.26}$$

Following Proops *et al.* (1993, pp.241, 144), solving this yields:

$$\dot{f}_{ij} = \left[\frac{w_{ij}}{\sum_{i=1}^{n} \sum_{j=1}^{k} w_{ij}^2} \right] R_F \tag{6.27}$$

The following sections apply these results to New Zealand, using the data described in the previous chapter.

6.2 Minimum Disruption Calculations

This section applies to New Zealand the minimum disruption approach described above. The first subsection considers final demand changes while the second subsection examines changes in fuel use.

6.2.1 Disruptions to Final Demands

First, the basic results relating to carbon intensities, along with final demands and employment weights for each industry, are reported in Table 6.1. The main results regarding final demand changes are provided in Table 6.2, which gives the annual changes to the elements of the final demand vector, y, which minimise disruptions to final demand while satisfying the constraints described. All values are expressed in percentage terms.

The carbon intensities are measured in terms of the carbon content per dollar of final demand. It is not surprising that Petroleum and Industrial Chemical Manufacturing (IGC Code 18), which demands the greatest quantity of fuel across all industries, recorded by far the highest carbon content of

3.64 tonnes of carbon dioxide per dollar. Rubber, Plastic and Other Chemical Product Manufacturing (IGC Code 19) and Basic Metal Manufacturing (IGC Code 21), which respectively demand the largest quantities of natural gas and coal, record similarly high carbon contents of 1.83 and 1.40 tonnes of carbon dioxide per dollar. The only other industry to record a carbon content in excess of 1, is Electricity Generation and Supply (IGC Code 26), with a value of 1.21.

Carbon Dioxide Emissions Reduction Target

The column of Table 6.2 labelled 'R Only' represents the results of the minimum disruption approach where the only constraint imposed is a 1 percentage point reduction in total carbon dioxide emissions. The changes in final demand required to achieve, for example, a 2 percentage point reduction in emissions are simply double those for the 1 per cent case. With no constraint imposed on growth or employment, all industries are required to reduce their final demand. These annual reductions are proportional to the carbon dioxide emissions shares of each industry, as seen from equation (6.13), which in turn depend on final demands as well as carbon intensities. There is no simple relationship between carbon intensities and required reductions in final demand, as shown in Figure 6.1. The number corresponding to each dot in the figure indicates the Industry Group Classification Code (though it is only possible to show a proportion of these numbers). Nevertheless, the largest required annual rate of reduction in final demand is for Petroleum and Industrial Chemical Manufacturing (IGC Code 18) at -2.141 per cent, followed by Rubber, Plastic and Other Chemical Product Manufacturing (IGC Code 19) at -1.491 per cent and Construction (IGC Code 29) at -1.462 per cent. Basic Metal Manufacturing (IGC Code 21) has the third highest carbon intensity but requires a much smaller reduction in final demand than several industries with lower intensities, because of its low weight. As mentioned earlier, these reductions should not be viewed as realistic values to be pursued, but instead

Table 6.1: Final Demands, Carbon Intensities and Employment Weights

IGC Code	IGC Description	Final Demand	Carbon Intensity	Employment Weight
1	Horticulture and Fruit Growing	896,214	0.96	0.017
2	Livestock and Cropping Farming	213,229	0.40	0.034
3	Dairy Cattle Farming	213,893	0.40	0.017
4	Other Farming	161,922	0.58	0.001
5	Services to Agriculture, Hunting and Trapping	111,614	0.68	0.007
6	Forestry and Logging	1,127,374	0.34	0.005
7	Fishing	173,891	0.68	0.002
8	Mining and Quarrying	367,660	0.41	0.003
9	Oil and Gas Exploration and Extraction	229,624	0.23	0.000
10	Meat and Meat Product Manufacturing	4,150,526	0.41	0.015
11	Dairy Product Manufacturing	4,174,399	0.58	0.006
12	Other Food Manufacturing	3,370,380	0.43	0.015
13	Beverage, Malt and Tobacco Manufacturing	1,171,464	0.31	0.003
14	Textile and Apparel Manufacturing	1,854,639	0.25	0.016
15	Wood Product Manufacturing	877,534	0.39	0.010
16	Paper and Paper Product Manufacturing	1,357,094	0.40	0.006
17	Printing, Publishing and Recorded Media	594,218	0.28	0.015
18	Petroleum and Industrial Chemical Manufacturing	1,069,290	3.64	0.003
19	Rubber, Plastic and Other Chemical Product Manufacturing	1,478,374	1.83	0.011
20	Non-Metallic Mineral Product Manufacturing	144,620	0.66	0.004
21	Basic Metal Manufacturing	671,546	1.40	0.005
22	Structural, Sheet and Fabricated Metal Product Manufacturing	761,224	0.37	0.017
23	Transport Equipment Manufacturing	1,629,210	0.23	0.006
24	Machinery and Equipment Manufacturing	2,805,651	0.29	0.019
25	Furniture and Other Manufacturing	977,413	0.29	0.011
26	Electricity Generation and Supply	1,256,515	1.21	0.005
27	Gas Supply	188,335	0.36	0.001
28	Water Supply	720	0.26	0.001
29	Construction	8,246,331	0.32	0.066
30	Wholesale Trade	7,874,809	0.24	0.049
31	Retail Trade	8,105,204	0.24	0.130
32	Accommodation, Restaurants and Bars	2,859,420	0.26	0.044
33	Road Transport	456,138	0.35	0.017
34	Water and Rail Transport	693,698	0.70	0.005
35	Air Transport, Services to Transport and Storage	3,001,753	0.86	0.019
36	Communication Services	1,706,165	0.07	0.018
37	Finance	1,181,042	0.05	0.022
38	Insurance	1,205,743	0.06	0.004
39	Services to Finance and Insurance	50,149	0.06	0.008
40	Real Estate	3,053,166	0.06	0.012
41	Ownership of Owner-Occupied Dwellings	8,693,724	0.07	0.000
42	Equipment Hire and Investors in Other Property	249,195	0.12	0.000
43	Business Services	1,561,393	0.10	0.090
44	Central Government Administration, Defence, Public Order and Safety Services	5,158,249	0.19	0.044
45	Local Government Administration Services and Civil Defence	2,537,488	0.17	0.014
46	Education	4,272,040	0.10	0.076
47	Health and Community Services	5,793,658	0.15	0.072
48	Cultural and Recreational Services	2,047,472	0.11	0.022
49	Personal and Other Community Services	1,158,033	0.14	0.031

Table 6.2: Minimum Disruption Changes to Final Demands

| IGC Code | R = −0.01 | | | R = −0.02 | | |
	R Only	G = 0.02	G = 0.02 E = 0.02	G = 0.02	G = 0.015 E = 0.015	G = 0.02 E = 0.02
1	-0.472	-1.3425	-0.7122	-2.0309	-1.2052	-1.3886
2	-0.047	0.0077	1.3626	-0.0260	1.3268	1.3320
3	-0.047	0.0096	0.6760	-0.0235	0.6405	0.6460
4	-0.051	-0.0715	-0.0837	-0.1278	-0.1302	-0.1377
5	-0.042	-0.0811	-0.0852	-0.1326	-0.1254	-0.1354
6	-0.208	0.2545	0.1646	0.1615	0.0286	0.0880
7	-0.065	-0.1255	-0.1379	-0.2053	-0.1999	-0.2153
8	-0.083	0.0057	-0.0225	-0.0553	-0.0862	-0.0783
9	-0.029	0.1206	0.1014	0.1291	0.0909	0.1133
10	-0.945	0.0335	-0.2953	-0.6680	-1.0210	-0.9370
11	-1.324	-1.8512	-2.1799	-3.3065	-3.3793	-3.5762
12	-0.795	-0.1136	-0.3781	-0.7392	-1.0026	-0.9553
13	-0.198	0.3569	0.2619	0.2971	0.1437	0.2193
14	-0.258	0.8435	0.6995	0.8596	0.5814	0.7427
15	-0.188	0.0667	0.0015	-0.0580	-0.1373	-0.1106
16	-0.297	0.0728	-0.0344	-0.1320	-0.2563	-0.2196
17	-0.090	0.2337	0.1944	0.2244	0.1471	0.1934
18	-2.141	-9.5474	-9.5919	-13.5292	-12.1604	-13.5655
19	-1.491	-5.8031	-5.8915	-8.3660	-7.5995	-8.4377
20	-0.052	-0.0958	-0.1042	-0.1588	-0.1538	-0.1654
21	-0.516	-1.8257	-1.8692	-2.6676	-2.4431	-2.7028
22	-0.155	0.0981	0.0473	0.0061	-0.0634	-0.0341
23	-0.202	0.8661	0.7338	0.9300	0.6615	0.8218
24	-0.452	0.9610	0.7407	0.8601	0.4837	0.6806
25	-0.153	0.3566	0.2828	0.3301	0.1985	0.2704
26	-0.837	-2.7632	-2.8508	-4.0787	-3.7616	-4.1503
27	-0.037	0.0307	0.0157	0.0105	-0.0099	-0.0017
28	0.000	0.0003	0.0008	0.0003	0.0007	0.0008
29	-1.462	2.1587	1.5212	1.5971	0.5994	1.0789
30	-1.031	3.8996	3.2738	4.0945	2.8520	3.5844
31	-1.086	3.8902	3.3003	4.0416	2.8326	3.5684
32	-0.412	1.2253	1.0166	1.2202	0.8150	1.0526
33	-0.088	0.0819	0.0557	0.0359	-0.0051	0.0159
34	-0.266	-0.5385	-0.5891	-0.8722	-0.8462	-0.9133
35	-1.424	-3.7048	-3.9212	-5.6955	-5.3757	-5.8716
36	-0.063	1.6531	1.5192	2.0168	1.6290	1.9084
37	-0.032	1.2017	1.1154	1.4764	1.2054	1.4074
38	-0.039	1.1942	1.0936	1.4615	1.1779	1.3792
39	-0.002	0.0497	0.0507	0.0608	0.0540	0.0624
40	-0.109	2.9764	2.7226	3.6345	2.9243	3.4269
41	-0.311	8.4695	7.7241	10.3411	8.2982	9.7282
42	-0.016	0.2059	0.1847	0.2448	0.1919	0.2274
43	-0.082	1.3895	1.3170	1.6733	1.3841	1.6218
44	-0.533	3.2718	2.8666	3.6848	2.7687	3.3556
45	-0.241	1.7173	1.5127	1.9634	1.4917	1.7965
46	-0.239	3.7313	3.4180	4.4797	3.5902	4.2290
47	-0.474	4.3032	3.8607	5.0170	3.9066	4.6597
48	-0.121	1.7534	1.5937	2.0983	1.6680	1.9689
49	-0.087	0.9006	0.8229	1.0593	0.8416	0.9982

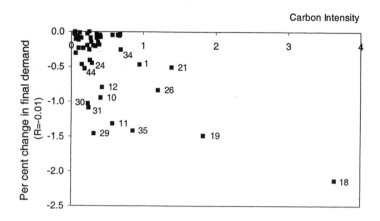

Figure 6.1: Carbon Intensities and Changes in Final Demands with Reductions in Carbon

as benchmarks against which later results may be compared.

Carbon Dioxide Emissions and GDP Growth Targets

Table 6.2 also reports the changes to final demand when 2 per cent growth in GDP is imposed in addition to the 1 percentage point reduction in carbon dioxide emissions. The two constraints exert opposing influences on final demand. The GDP growth constraint prompts increases in final demand, while the carbon dioxide constraint necessitates reductions.

The objective function requires minimising the sum of the square of the proportionate changes in final demand of each industry. To achieve the GDP growth constraint, increasing the final demands of industries which have relatively larger final demands, gives smaller proportionate changes, thereby minimising the objective function. Figure 6.2 clearly shows the positive correlation between the final demand of an industry and its associated required change in final demand. Similarly, in achieving the carbon constraint, industries whose outputs have higher carbon contents achieve greater reductions in emissions for given reductions in final demand.

An industry's required change in final demand is therefore determined by balancing the carbon intensity of its output against the level of final demand. Accordingly, Ownership of Owner-Occupied Dwellings (IGC Code 41), which has the largest final demand coupled with one of the smallest carbon contents is required to achieve the largest increase in final demand of 8.4695 per cent. Similarly, Health and Community Services (IGC Code 47), Wholesale Trade (IGC Code 30), Retail Trade (IGC Code 31) and Education (IGC Code 46) are all required to achieve substantial increases in final demand. All four of these industries may be classified as service industries which produce low carbon dioxide emissions, yet have high levels of final demand. The changes in final demand required by Retail and Wholesale Trade (IGC Codes 30 and 31 respectively) and by Construction (IGC Code 29) contrast substantially with those required in the absence of a growth constraint.

Regarding industries required to reduce their final demand, Petroleum and Industrial Chemical Manufacturing (IGC Code 18) and Rubber, Plastic and Other Chemical Product Manufacturing (IGC Code 19), which have the two highest carbon intensities, require the greatest reductions in final demand of respectively -9.5474 and -5.8031 per cent. These are of course larger than when there is no GDP constraint, to compensate for the positive growth of other industries.

Table 6.2 shows the required changes to final demands when the required aggregate reduction in carbon dioxide emissions is raised from 1 to 2 per cent, holding the GDP growth constraint constant. The addition of a GDP growth target removes the simple relationship between the proportional reductions in carbon dioxide emissions by each industry and the required aggregate percentage reduction in emissions. Variations in the changes to final demand which arise from raising the emissions constraint are displayed in Figure 6.3. If the points were all to lie on the 45 degree line, the higher emissions

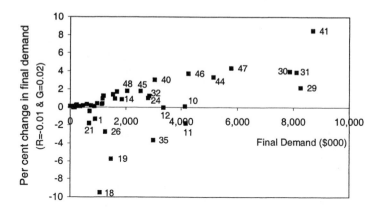

Figure 6.2: Final Demands and Changes in Final Demands with Carbon Dioxide Emissions and GDP Growth Targets

constraint would have no effect. However, as Figure 6.3 shows, the higher constraint requires greater reductions to be achieved in final demand. Consequently, increases in final demand must also be accentuated so as to achieve the growth constraint. These two effects combine to increase the spread of the distribution, thereby increasing the costs of disruption. However, the relative positions of the industries are seen to change only slightly.

Carbon Dioxide Emissions, GDP Growth and Employment Growth Targets

Both employment and GDP growth targets, in addition to the 1 percentage point reduction in carbon dioxide emissions, were used to generate results also shown in Table 6.2. A 2 per cent growth constraint on both GDP and employment was also imposed by Proops *et al.* (1993, p.252) 'so that the growing productivity of labour [could] be taken into account, without needing the labour coefficients to be altered'. As in Figure 6.3, Figure 6.4

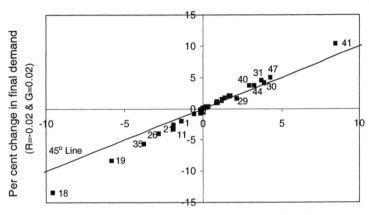

Figure 6.3: Changes in Final Demands and Raising the CO_2 Reduction Target

displays the impact on the required changes to final demands caused by the
employment constraint.

The additional employment constraint is seen to cause very little variation to the required changes in final demand. This should not be surprising
as those industries which have the largest final demands and consequently
employ the greatest proportion of workers also require the largest increases
in final demands to achieve 2 per cent growth in GDP. Furthermore, in
achieving this growth, a certain level of growth in employment is essential.
Consequently, making the employment constraint explicit makes very little
difference to the required changes in final demand.

Shown in the final two columns of Table 6.2, and contrasted in Figure
6.5, are the minimum disruption changes to final demand which arise from
respectively 1.5 and 2 per cent growth targets for GDP and employment,
holding constant a 2 per cent reduction in carbon dioxide emissions. The
higher growth rate of 2 per cent necessitates greater increases in final de-

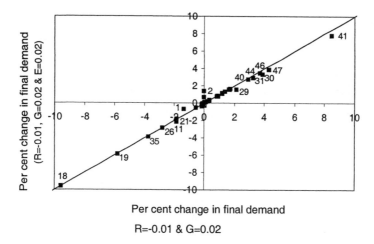

Figure 6.4: Changes in Final Demands and Adding an Employment Growth Target

mands, which are sought from those industries which already required the largest increases in the case of the 1.5 per cent growth rate. The resulting rise in carbon dioxide emissions is countered primarily by Petroleum and Industrial Chemical Manufacturing (IGC Code 18) and Rubber, Plastic and Other Chemical Product Manufacturing (IGC Code 19), which are required to further reduce their final demands by 1.4051 and 0.8382 per cent respectively. These changes at the extremes of the distribution again increase the spread, which leads to further increases in the cost of adjustment.

This result is magnified for the required changes to final demand in the case of 1 and 2 per cent reductions in carbon dioxide emissions, holding constant 2 per cent growth rates in GDP and employment. These are illustrated in Figure 6.6. Achieving the 1 percentage point increase in the reduction in carbon dioxide emissions requires relatively greater changes in final demands than are required to achieve the 0.5 percentage point increase in both growth rates.

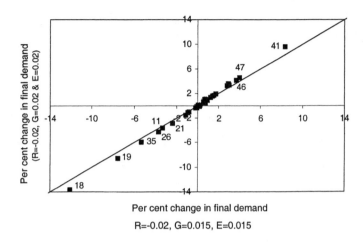

Figure 6.5: Changes in Final Demands and Raising the GDP and Employment Growth Targets

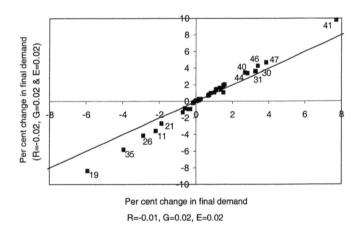

Figure 6.6: Changes in Final Demands and Raising the CO_2 Reduction Target with Growth and Employment Targets

6.2.2 Disruptions to Fuel-Use Coefficients

This subsection examines the annual minimum disruption changes to fuel-use necessary to reduce carbon dioxide emissions by 1 percentage point. The elements of the F matrix, which describe the quantity of fuel required per unit of gross output, vary subject only to the constraint on the reductions in carbon dioxide emissions being achieved. Consequently, the changes given in Tables 6.3 and 6.4 are all non-positive values, which are again expressed in percentage terms. The changes required for a 2 per cent reduction in carbon dioxide emissions are simply double those shown in Table 6.3 and 6.4, and for this reason are not reported.

The largest annual rate of change required is in the use of crude petroleum by Petroleum and Industrial Chemical Manufacturing (IGC Code 18). The only other required change over 1 per cent is in the use of natural gas by Rubber, Plastic and Other Chemical Product Manufacturing (IGC Code 19). All other changes are either zero or negligible, suggesting that achieving a 1 percentage point reduction in carbon dioxide emissions purely through fuel substitution is feasible.

6.3 A Carbon Tax and Minimum Disruption Changes

The above approach has produced changes in final demands for each industry which satisfy a required aggregate reduction in carbon dioxide emissions while minimising the value of a cost function (the sum of squared proportional changes in final demands). The analysis begs the question of how reductions may in practice be achieved in a market system using, for example, a carbon tax. Such a tax, imposed on carbon dioxide emissions, would be expected to give rise to a set of price changes, the extent depending on the carbon intensity of each good. The overall required reduction in carbon dioxide

Table 6.3: Percentage Change in Fuel-Use Coefficients: Part 1

IGC Code	IGC Description	Percentage Changes in the F Matrix			
		Coal	Lignite	Crude Petroleum	Natural Gas
1	Horticulture and fruit growing	0.0000	0.0000	0.0000	0.0000
2	Livestock and cropping farming	0.0000	0.0000	0.0000	0.0000
3	Dairy cattle farming	0.0000	0.0000	0.0000	0.0000
4	Other farming	0.0000	0.0000	0.0000	0.0000
5	Services to agriculture, hunting and trapping	0.0000	0.0000	0.0000	-0.0060
6	Forestry and logging	0.0000	0.0000	0.0000	0.0000
7	Fishing	0.0000	0.0000	0.0000	-0.0100
8	Mining and quarrying	-0.0110	0.0000	0.0000	0.0000
9	Oil & gas exploration & extraction	-0.0070	0.0000	0.0000	0.0000
10	Meat and meat product manufacturing	-0.0530	-0.0080	0.0000	-0.0160
11	Dairy product manufacturing	-0.1350	-0.0200	0.0000	-0.0610
12	Other food manufacturing	-0.0130	-0.0020	0.0000	-0.0360
13	Beverage, malt and tobacco manufacturing	-0.0040	-0.0010	0.0000	-0.0120
14	Textile and apparel manufacturing	-0.0130	-0.0020	0.0000	-0.0130
15	Wood product manufacturing	-0.0070	-0.0010	0.0000	-0.0130
16	Paper & paper product manufacturing	-0.0130	-0.0020	0.0000	-0.0360
17	Printing, publishing & recorded media	-0.0060	-0.0010	0.0000	-0.0160
18	Petroleum and industrial chemical manufacturing	0.0000	0.0000	-2.5730	0.0000
19	Rubber, plastic and other chemical product manufacturing	-0.0070	-0.0010	0.0000	-1.1790
20	Non-metallic mineral product manufacturing	-0.1000	-0.0150	0.0000	-0.0150
21	Basic metal manufacturing	-0.3240	0.0000	0.0000	-0.1090
22	Structural, sheet and fabricated metal product manufacturing	0.0000	0.0000	0.0000	-0.0020
23	Transport equipment manufacturing	-0.0010	0.0000	0.0000	-0.0040
24	Machinery & equipment manufacturing	-0.0010	0.0000	0.0000	-0.0070
25	Furniture and other manufacturing	-0.0020	0.0000	0.0000	-0.0020
26	Electricity generation and supply	-0.1240	0.0000	0.0000	-0.6980
27	Gas supply	-0.0050	0.0000	0.0000	0.0000
28	Water supply	0.0000	0.0000	0.0000	0.0000
29	Construction	0.0000	0.0000	0.0000	-0.0020
30	Wholesale trade	-0.0180	-0.0010	0.0000	-0.0050
31	Retail trade	-0.0220	-0.0010	0.0000	-0.0140
32	Accommodation, restaurants and bars	-0.0010	0.0000	0.0000	-0.0130
33	Road transport	0.0000	0.0000	0.0000	-0.0030
34	Water and rail transport	0.0000	0.0000	0.0000	-0.0040
35	Air transport, services to transport and storage	-0.0010	0.0000	0.0000	-0.0170
36	Communication services	0.0000	0.0000	0.0000	-0.0010
37	Finance	0.0000	0.0000	0.0000	-0.0010
38	Insurance	0.0000	0.0000	0.0000	-0.0010
39	Services to finance and insurance	0.0000	0.0000	0.0000	0.0000
40	Real estate	0.0000	0.0000	0.0000	-0.0020
41	Ownership of owner-occupied dwellings	-0.0010	0.0000	0.0000	-0.0060
42	Equipment hire and investors in other property	0.0000	0.0000	0.0000	0.0000
43	Business services	0.0000	0.0000	0.0000	-0.0010
44	Central government administration, defence, public order and safety services	-0.0120	-0.0010	0.0000	-0.0040
45	Local Government administration services and Civil Defence	-0.0010	0.0000	0.0000	-0.0050
46	Education	-0.0290	-0.0020	0.0000	-0.0070

Table 6.4: Percentage Change in Fuel-Use Coefficients: Part 2

IGC Code	IGC Description	Percentage Changes in the F Matrix				
		LPG	Petrol	Diesel	Fuel Oil	Aviation Fuels & Kerosene
1	Horticulture and fruit growing	0.0000	-0.0870	-0.1610	0.0000	-0.0010
2	Livestock and cropping farming	0.0000	-0.0210	-0.0380	0.0000	0.0000
3	Dairy cattle farming	0.0000	-0.0210	-0.0380	0.0000	0.0000
4	Other farming	0.0000	-0.0160	-0.0290	0.0000	0.0000
5	Services to agriculture, hunting and trapping	0.0000	-0.0110	-0.0720	-0.0070	0.0000
3	Forestry and logging	0.0000	-0.0110	-0.0280	0.0000	0.0000
7	Fishing	0.0000	0.0000	-0.0810	-0.0110	0.0000
3	Mining and quarrying	0.0000	-0.0030	-0.0240	-0.0030	0.0000
3	Oil & gas exploration & extraction	0.0000	-0.0020	-0.0150	-0.0020	0.0000
10	Meat and meat product manufacturing	-0.0060	-0.0070	-0.0020	-0.0030	0.0000
11	Dairy product manufacturing	-0.0010	0.0000	-0.0270	-0.0090	0.0000
12	Other food manufacturing	-0.0080	-0.0250	-0.0160	-0.0140	0.0000
13	Beverage, malt and tobacco manufacturing	-0.0030	-0.0090	-0.0060	-0.0050	0.0000
14	Textile and apparel manufacturing	-0.0010	-0.0020	-0.0090	-0.0070	0.0000
15	Wood product manufacturing	-0.0010	0.0000	-0.0030	-0.0130	0.0000
16	Paper & paper product manufacturing	-0.0020	0.0000	-0.0010	-0.0250	0.0000
17	Printing, publishing & recorded media	-0.0010	0.0000	-0.0010	-0.0110	0.0000
18	Petroleum and industrial chemical manufacturing	0.0000	0.0000	0.0000	0.0000	0.0000
19	Rubber, plastic and other chemical product manufacturing	-0.0030	-0.0020	-0.0440	-0.0110	0.0000
20	Non-metallic mineral product manufacturing	-0.0100	0.0000	-0.0060	-0.0020	0.0000
21	Basic metal manufacturing	-0.0060	0.0000	-0.0030	-0.0420	0.0000
22	Structural, sheet and fabricated metal product manufacturing	-0.0010	-0.0010	-0.0080	-0.0010	0.0000
23	Transport equipment manufacturing	-0.0030	-0.0020	-0.0170	-0.0020	0.0000
24	Machinery & equipment manufacturing	-0.0050	-0.0030	-0.0300	-0.0030	0.0000
25	Furniture and other manufacturing	0.0000	-0.0020	0.0000	0.0000	0.0000
26	Electricity generation and supply	0.0000	-0.0010	-0.0020	0.0000	0.0000
27	Gas supply	0.0000	-0.0020	-0.0120	-0.0020	0.0000
28	Water supply	0.0000	0.0000	-0.0010	0.0000	0.0000
29	Construction	-0.0090	-0.0340	-0.1280	0.0000	-0.0030
30	Wholesale trade	-0.0050	-0.1690	-0.0140	-0.0010	0.0000
31	Retail trade	-0.0060	-0.1940	-0.0140	-0.0010	0.0000
32	Accommodation, restaurants and bars	-0.0060	-0.0120	-0.0030	-0.0100	0.0000
33	Road transport	0.0000	-0.0190	-0.0390	-0.0060	-0.0640
34	Water and rail transport	0.0000	-0.0280	-0.0600	-0.0090	-0.0970
35	Air transport, services to transport and storage	0.0000	-0.1230	-0.2580	-0.0400	-0.4200
36	Communication services	0.0000	-0.0140	-0.0100	0.0000	0.0000
37	Finance	0.0000	-0.0030	0.0000	-0.0010	0.0000
38	Insurance	0.0000	-0.0030	0.0000	-0.0010	0.0000
39	Services to finance and insurance	0.0000	0.0000	0.0000	0.0000	0.0000
40	Real estate	0.0000	-0.0070	0.0000	-0.0020	0.0000
41	Ownership of owner-occupied dwellings	0.0000	-0.0190	0.0000	-0.0060	0.0000
42	Equipment hire and investors in other property	0.0000	-0.0010	0.0000	0.0000	0.0000
43	Business services	0.0000	-0.0030	0.0000	-0.0010	0.0000

emissions would thus be achieved largely by reductions in consumer demands arising from the price changes. The pattern of changes in final demands therefore depends on the carbon intensities, combined with all the own-price and cross-price demand elasticities.

Such a tax is unlikely to produce changes that coincide precisely with minimum disruption changes, even taking the closest case considered above, that is the benchmark situation where no employment or GDP growth constraint is imposed. This is easily seen in the extreme case where the carbon intensity of only one industry is positive. A carbon tax would only raise the price of that industry's output, but would affect the final demands of the other industries depending on the size of the aggregate cross-price demand elasticities. In contrast, the minimum disruption change would involve a reduction in the output of only the polluting industry.

The relationship between the two sets of changes can be examined in more detail as follows. Consider the use of a carbon tax imposed at the rate α, which is expressed as an amount per tonne of carbon dioxide. This is equivalent to an *ad valorem* tax-exclusive indirect tax rate on the output of industry i of $\tau_i = \alpha c_i$, where c_i is the carbon dioxide intensity of the industry's output as defined above. This implies a set of proportional price changes of $\dot{p}_i = \tau_i$. Define η_{ij} as the aggregate demand elasticity of good i with respect to a change in the price of good j. The proportional changes in final demands (remembering that these are measured in terms of expenditures), may be denoted by $\dot{y}_i^C$, and are given by:

$$
\begin{aligned}
\dot{y}_i^C &= \dot{p}_i + \sum_{j=1}^{n} \eta_{ij}\dot{p}_j \\
&= \alpha \left(c_i + \sum_{j=1}^{n} \eta_{ij}c_j \right)
\end{aligned}
\tag{6.28}
$$

If, as before, $w_i = c_i y_i / \sum_{j=1}^{n} c_j y_j$ is the share of carbon dioxide emissions produced by industry i, the carbon tax rate that achieves the desired proportional reduction of R in aggregate emissions is given by solving for α from:

$$R = \sum_{i=1}^{n} w_i \dot{y}_i^C \qquad (6.29)$$

Substituting for $\dot{y}_i^C$ and rearranging gives:

$$\alpha = \frac{R}{\sum_{i=1}^{n} w_i \left(c_i + \sum_{j=1}^{n} \eta_{ij} c_j \right)} \qquad (6.30)$$

Hence the proportional reductions arising from the carbon tax can be expressed as $\dot{y}_i^C = R\delta_i$ where:

$$\delta_i = \frac{\left(c_i + \sum_{j=1}^{n} \eta_{ij} c_j \right)}{\sum_{i=1}^{n} w_i \left(c_i + \sum_{j=1}^{n} \eta_{ij} c_j \right)} \qquad (6.31)$$

By contrast, the minimum disruption changes are given, from above, by $\dot{y}_i^M = R\phi_i$, where:

$$\phi_i = \frac{w_i}{\sum_{i=1}^{n} w_i^2} \qquad (6.32)$$

The two sets of reductions are similar only in the unlikely situation where:

$$w_i \approx c_i + \sum_{j=1}^{n} \eta_{ij} c_j \qquad (6.33)$$

Allowance for GDP growth clearly introduces a role for aggregate income elasticities, further complicating the differences between the sets of final demand changes which achieve equivalent reductions in carbon dioxide emissions.

Nevertheless, there is likely to be a positive correlation between the two sets of changes, given that they are both heavily influenced by the carbon dioxide intensities. The minimum disruption changes are determined by the carbon intensities, modified by the influence of the share terms, w_i; the influence of those intensities is shown in Figure 6.1. The carbon tax changes are

determined by the same intensities, which affect price changes, modified by
the demand elasticities, and some high-intensity goods may have relatively
low elasticities.

However, in principle a differential set of carbon taxes could be used
to ensure that the reductions arising from demand adjustments correspond
precisely to minimum disruption adjustments. Again, where no further constraints are imposed, equating the sets of changes gives the matrix equation:

$$[I + \eta]\,\hat{\alpha}c = \dot{y}^M \tag{6.34}$$

where I is the unit matrix, $\hat{\alpha}$ is a square matrix with the vector of αs along
the leading diagonal, η is a matrix of demand elasticities and c and $\dot{y}^M$ are
column vectors. The vector of required carbon tax rates can then be obtained
from:

$$\hat{\alpha}c = [I + \eta]^{-1}\,\dot{y}^M \tag{6.35}$$

These results could be used to investigate the extent to which carbon tax rates
would need to differ among sectors in order to produce minimum disruption
changes.

6.4   Conclusions

This chapter has examined the nature of the least disruptive changes in the
New Zealand economy that are necessary to achieve a target annual rate of
reduction in carbon dioxide emissions, using a cost function that depends
on the sum of the squares of the proportionate changes in final demands.
The chapter followed the methods first developed by Proops *et al.* (1993),
and concentrates on changes in final consumer demands and changes in the
quantities and mixture of fossil fuels used by industries. A situation in which
target emission levels are achieved by reducing all final demands would imply
an increase in aggregate unemployment and a negative growth rate of GDP.
To overcome this problem, constraints on GDP and employment growth were

imposed, implying that the final demands of some industries need to increase while other industries decline.

The magnitude of an industry's required change in final demand was found to be determined by the relative efficiency with which it could achieve the stated constraints. The carbon intensity of an industry's output was balanced against its employment weight and value of final demand. The small orders of magnitude which resulted from these calculations suggest that reducing carbon dioxide emissions is economically feasible. That is, reductions can be achieved while maintaining acceptable levels of key macroeconomic variables if structural change can be encouraged in the areas indicated by this study. Further employment was found to be essential in achieving the growth constraint. Consequently, the addition of an employment constraint was found to make a negligible difference to the changes in final demand. Raising the magnitudes of the constraints was found to increase the spread of the distribution, thereby increasing the costs of adjustment. An increase in the carbon constraint of 1 percentage point was found to increase this cost more than increasing each of the growth constraints by 0.5 percentage points.

The required changes in the fuel-use coefficients were also small, with only two industries required to reduce specific fuel demands by more than 1 per cent to achieve a 1 per cent reduction in carbon dioxide emissions. Again, this supports the conclusion that such reductions in carbon dioxide emissions are feasible. The chapter also compared the nature of reductions obtained using a carbon tax with minimum disruption changes, and showed that, in principle, the required changes could be achieved using a differential set of carbon taxes.

Part IV

Tax Revenue

Chapter 7

The Revenue Elasticity of NZ Taxes

This chapter turns to the question of how tax revenues can be expected to change over time. It provides estimates for New Zealand of the built-in flexibility, or revenue elasticity, of income and consumption taxes. The latter comprise the Goods and Services Tax and excise taxes. Values at individual and aggregate levels are reported. These are obtained using convenient analytical expressions which have the advantage that they can be evaluated readily from relatively little information about the tax structure, income distribution and budget shares. Furthermore, the main factors affecting the size of the elasticities can be identified using meaningful and easily interpreted decompositions of the revenue elasticities. The approach, involving explicit modelling of the tax structure, contrasts with the use of regression analyses, of time series data on tax revenues and income, which are sometimes used to produce aggregate elasticities. Some comparisons of aggregate income tax revenue elasticities based both on regressions and on tax-share weighted individual values are given in Giorno *et al.* (1995), although they do not include New Zealand.

Detailed official forecasts of tax revenues in New Zealand are frequently made, though for various reasons these do not always involve the explicit calculation of revenue elasticities. Few independent estimates for New Zealand

119

appear to have been published. However, various elasticities are given by van den Noord (2000) for OECD countries, who reports (2000, p.19) elasticities of personal and indirect taxes, with respect to changes in GDP, of 1.2 for both sets of taxes in New Zealand. The value of 1.2 for indirect taxes, which appears to be based on regression analysis, seems unrealistically high, given the values reported in the present chapter.

The neglect of built-in flexibility measures may reflect a perception that, in the presence of lower rates of inflation in recent years, a flattening of the income tax structure and a broad-based consumption tax, fiscal drag is no longer significant. However, as the analysis below shows, the issue is more complex than this simple view would suggest. It is also useful to identify the various influences on the size of New Zealand tax revenue elasticities.

Section 7.1 sets out the relevant conceptual expressions for income and consumption tax revenue elasticities at the individual level. Subsection 7.1.2 provides some estimates based on the 2001 tax structure. Section 7.2 defines aggregate revenue elasticity expressions, with empirical estimates in subsection 7.2.2. These estimates use the standard assumption that all incomes increase by the same proportion from year to year. Subsection 7.2.3 models the more realistic case of non-equiproportional income changes. The computation of aggregate elasticities requires information about the distribution of taxable income. One approach to income tax revenue forecasting is to use a purely numerical approach based on a large sample survey, or preferably longitudinal data on consecutive years, of taxable income. However, the aim of the present chapter is to offer a modelling approach which provides an understanding of the determinants of revenue elasticities, and which requires only limited data which are available to all researchers. It is then possible to examine the sensitivity of, say, income tax revenue elasticities to changes in the dynamic process of income changes from year to year, or the effects on consumption tax revenue elasticities of changes in expenditure patterns.

7.1 Individual Revenue Elasticities

This section examines tax revenue elasticities for individuals. The variation in individual elasticities with income provides a useful independent indication of the local progressivity of the tax structure, and of course the individual elasticities provide the basic components on which aggregate values are based: for further details of elasticity formulae, see Creedy and Gemmell (2002, 2003). The appropriate formulae are given in subsection 7.1.1, and empirical estimates for the 2001 tax structure in New Zealand are reported in subsection 7.1.2.

7.1.1 Elasticity Formulae

Suppose T_{y_i} denotes the income tax paid by individual i with a nominal income of y_i. Changes in nominal income with respect to nominal tax allowances affect built-in flexibility.[1] The revenue elasticity of the income tax with respect to a change in individual income, η_{T_y,y_i}, is defined as:

$$\eta_{T_y,y_i} = \frac{dT(y_i)/dy_i}{T(y_i)/y_i} = \frac{mtr_i}{atr_i} \qquad (7.1)$$

where mtr_i is the marginal tax rate and atr_i is the average tax rate faced by i. Here, the first subscript of the revenue elasticity, η, refers to the type of tax revenue considered (so that in the present case of the individual elasticity, the i subscript on this subscript is dropped for convenience) and the second subscript refers to the income (or tax base) that is considered to change. In a progressive tax structure, $mtr_i > atr_i$ for all i, so that $\eta_{T_y,y_i} > 1$. This elasticity is also a local measure of progressivity: it is the concept of liability progression defined by Musgrave and Thin (1948).

Consider an individual with gross income of y_i and facing a multi-step income tax function, such that if $0 < y_i \leq a_1$, the tax paid is $T_{y_i} = t_0 y_i$; if

---

[1] The exception is where the tax function is homogeneous of degree one in income and allowances, and both are indexed similarly.

$a_1 < y_i \leq a_2$, tax paid is $T_{y_i} = t_0 a_1 + t_1 (y_i - a_1)$; if $a_2 < y_i \leq a_3$, tax paid is $T_{y_i} = t_0 a_1 + t_1 (a_2 - a_1) + t_2 (y_i - a_2) = t_2 y_i - a_1 (t_1 - t_0) - a_2 (t_2 - t_1)$, and so on. Hence if y_i falls into the kth tax bracket, so that $a_k < y_i \leq a_{k+1}$, and $a_0 = 0$, income tax can be expressed for $k \geq 1$ as:

$$
\begin{aligned}
T_{y_i} &= t_k y_i - \sum_{j=1}^{k} a_j (t_j - t_{j-1}) \\
&= t_k (y_i - a_k')
\end{aligned}
\tag{7.2}
$$

where $a_k' = \sum_{j=1}^{k} a_j (t_j - t_{j-1}) / t_k$. Hence the tax paid under a multi-step function is equivalent to that paid with a single-step tax structure having a marginal rate, t_k, imposed on the individual's income in excess of an effective threshold of a_k'.

If there is a range of income-related allowances, for example when there is tax relief for mortgage interest payments or pension contributions, it is necessary to introduce the concept of the income elasticity of effective thresholds, η_{a_k', y_i}. Creedy and Gemmell (2003) show that, for the multi-step tax function, the individual elasticity is:

$$
\eta_{T_y, y_i} = 1 + \left(\frac{a_k'}{y_i - a_k'} \right) \left(1 - \eta_{a_k', y_i} \right)
\tag{7.3}
$$

This result shows that the individual revenue elasticity must exceed unity if $\eta_{a_k', y_i} < 1$. A positive value of η_{a_k', y_i} can be expected. For example, Creedy and Gemmell (2003) found that η_{a_k', y_i} takes values around 0.4 for the UK, but varies significantly over time in response to changes in the tax deductability of various income-related reliefs such as those for families, pensions and mortgages. The value of η_{a_k', y_i} is of course unlikely to exceed unity.

To derive the individual revenue elasticity for consumption taxes, define z_i as individual i's net income, so that:

$$
\begin{aligned}
z_i &= y_i - T_{y_i} \\
&= a_k' t_k + y_i (1 - t_k)
\end{aligned}
\tag{7.4}
$$

Suppose a proportion, γ_i, of z_i is consumed, so that total consumption expenditure, m_i, is $\gamma_i z_i$. In general, γ_i can vary with z_i and hence with y_i, and can exceed unity over some ranges of z_i, as discussed below.

If the tax-exclusive *ad valorem* indirect tax rate imposed on the ℓth good (for $\ell = 1, ..., n$) is v_ℓ, the equivalent tax-inclusive rate is $v'_\ell = v_\ell / (1 + v_\ell)$. Define $w_{i\ell}$ as person i's budget share of the ℓth good. The consumption tax paid by person i on good ℓ can be written as:

$$T_{v_{\ell,n}} = v'_\ell w_{i\ell} m_i = v'_\ell w_{i\ell} \gamma_i z_i \tag{7.5}$$

It is required to obtain the consumption tax revenue elasticity for each good, that is, $\eta_{T_{v_\ell}, y_i}$. Writing $m_{i\ell} = w_{i\ell} m_i$ as expenditure on the ith good, the following relationships are easily obtained:

$$\begin{array}{lll}
m_{i\ell} = w_{i\ell} m_i & \text{implies:} & \eta_{m_{i\ell}, m} = 1 + \eta_{w_{i\ell}, m_i} \\
m_i = \gamma_i z_i & \text{implies:} & \eta_{m_i, z_i} = 1 + \eta_{\gamma_i, z_i} \\
T_{v_{i\ell}} = v'_\ell m_{i\ell} & \text{implies:} & \eta_{T_{v_{i\ell}}, m_{i\ell}} = 1
\end{array} \tag{7.6}$$

Differentiating (7.5) with respect to income, y_i, and using the relationships in (7.6), it can be shown that:

$$\eta_{T_{v_\ell}, y_i} = \left(1 + \eta_{w_{i\ell}, m_i}\right) \left(1 + \eta_{\gamma_i, z_i}\right) \eta_{z_i, y_i} \tag{7.7}$$

where η_{z_i, y_i} is the elasticity of disposable income, z_i, with respect to y_i. Three elasticities appear on the right hand side of (7.7). The first term in parentheses on the right hand side of (7.7) can be expressed in terms of $e_{i\ell}$, the total expenditure elasticity of demand for the ℓth good by person i, since:

$$e_{i\ell} = 1 + \eta_{w_{i\ell}, m_i} \tag{7.8}$$

The last term in (7.7), η_{z_i, y_i}, is the familiar measure of residual progression and can be written as:

$$\eta_{z_i, y_i} = \eta_{(y_i - T_{y_i}), y_i} = \frac{1 - mtr_i}{1 - atr_i} \tag{7.9}$$

Combining (7.7), (7.8) and (7.9) it follows that:

$$\eta_{T_{v_\ell},y_i} = e_{i\ell}\left(1 + \eta_{\gamma_i,z_i}\right)\left(\frac{1 - mtr_i}{1 - atr_i}\right) \tag{7.10}$$

Hence the consumption tax revenue elasticity for good ℓ can be decomposed into three terms, reflecting the total expenditure elasticity for good ℓ, the way in which the proportion of disposable income consumed by i changes with income, and the degree of residual progression determined by individual i's marginal and average income tax rates.

The consumption tax revenue elasticity for all goods combined, for person i, η_{T_v,y_i}, can be obtained directly from the expression for the consumption tax paid on all goods, T_{v_i}. Aggregating (7.5) over n goods gives:

$$\begin{aligned} T_{v_i} &= \sum_{\ell=1}^{n} T_{v_{\ell,n}} \\ &= m_i \sum_{\ell=1}^{n} v'_\ell w_{i\ell} \end{aligned} \tag{7.11}$$

Differentiation of (7.11) therefore reveals that η_{T_v,y_i} is given by:

$$\eta_{T_v,y_i} = \left(1 + \eta_{\gamma_i,z_i}\right)\left(\frac{1 - mtr_i}{1 - atr_i}\right)\left\{\sum_{\ell=1}^{n}\left(\frac{T_{i\ell}}{T_{v_i}}\right)e_{i\ell}\right\} \tag{7.12}$$

The only difference, compared with the revenue elasticity for a single good in (7.10), is that the tax-share weighted expenditure elasticity appears in (7.12). To calculate the weighted elasticity, it is necessary to distinguish only between goods facing different *ad valorem* tax rates.

The elasticity of the consumption proportion with respect to income, η_{γ_i,z_i}, also varies with incomes if saving rates vary across disposable income levels. While a non-proportional relationship is generally accepted for cross-sectional income differences and, to a lesser extent, for time series changes over the short term, changes in the consumption proportion over the long run are probably best regarded as proportional.

The possibility of a non-proportional relationship is modelled by using the specification:

$$m_i = a\,(z_i + b) \tag{7.13}$$

The over-spending at low income levels can be viewed in terms of the existence of transfer payments and consumption out of savings. For this case, it can be shown that $1 + \eta_{\gamma_i, z_i}$ in (7.12) is equal to $z/(z + b)$. Hence for a proportional consumption function (including zero savings, where $a = 1$), $b = 0$, $1 + \eta_{\gamma_i, z_i} = 1$. The elasticity therefore depends on the three terms as follows:

$$\eta_{T_v, y_i} = \left(\frac{z}{z+b}\right)\left(\frac{1 - mtr_i}{1 - atr_i}\right)\left\{\sum_{\ell=1}^{n}\left(\frac{T_{i\ell}}{T_{v_i}}\right)e_{i\ell}\right\} \tag{7.14}$$

The first two bracketed terms of equation (7.14) are less than or equal to unity, but the third component, shown in curly brackets, may exceed unity for some income levels and tax structures. However, η_{T_v, y_i} tends towards unity as income increases. This is because all expenditure elasticities converge towards unity, along with the first two terms in (7.14), although the convergence may not be monotonic.

7.1.2 Estimates of Individual Revenue Elasticities

This subsection shows how individual revenue elasticities can be expected to vary across income levels in New Zealand. The New Zealand income tax structure in 2001 has marginal tax rates of 0.15, 0.21, 0.33 and 0.39 applying above income thresholds of 0, \$9500, \$38000 and \$60000. There is thus no initial tax-free allowance. These are the effective rates and thresholds, allowing for the existence of the Low-Income Rebate. These values are used to calculate effective allowances, a'_k. In New Zealand there are virtually no deductions or allowances. Hence the set of tax thresholds does not change with individuals' incomes, and it is appropriate to set $\eta_{a'_k, y_i} = 0$ in (7.3).

Consumption tax revenue elasticity calculations require estimates of the *ad valorem*-equivalent indirect tax rates. Most goods are taxed at the 12.5

per cent Goods and Services Tax rate. However some expenditures, such as rent and overseas travel, are exempt from GST. Furthermore a number of excise taxes produce very different effective tax rates on goods such as fuel, alcohol and tobacco. The consumption tax rates used are given in chapter 2.

It is necessary to have information about the total expenditure elasticities, at different expenditure levels, of the relevant commodity groups. It is not possible, even if separate income-unit data from budget studies were available, to produce precise individual values since estimates must be based on the cross-sectional variation in budget shares as total expenditure varies.[2] The question therefore arises of the level of disaggregation to be used. The estimates reported here are based on an overall distribution of taxable income and use published budget share data derived from average expenditures for a range of goods and income groups, from the 2000-2001 Household Expenditure Survey (HES); further details of the method used are discussed in Appendix D. These are for all households combined, rather than considering different household types separately; however, the methods could be applied to more disaggregated data, where available.

Finally, consumption function parameters, a and b in (7.13), are required. In view of the considerable difficulty in obtaining reliable information about savings functions, three consumption function cases were examined. These are the no savings case with $a = 1$, $b = 0$, the proportional savings case where $a = 0.95$, $b = 0$, and the non-proportional case with $a = 0.85$, $b = 3000$. The proportional case assumes that 95 per cent of disposable income is spent, while the non-proportional case implies an average propensity to consume of 0.95 at \$30,000, which is a little above the arithmetic mean income level.[3]

---

[2]It must, as always, be acknowledged that the cross-sectional variations may not necessarily reflect the adjustments to total expenditure changes that would take place over time.

[3]The use of a single set of a and b parameters again reflects the high level of aggregation used here, where no attempt is made to distinguish different transfer payments according to household composition.

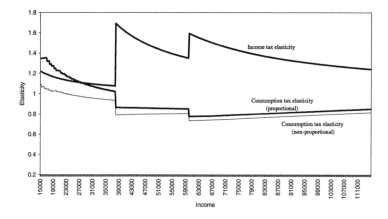

Figure 7.1: Individual Tax Revenue Elasticities

Figure 7.1 shows how the income and consumption tax revenue elasticities
(all goods) vary across income levels. This displays the standard property
whereby the income tax elasticity generally declines as income rises, with
discrete jumps taking place as individuals cross the tax thresholds, reflecting
the sharp increase in the marginal rate of income tax.

For the consumption tax elasticity, two examples of the proportional and
non-proportional cases are shown. As shown in subsection 7.1.1, the shapes
of these profiles reflect the three combined effects of the progressivity of the
income tax, saving habits and differing expenditure elasticities across goods
(combined with their associated *ad valorem* rates). Income tax progressivity
tends to induce a mirror image effect in the consumption tax profile via
changes in disposable incomes. For example, discrete declines are evident
in the consumption tax elasticity profiles in Figure 7.1 at the income tax
thresholds and, at higher income levels, elasticities tend to rise.

However, at lower income levels consumption tax revenue elasticities also
decline, rather than showing a mirror image of the decline in the income

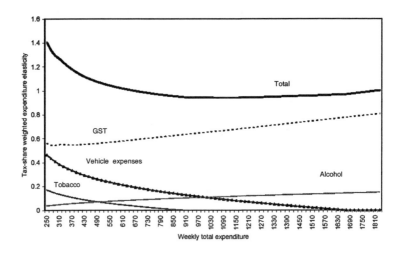

Figure 7.2: Tax-Share Weighted Total Expenditure Elasticities

tax elasticity. This arises because of the dominant effect of declines in the tax-share weighted expenditure elasticities. These elasticities are shown in Figure 7.2, which reveals substantial declines in tax-share weighted expenditure elasticities for vehicles (mainly fuel) and tobacco as incomes increase from relatively low levels. Since these expenditures face especially high tax rates, changes in these tax-share weighted elasticities dominate changes in the weighted average at low income levels. Figure 7.1 also reveals that the elasticities produced by the non-proportional consumption function relationship are generally slightly lower, by about 0.1 to 0.2 percentage points, than the proportional equivalents.

7.2   Aggregate Revenue Elasticities

This section examines aggregate tax revenue elasticities, which are the most relevant from the point of view of tax forecasting and planning, along with possible automatic stabilisation properties of the tax structure. Subsection 7.2.1 presents the basic formulae required and subsection 7.2.2 reports results for New Zealand in the case of equiproportional income changes. The implications of non-equiproportional income changes are examined in subsection 7.2.3.

7.2.1 Elasticity Formulae

Aggregate revenue elasticities can readily be expressed as a tax weighted sum of the individual elasticities. Letting T_Y and Y denote respectively total income tax revenue and total income, the aggregate income tax revenue elasticity is:

$$\eta_{T_Y,Y} = \sum_{i=1}^{N} \left(\frac{T_{y_i}}{T_Y} \right) \eta_{T_y,y_i} \eta_{y_i,Y} \tag{7.15}$$

Evaluation of the aggregate elasticity therefore requires, in addition to information about the income distribution (for computation of the income tax shares T_{y_i}/T_Y), knowledge of the extent to which individuals' incomes change when aggregate income changes, reflected in the term $\eta_{y_i,Y}$, where the condition $\frac{1}{N}\sum_{i=1}^{N}\eta_{y_i,Y} = 1$ must hold. A typical simplifying assumption is that all incomes increase by the same proportion, so that $\eta_{y_i,Y} = 1$ and the aggregate income tax revenue elasticity is a simple tax-share weighted average of individual values.

The aggregate consumption tax elasticity can be calculated, following (7.15), using:

$$\eta_{T_V,Y} = \sum_{i=1}^{N} \left(\frac{T_{v_i}}{T_V} \right) \eta_{T_v,y_i} \eta_{y_i,Y} \tag{7.16}$$

where T_V is aggregate consumption tax revenue. Furthermore, since total revenue is $T = T_Y + T_V$, the elasticity of total revenue with respect to aggregate income can be found as a tax-share weighted average of the income and consumption tax revenue elasticities.

7.2.2   Estimates of Aggregate Revenue Elasticities

This subsection uses the analytical expressions in subsection 7.2.1, along with the assumption of equiproportional income changes, to examine how aggregate revenue elasticities vary with aggregate income levels in New Zealand.

As mentioned above, one approach would be to use detailed information, in the form of a large dataset containing data on individual taxable incomes. Some studies use an entirely numerical approach, by imposing small income increases on each individual in the dataset and examining the resulting tax changes, rather than using explicit formulae such as those given above. However, the method used here (since such individual data are available only to a highly restricted group of users in New Zealand) is to parameterise the distribution, based on grouped income distribution data, and then to produce a simulated distribution of incomes by taking random draws from the fitted distribution.

Appendix D shows the New Zealand grouped income distribution in 2001, and discusses the application of a lognormal distribution to summarise the data.[4] It was found that a mean and variance of the logarithms of incomes of $\mu = 9.85$ and $\sigma^2 = 0.7$ provide a reasonable approximation to parameterise a lognormal income distribution. These values imply an arithmetic mean income of \$26,903: in the lognormal case, the arithmetic mean income is derived as $\bar{y} = \exp\{\mu + \sigma^2/2\}$. Each aggregate revenue elasticity is obtained using a simulated population of 20,000 individuals, drawn at random from the distribution. As the results reported here assume that all incomes increase by the same proportion, the relative dispersion of incomes remains constant

---

[4]In Giorno *et al.* (1995), aggregate income tax revenue elasticities were obtained by fitting lognormal distributions, using information for each country about only the ratios of the first and ninth deciles to the median income. Values of individual elasticities were computed at 16 points on the income distribution. An aggregate elasticity was obtained as the ratio of average (income weighted) marginal rates to that of average (income weighted) average tax rates. The weights were obtained from the first moment distribution of the associated lognormal distribution. Unfortunately the ratio of averages is not equivalent to the average of ratios, which is the required measure.

as incomes change over time. The non-equiproportional case is examined below.

Figure 7.3 shows aggregate elasticity profiles for income and all consumption taxes (for the non-proportional consumption case), and for total tax revenues, as incomes increase over a wide range of average income levels. The 20k values were selected randomly from an initial distribution with a lower mean of logarithms than the 2001 distribution. The average income increase, with a fixed variance of logarithms of income, was achieved by increasing all incomes by a fixed proportion each year. The non-equiproportional case involves a more complex process of income change, as shown below. This wide range, either side of the 2001 average, has been chosen to examine the sensitivity of the elasticities to extremes, even though revenue forecasts over such an effectively long time period are most unlikely to be made on the assumption of fixed thresholds.

A strong feature of these profiles is that the elasticities are relatively stable, despite the wide range of average incomes considered, involving a substantial movement of individuals from the lower income tax ranges to a situation in which a significant proportion of the income distribution faces the highest marginal income tax rate. For the highest average income shown, about one quarter of taxpayers are above the top threshold. The slight tendency of the income tax elasticity to rise and then decline at higher average income levels is associated with this systematic upward movement of individuals through the thresholds as average income increases. The income and consumption tax elasticities are slightly below 1.3 and 0.9 respectively throughout the range. This result for the aggregate income tax revenue elasticity is consistent with the value obtained by Bell (2003), which uses a numerical approach with a very large sample of individual data from tax records, to which equiproportional increases are applied.

Figure 7.4 shows how consumption tax elasticities depend on assumed saving behaviour. Revenue elasticity estimates are noticeably higher for the

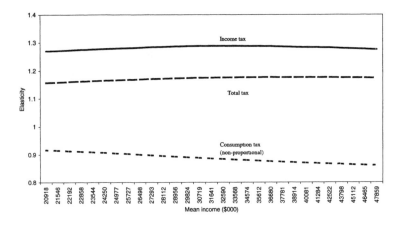

Figure 7.3: Aggregate Tax Revenue Elasticities

proportional consumption and 'no savings' cases (profiles A and B), but decline more rapidly as income rises, compared to the non-proportional case in profile C. For example, at mean income levels of around $30,000, elasticities of about 1.0 and slightly below 0.9 are obtained from profiles A and C respectively. Figure 7.4 also suggests that the effect on the revenue elasticity of ignoring savings is not substantial provided, when income increases, the proportion of income consumed remains approximately constant.

7.2.3   Non-Equiproportional Income Changes

This subsection relaxes the assumption of equiproportional income changes, used in the previous subsection and in the vast majority of studies. In line with the present approach of using parametric specifications at a fairly high level of aggregation, subsection 7.2.3 presents a function to describe the systematic variation in $\eta_{y_i,Y}$ with y_i. Subsection 7.2.3 presents revised aggregate elasticities based on estimates of the dynamic specification.

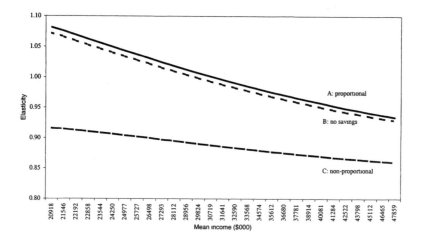

Figure 7.4: Aggregate Consumption Tax Revenue Elasticities

A specification

It is convenient to specify a functional form for the variation in $\eta_{y_i,Y}$ with y_i. A suitable form, involving just one parameter, is:

$$\eta_{y_i,Y} = 1 - (1 - \beta)(\log y_i - \mu) \tag{7.17}$$

where μ is the mean of logarithms of income (the logarithm of geometric mean income).[5] This means that if $\beta < 1$ and y_i is less than geometric mean income, the elasticity, $\eta_{y_i,Y}$, is greater than unity, and *vice versa*, so that (7.17) involves equalising changes. If $\beta > 1$, income changes are disequalising. This specification can thus be used to examine the sensitivity of aggregate revenue elasticity measures to variations in the standard assumption of $\eta_{y_i,Y} = 1$. For non-equiproportional changes, the aggregate revenue elasticity can be less than 1; for example it is zero if the only incomes which increase are below a tax-free threshold and none crosses the threshold.

---

[5] In the case of lognormal income distributions, this is also the median income.

In examining changes in total income arising from non-equiproportional changes, according to equation (7.17), it is also useful, when increasing the 20,000 simulated incomes from one year to the next, to impose random proportional income changes, in addition to the systematic equalising or disequalising tendency reflected in β. Without such changes, annual income inequality changes too rapidly. The specification in (7.17) is consistent with the following dynamic process. Let y_{it} denote individual i's income in period t, and let μ_t denote the mean of logarithms in period t, with $g_t = \exp(\mu_t)$ as the geometric mean. The generating process can be written as:

$$y_{i2} = \left(\frac{y_{i1}}{g_1} \right)^\beta \exp(\mu_2 + u_i) \tag{7.18}$$

where u_i is $N(0, \sigma_u^2)$. Equation (B.1) can be rewritten as:

$$(\log y_{i2} - \mu_2) = \beta(\log y_{i1} - \mu_1) + u_i \tag{7.19}$$

Hence the variance of logarithms of income in period 2, σ_2^2, is given by

$$\sigma_2^2 = \beta^2 \sigma_1^2 + \sigma_u^2 \tag{7.20}$$

The variance of logarithms is therefore constant when $\sigma_u^2 = \sigma_1^2(1 - \beta^2)$. In general, the variance of logarithms of income increases if the regression coefficient, β, exceeds the correlation between log-incomes in the two periods. If $\beta < 1$, the variance of logarithms of incomes eventually becomes stable at $\sigma_u^2/(1 - \beta^2)$. On dynamic income specifications, see Creedy (1985).

Aggregate Elasticities

Estimation of equation (7.19) was carried out for a range of pairs of consecutive years during the 1990s, using information from large samples of IR5 and IR3 filers.[6] The results suggest a relatively stable value of β of around

---

[6]The regressions were kindly carried out by Matthew Bell.

0.85. This reflects a substantial degree of regression towards the (geometric) mean; indeed, with no random component of income change this would have the effect of halving income inequality in as little as three years.[7] If $\beta = 0.85$ is combined with $\sigma_u^2 = 0.194$, the variance of logarithms of income remains constant over time.[8] These values produce an aggregate income tax revenue elasticity, at 2001 mean income, of about 1.11. For the proportional and non-proportional consumption functions respectively, the aggregate consumption tax revenue elasticities are 0.93 and 0.83, giving corresponding total tax revenue elasticities of 1.05 and 1.03 respectively. Again, using a purely numerical approach to income tax elasticities, using a large sample of longitudinal income data, Bell (2003) found a very similar elasticity.

Regression towards the geometric mean therefore reduces the aggregate revenue elasticities. This arises because, for those above the geometric mean income, the value of $\eta_{T_y,y_i}\eta_{y_i,Y}$ is reduced, and *vice versa* for those below the geometric mean. The aggregate elasticity, from (7.15), is a tax-share weighted average of these terms, and in view of the fact that T_{y_i}/T_Y increases as y increases, the lower values of $\eta_{T_y,y_i}\eta_{y_i,Y}$ at the upper income levels dominate.

To give some idea of the sensitivity of results to the variation in β, consider a value of $\beta = 0.9$, which requires $\sigma_u^2 = 0.133$ for a stable degree of income inequality. The aggregate income tax elasticity, again at 2001 mean income, is now 1.17, while the consumption tax elasticities are 0.96 and 0.85 for proportional and non-proportional consumption functions (giving total revenue elasticities of 1.11 and 1.07).

---

[7]The degree of regression is expected to be lower for separate cohorts or age groups. Part of the overall regression reported here arises from the systematic component of change associated with age-earnings profiles.

[8]This value is in fact similar to that estimated for IR3 filers, though the values obtained for IR5 filers were lower, at about 0.1. Given that these samples do not constitute all taxpayers, and in practice inequality is relatively stable, it is appropriate here to model a stable variance of logarithms.

7.3   Conclusions

This chapter has examined the revenue responsiveness properties of New Zealand income and consumption taxes, based on the 2001 tax structure and expenditure patterns. Using analytical expressions for revenue elasticities at the individual and aggregate levels, together with a simulated income distribution, values for New Zealand were obtained. Treating income growth as equiproportional, these suggest that the aggregate income and consumption tax revenue elasticities are both fairly constant as mean income increases, at around 1.3 and 1.0 respectively. This latter estimate assumes that increases in disposable income are accompanied by approximately proportional increases in total expenditure. Allowing for non-equiproportional income growth reduces revenue elasticities to around 1.1 (income tax) and 0.93 (consumption taxes). If there is a tendency for the savings proportion to increase as disposable income increases, a somewhat lower total consumption tax revenue elasticity, of around 0.85 to 0.90, is obtained at mean income levels which approximate current levels in New Zealand. Examination of the tax-share weighted expenditure elasticities for various goods also revealed that, despite the adoption of a broad-based GST at a uniform rate in New Zealand, the persistence of various excises has an important effect on the overall consumption tax revenue elasticity, especially for individuals at relatively low income levels.

Part V

Some Measurement Issues

Chapter 8

Indirect Taxation and Progressivity

The progressivity of indirect taxes is often examined by computing the variation in the amount of tax paid, expressed as a ratio of household expenditure, as household expenditure increases. If this ratio increases over a range of total expenditure levels, the taxes are said to be 'locally tax-progressive'. This accords with the standard idea that a tax is locally progressive if the average tax rate increases as the tax base increases. Typically no demand changes are modelled. Such an approach may be contrasted with the determination of whether indirect taxes are 'locally welfare-progressive', whereby the ratio of a measure of the welfare impact (such as the equivalent variation) to total expenditure rises with total expenditure. The evaluation of such welfare changes requires the use of utility or expenditure functions, as in Parts II and III above.

It would be extremely convenient if the condition under which indirect taxes are tax-progressive were to coincide with that required for welfare-progressivity, in view of the relative ease of obtaining tax-progressivity measures. The aim of this chapter is to investigate whether such agreement necessarily arises when preference heterogeneity is allowed, such that the parameters of utility functions are specified to vary with total expenditure in a way that is consistent with observed variations in budget shares.

In the simplest case of a tax or tax change imposed on a single good, it is locally tax progressive if it is imposed on a luxury good, for which the total expenditure (or 'income') elasticity exceeds unity. As total expenditure rises, the budget share attributed to the luxury good rises and consequently so must the average tax rate. Variations in the degree of tax-progressivity over a range of total expenditure levels depend only on the variation in the budget share of the taxed good. However, the degree of welfare loss depends on, among other things, the compensated price elasticity of demand for the good. Thus welfare-progressivity is not solely dependent on the variation in the budget share of the taxed good, so that the two measures of progressivity can possibly differ.

It is important to clarify the relationship between the two measures of progressivity in view of the widespread use of the tax revenue alone and the emphasis given to tax progression in debates regarding indirect taxation. For example, many exemptions from broad-based taxes are based explicitly on distributional grounds. Furthermore, selective indirect taxes such as excises imposed on tobacco, alcohol and petrol are often thought to be regressive. The implications of environmental taxes, such as a carbon tax, for progressivity are also hotly debated.

Section 8.1 derives the progressivity condition in terms of tax revenue. Section 8.2 examines the case where the parameters of the direct utility function of a demand system are assumed to remain fixed as total expenditure varies. This assumption restricts households to have the same basic preferences. Welfare-progressivity is examined for the Linear Expenditure System (LES), where expressions for the welfare changes are readily obtained, and have been used in earlier chapters of this book. Fixing the parameters of the direct utility functions implies a particular form of variation in the budget shares of each good as total expenditure rises. This implied variation is shown in section 8.3. A more general form of variation in budget shares has been found to be useful in Parts II and III above. The imposition of this leads the parameters of the direct utility function to vary with total expenditure, allowing for heterogeneous preferences among households and therefore more realistic analysis. Section 8.4 uses data obtained from New Zealand's Household Economic Surveys (HES) to provide empirical examples of cases where the directions of tax and welfare disproportionality conflict for the case of a tax imposed on a single good and New Zealand's indirect tax structure as a whole.

8.1 Tax Revenue and Progressivity

The Musgrave–Thin (1948) measure of local liability progression (that is, progression at a particular level of total expenditure) is the elasticity of tax paid with respect to total expenditure, η.[1] This section shows how this measure depends on total expenditure elasticities. Let m denote a household's total expenditure and $w_i = p_i x_i / \sum_{i=1}^{n} p_i x_i$ the budget share devoted to the ith good, with p_i and x_i the price and quantity demanded of the good respectively. If t_i is the tax-inclusive *ad valorem* tax rate on the ith good, total indirect tax revenue is:

$$T = m \sum_{i=1}^{n} t_i w_i \qquad (8.1)$$

Letting $\dot{w}_i = \frac{dw_i}{dm} \frac{m}{w_i}$ denote the elasticity of the budget share with respect to total expenditure, differentiation of (F.1) gives:

$$\eta = 1 + \sum_{i=1}^{n} \left(\frac{t_i w_i}{\sum_i t_i w_i} \right) \dot{w}_i \qquad (8.2)$$

The total expenditure elasticity, the proportional increase in consumption as a ratio of the proportional increase in total expenditure, is given by $e_i = 1 + \dot{w}_i$. Letting $\varphi_i = t_i w_i / \sum_i t_i w_i$ denote the proportion of tax revenue

---

[1]As discussed in chapter 7, it is equivalent to the ratio of the marginal to the average tax rate, and is also equal to the built-in flexibility of the tax structure at the particular total expenditure level.

resulting from good i, equation (F.2) becomes:

$$\eta = 1 + \sum_{i=1}^{n} \varphi_i \left(e_i - 1\right) \tag{8.3}$$

Hence a progressive system, for which the elasticity η must be greater than unity, generally requires luxuries to be taxed more heavily than necessities, although this need not be the case for every good, depending on its tax share. If taxation is imposed on only one good, say good k, then (8.3) simplifies to $\eta = e_k$ and the Musgrave–Thin local progressivity measure is given by the total expenditure elasticity alone. Hence the determination of whether a tax structure is 'tax progressive' over any particular range of total expenditure is quite straightforward, and requires information only about the variation in budget shares with total expenditure.

8.2   Welfare Changes with Fixed Parameters

This section examines welfare-progressivity for the case where the parameters of the utility function are fixed, thereby imposing homogeneous preferences on all households. The analysis proceeds by imposing a tax on a single commodity. The equivalent variation, EV, resulting from the tax is derived. Then the expression for EV/m is differentiated with respect to total expenditure, m, while holding the parameters of the direct utility function constant. Welfare-progressivity requires the derivative to be strictly positive.

As discussed in earlier chapters and in Appendix C, the Linear Expenditure System has direct utility functions of the form:[2]

$$U = \prod_{i=1}^{n} (x_i - \gamma_i)^{\beta_i} \tag{8.4}$$

where γ_i is the minimum necessary level of consumption, or 'committed consumption', so that $x_i > \gamma_i$. The parameters β_i are constrained such that

---

[2]For details of the LES see, for example, Brown and Deaton (1973), Powell (1974) and Creedy (1998a, b). Muellbauer (1974) used the fixed parameter LES to examine the distributional effects of inflation in the UK.

$0\beta_i 1$ and $\sum_{i=1}^{n} \beta_i = 1$. Define $C = \sum_{i=1}^{n} p_i \gamma_i$ as total committed expenditure. The demand functions are found to be:

$$x_i = \gamma_i + \frac{\beta_i}{p_i} \left(m - \sum_j p_j \gamma_j \right) \tag{8.5}$$

Differentiating with respect to total expenditure gives $dx_i/dm = \beta_i/p_i$, so that the total expenditure elasticity, e_i, is given by:

$$e_i = \frac{\beta_i}{w_i} \tag{8.6}$$

It can be shown that when prices change from p^0 to p^1, the equivalent variation is:

$$EV = m - C^0 \left[1 + \frac{B^0}{B^1} \left(\frac{m}{C^0} - \frac{C^1}{C^0} \right) \right] \tag{8.7}$$

This can be simplified as follows. If $\dot{p}_i$ denotes the proportionate change in the price of the good, then $C^1/C^0 = 1 + \sum_{i=1}^{n} s_i \dot{p}_i$ where $s_i = (p_i^0 \gamma_i) / \sum_{i=1}^{n} p_i^0 \gamma_i$. The term B^1/B^0 simplifies to:

$$B^1/B^0 = \prod_{i=1}^{n} \left(p_i^1/p_i^0 \right)^{\beta_i} = \prod_{i=1}^{n} (1 + \dot{p}_i)^{\beta_i} \tag{8.8}$$

Consider imposing a tax on good k only, giving rise to a proportionate change in the price of the good, $\dot{p}_k$, with $\dot{p}_i = 0$ for all other goods. The term C^1/C^0 simplifies to $C^1/C^0 = 1 + s_k \dot{p}_k$ and B^1/B^0 becomes $(1 + \dot{p}_k)^{\beta_k}$. Let $c_k = p_k^0 \gamma_k$ denote the initial level of committed expenditure on good k. Hence the equivalent variation as a proportion of total expenditure is:

$$\frac{EV}{m} = 1 - \frac{C^0}{m} - (1 + \dot{p}_k)^{-\beta_k} \left(1 - \frac{C^0}{m} - \frac{c_k}{m} \dot{p}_k \right) \tag{8.9}$$

Differentiating equation (8.9) with respect to total expenditure, while holding the parameters of the direct utility function, β_k and γ_k constant, using the result from equation (8.6) that $\beta_i = e_i w_i$, and simplifying (as explained in Appendix E) gives the familiar condition that welfare-progressivity requires $e_k > 1$. This is the same condition required for local tax-progressivity.

8.3   Welfare Changes with Variable Parameters

The above analysis has held the parameters of the direct utility functions constant while considering the variation in the equivalent variation with total expenditure. It is possible to show that other demand systems produce the convenient result that tax-progressivity and welfare-progressivity require the same simple elasticity condition; the Almost Ideal Demand System (AIDS) is examined in Appendix F. However, the assumption of fixed parameters (independent of total expenditure) is unlikely to be satisfied. This section therefore shows how the specification of the demand model can be modified to allow for preference heterogeneity, and considers the implications for welfare-progressivity.

8.3.1   Budget Shares

It is useful to explore the implied relationship between the budget share attributed to each good and the level of total expenditure. It has been seen that $\beta_i = e_i w_i$, and combining this with the fact that in general, as mentioned in section 8.2, e_i is linked to the elasticity of the budget share with respect to total expenditure, whereby $e_i = 1 + \dot{w}_i$, gives:

$$\beta_i = w_i \left(1 + \dot{w} \right) = w_i + m \frac{dw_i}{dm} \tag{8.10}$$

so that:

$$\beta_i = \frac{d \left(m w_i \right)}{dm} \tag{8.11}$$

The solution to this differential equation is:

$$m w_i = m \beta_i + d_i \tag{8.12}$$

where d_i is a constant of integration. The budget share is therefore related to total expenditure according to:

$$w_i = \beta_i + \frac{d_i}{m} \tag{8.13}$$

However, more general forms have often been used in empirical studies of the variation in budget shares with total expenditure. For example, the form used in previous sections has been found to provide a good fit to a wide variety of data, and is the following:

$$w_i = \delta_{1i} + \delta_{2i} \log m + \frac{\delta_{3i}}{m} \qquad (8.14)$$

The parameters, δ_{1i}, δ_{2i} and δ_{3i} can be estimated by regressing budget shares for good i, obtained from sample surveys, on total expenditure levels. The adding up condition, $\sum_i w_i = 1$ is automatically satisfied by ordinary least squares estimates of each budget share equation, estimated separately. Using this specification, the total expenditure elasticity for good i, using $e_i = 1 + \dot{w}_i$, is:

$$e_i = \frac{(\delta_{1i} + \delta_{2i}(1 + \log m))}{(\delta_{1i} + \delta_{2i} \log m + \frac{\delta_{3i}}{m})} \qquad (8.15)$$

This more general budget share relationship leads the parameters, β_i, of the LES to be functions of total expenditure, m, which in turn allows for heterogeneous preferences among households. Thus:

$$\beta_i = \delta_{1i} + \delta_{2i}(1 + \log m) \qquad (8.16)$$

Using the results in Appendix E, the parameter γ_i can also be expressed as a function of total expenditure, although it is somewhat less simple than for β_1. The consequence of this modification for welfare-progressivity is explored in the following subsection.

8.3.2 The Modified Linear Expenditure System

It has been seen that in the LES, the parameter, β_i, can be expressed as a function of m by substituting the above expression for e_i into $\beta_i = e_i w_i$. Using this result to replace β_i in the expression for EV/m in equation (8.4), differentiating and then simplifying, leads the required condition for welfare-progressivity to become:

$$\delta_{2k} < \frac{\xi(e_k - 1)}{\dot{p}_k(\xi + e_k)} \qquad (8.17)$$

where ξ is the Frisch parameter, defined as the elasticity of marginal utility of total expenditure with respect to total expenditure; see Frisch (1959). For necessities, the constraint $|\xi| > 1$ ensures total committed expenditure on each good is non-negative, whereas for luxuries it is required to have $|\xi| > e_k$. For details of the derivation, see Appendix E.

Identifying good k as a luxury good is no longer sufficient to establish welfare-progressivity. Similarly, taxing a necessity is not sufficient to ensure welfare-regressivity. It is not surprising that the condition depends crucially on the parameter, δ_{2k}, as this is the additional parameter introduced into the LES budget share relationship, compared with the fixed parameter case. Setting this parameter to zero leads to the condition derived for the fixed parameter case, namely that $e_k > 1$. The condition shown in equation (8.17) is explored below in further detail for necessities and luxuries in turn.

8.3.3   The Conditions for Welfare Progressivity

Inspection of the condition in (8.17) shows that welfare-progressivity requires δ_{2k} to be negative. For luxury goods, for which $e_k > 1$, the condition $\delta_{2k} < 0$ is also sufficient for (8.17) always to hold. However, for necessities, for which $e_k > 1$, the condition in (8.17) can be satisfied only if δ_{2k} is negative and sufficiently large in absolute size. Conversely, where $e_k < 1$ (8.17) is not satisfied for any positive δ_{2k}, so that $\delta_{2k} > 0$ is sufficient for welfare-regressivity. For luxuries δ_{2k} must be positive and sufficiently large to satisfy (8.17).

These conditions are illustrated in Figure 8.1, which plots the relationship $\delta_{2k} = \frac{\xi}{\bar{p}_k} \frac{(e_k-1)}{(\xi+e_k)}$ in a graph with δ_{2k} on the vertical axis and e_k on the horizontal axis. Any point lying above this line indicates that the tax imposed on good k is welfare-regressive, while any point lying below the line indicates welfare-progressivity. This line is contrasted against the dotted line positioned at $e_k = 1$ which determines the tax-disproportionality of the indirect tax. There

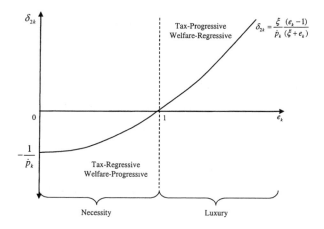

Figure 8.1: Tax- and Welfare-Disproportionality in the Extended LES

are therefore two areas in which tax- and welfare-disproportionality can conflict.[3]

The conditions in this subsection have been expressed in terms of the total expenditure elasticity of the good, e_k, so that a direct comparison with the simple condition for tax-progressivity can be made. However, e_k depends on total expenditure, m, and the parameters, $\delta_{1k}, \delta_{2k}, \delta_{3k}$, of the budget share relationship, so it may be argued that a more complete expression would establish the precise ranges of total expenditure over which tax-progressivity and welfare-progressivity simultaneously arise. This is cumbersome analytically, although, as shown in the following section, ranges can be obtained numerically using the above conditions.

8.4 Empirical Examples

This section provides empirical examples of such cases where tax-progressivity and welfare-progressivity conflict, using New Zealand data. The first subsec-

---

[3]Raising the tax rate imposed on the good shifts the curve upward, while lowering the degree of convexity. The curve continues to pass through the point (1,0).

tion considers the case of imposing a tax on a single good, while the second subsection compares the progressivity measures for the indirect tax system as a whole.

The measure of equivalent variation in the extended LES is computed using data collected from households who participated in the 1995, 1996, 1997, 1998 and 2001 Household Economic Surveys (HES). As discussed in Part I, the weekly total expenditure data were adjusted to 2001 prices using the consumer price index (CPI). There were very few changes in indirect tax rates over this period. The surveys were then pooled to form one large database, providing approximately 13,500 households. Each household was placed into one of 18 demographic groups, shown in chapter 2, which were further sub-divided into smoking and non-smoking households. A positive weekly expenditure on tobacco was sufficient for a household to be designated as a smoking household. The division into smoking and non-smoking households was found to improve substantially the fit of the estimated budget share relationships. The budget shares were regressed on total expenditure levels for 22 commodity groups in turn; these are listed in chapter 2, which also shows the existing effective indirect taxes in New Zealand. Thus, a total of 792 ($= 22 \times 18 \times 2$) regressions were performed. The following results were obtained using a value of $\xi = -2$.[4]

8.4.1   A Single Tax

First, a tax increase (on top of existing taxes) of 10 per cent was imposed on each commodity group in turn, and the conditions were examined for a range of total expenditure levels; these were allowed to vary in $1 increments from $200 to $1500 per week. The conditions for tax- and welfare-progressivity were found to conflict in a total of 250 cases. Table 8.1 provides the num-

---

[4]Tulpule and Powell (1978) used a value of ξ=-1.82 when calculating elasticities at average income for Australia, based on the work of Williams (1978), and this value was adopted by Dixon *et al.* (1982) in calibrating a general equilibrium model. The slightly higher absolute value was used here to avoid some negative committed expenditures.

ber of conflicts which arose for each commodity group. The majority of conflicts occur where the tax revenue indicated local tax-regressivity, but the equivalent variation indicated welfare-progressivity. In these cases, the revenue collected from the tax as a fraction of total expenditure is falling, while the welfare loss from the tax as a fraction of total expenditure is rising. Intuitively, this may arise where the greater ability of households with higher total expenditure (in view of their larger supernumerary income) to substitute away from the good whose price has increased means that, despite the relatively smaller tax increase, the greater distortion to choices involves higher welfare losses.

Tables 8.2 and 8.3 provide further details of the demographic groups and the ranges of total expenditure over which conflicts occurred. As it is not possible to show all cases, only those where the range of total expenditure exceeded $2 are provided in the two tables. It is clear from these results that the possibility of conflicts between tax and welfare measures of local progressivity is far from negligible.

8.4.2 The Indirect Tax System

Having analysed the case of a single tax increase, the question arises as to whether a conflict between the direction of tax and welfare disproportionality could arise when considering a large number of indirect taxes combined, such as the effective current structure of indirect taxes in New Zealand.

It was found that a variety of situations exist where tax revenues from the current indirect tax structure indicate tax-regressivity, while the welfare losses from the taxes indicate progressivity. Figures 8.2 to 8.4 provide examples of this occurrence for three demographic groups. In each case, the current structure of indirect taxes, taken together, is tax-regressive over all ranges of total expenditure, but is welfare-progressive over higher ranges. Reliance on tax revenue alone thus gives an incomplete indication of progressivity.

Table 8.1: Conflicting Movements in Tax and Welfare Measures

Commodity Group	Overall	Tax-Regressive Welfare- Progressive	Tax-Progressive Welfare- Regressive
Rent	27	26	1
Other Expenditure	24	21	3
Vehicle Supplies etc	24	23	1
Household Equipment	23	19	4
Petrol	22	19	3
Services	21	9	12
Medical, Cosmetic etc	20	16	4
Alcohol	12	9	3
Public Transport in NZ	12	9	3
Food Outside Home	12	12	0
Household Services	11	6	5
Pay to Local Authorities	10	0	10
Furnishings	6	5	1
Food	5	4	1
Cigarettes and Tobacco	4	4	0
Children's Clothing	4	3	1
House Maintenance	4	1	3
Overseas Travel	3	0	3
Adult Clothing	3	1	2
Vehicle Purchase	2	1	1
Domestic Fuel and Power	1	0	1
Recreational Vehicles	0	0	0
Total	250	188	62

Table 8.2: Cases of Tax-Regressivity and Welfare-Progressivity

		Expenditure Range m		
	Rent			
S	Single Adult & 1 Child	376	-	381
	Single Adult & 2 Children	369	-	373
	Single Adult & 3 Children	413	-	420
	4+ Adults & No Children	1084	-	1089
	4+ Adults & 2+ Children	697	-	700
NS	Single Adult & 1 Child	285	-	288
	Single Adult & 2 Children	332	-	336
	Single Adult & 3 Children	247	-	250
	Single Adult & 4+ Children	441	-	448
	Other Expenditure			
S	Adult Couple and 3 Children	985	-	988
	3 Adults & No Children	831	-	834
	3 Adults and 2+ Children	1052	-	1055
NS	Adult Couple and 2 Children	947	-	951
	Adult Couple and 3 Children	1238	-	1242
	3 Adults & No Children	1094	-	1098
	3 Adults and 2+ Children	1175	-	1180
	4+ Adults & No Children	1011	-	1015
	Services			
S	3 Adults & No Children	981	-	986
NS	65+ Single	907	-	913
	Adult Couple and 2 Children	931	-	937
	3 Adults & 1 Child	1116	-	1124
	3 Adults and 2+ Children	1425	-	1435
	Food			
NS	Adult Couple $ 4+ Children	256	-	259
	4+ Adults & 2+ Children	293	-	296
	Food Outside Home			
NS	3 Adults & No Children	1441	-	1444

Table 8.3: Cases of Tax-Progressivity and Welfare-Regressivity

	Expenditure Range, m		
Food			
Single Adult & 4+ Children	698	-	704
Services			
4+ Adults & No Children	706	-	709
4+ Adults & 2+ Children	965	-	969
Rent			
Single Adult & 4+ Children	939	-	947

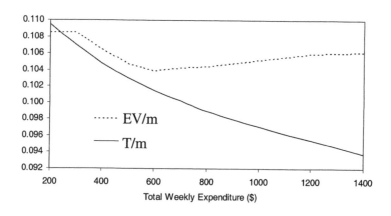

Figure 8.2: Tax-Disproportionality: 65+ Single Adults (Non-smoking)

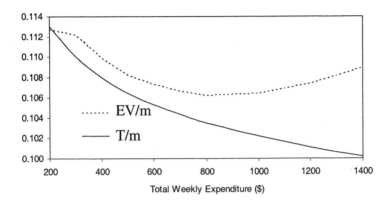

Figure 8.3: Disproportionality of Tax System: Single Adult, No Children (Non-smoking)

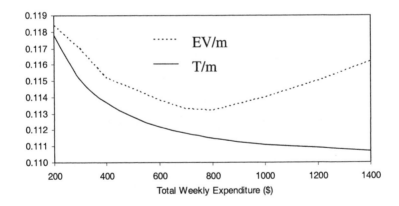

Figure 8.4: Disproportionality of Tax System: Adult Couple, One Child (Non-smoking)

8.5   Conclusions

This chapter has considered the disproportional effects of indirect taxation using two alternative measures, tax-progressivity and welfare-progressivity. In the context of an indirect tax imposed on a single good, welfare-progressivity requires the welfare loss from the tax as a fraction of total expenditure to rise with total expenditure. When the parameters of the direct utility function are held constant over all levels of total expenditure, it was shown that for the LES, the condition for welfare-progressivity is the same as that required for tax-progressivity, namely that the taxed good is a luxury. However, this constancy (or preference homogeneity) implies a particular pattern for the variation in budget shares with total expenditure, which is different for each demand system.

When parameters are allowed to vary, using a general budget share relationship applied to both models, enabling heterogeneous preferences amongst households, it was found that tax- and welfare-progressivity can conflict. (The AIDS demand system is examined in Appendix F.) The empirical application of these conditions to New Zealand data showed that many such cases can arise. Furthermore, conflicting results were obtained when examining the disproportionality of the effective indirect tax structure in New Zealand (allowing for GST and excise taxes). The majority of conflicts were found to arise where tax-regressivity existed at the same time as welfare-progressivity. The results show the importance of allowing for heterogeneous preferences in welfare analysis and further suggest that care should be taken when judging the effects of indirect taxes on the basis of tax revenue alone.

Chapter 9

The Income Unit and Income Concept

When examining the effects on inequality of indirect tax changes, in Parts II and III above, it was necessary to use adult equivalence scales and to decide on the unit of analysis, having chosen to use a money metric measure of household welfare. This chapter examines these aspects of inequality measurement, which arise essentially because populations consist of heterogeneous income units, in further detail. In practice the homogeneity required by inequality and poverty measures is achieved by forming, in the words of Ebert (1997, p.235), 'an (artificial) income distribution for a fictitious population'. The adjustment of household incomes (or money metric welfare measure) using an adult equivalence scale provides a measure of living standard that is comparable across households with differing compositions. The fictitious population is formed by defining a unit of analysis or income recipient, for whom the living standard applies. This chapter examines the sensitivity of several inequality and poverty measures to the choice of the adult equivalence scale and the unit of analysis.

Earlier empirical studies, using parametric equivalence scales and the individual as the unit of analysis, were carried out using UK data by Coulter *et al.* (1992), Banks and Johnson (1994) and Jenkins and Cowell (1994), who found a U or reverse-J shaped relationship between inequality and a parameter measuring economies of scale within households. The present chapter finds similar variations using New Zealand data and, in addition, considers alternative income units, drawing on discussions by Glewwe (1991), Decoster and Ooghe (2002) and Shorrocks (2004). Furthermore, this chapter provides further general analytical insights into the nature of the variations, by considering the relevant joint distributions in some detail. The finding that inequality and poverty can move in opposite directions is also clarified.

A further aim of the chapter is to examine the role of equivalence scales and the unit of analysis in the context of the reranking that arises from direct taxation, when moving from pre-tax to post-tax incomes. Some reranking in terms of unadjusted incomes is a deliberate aim of policy, but in terms of adult equivalent incomes any reranking opposes the vertical redistributive effect of a progressive tax structure. A reranking-minimising set of scales is identified.

The following analysis uses the convenient parametric scales introduced by Cutler and Katz (1992). A final aim of the present chapter is to investigate how well this specification approximates a wide range of equivalence scales. The use of parametric scales facilitates sensitivity analyses. Investigators typically report results for a very small range of equivalence scales, though these can actually have more influence on the conclusions than the inequality or poverty measures used. In considering alternatives it should of course always be borne in mind that, as Cowell and Mercader-Prats (1999, p. 423) state, 'it is fanciful to suppose that equivalence scales can be constructed without the introduction of fundamental value judgements'.

The chapter is arranged as follows. Section 9.1 defines the two-parameter functional form of the adult equivalence scale that is used to conduct the empirical analysis, and examines the use of the equivalent adult and the individual as alternative units of analysis. Earlier theoretical literature on these issues is also briefly discussed. Section 9.2 presents empirical comparisons of inequality for New Zealand for a variety of demographic groups. Analytical results are obtained concerning the effects on the correlation between living standards and household sizes of households' economies of scale in consumption, and the effect on measured inequality of the weight attached to children relative to adults.

Section 9.3 considers poverty measures, and examines the simultaneous increase in poverty and reduction in inequality that is found to occur when the economies of scale parameter is raised. Section 9.4 examines the effects of alternative equivalence scales and income units on the degree of reranking observed when comparing pre-tax and post-tax distributions. The extent of the reranking is strongly affected by the adult equivalence scales used. This section also reports reranking-minimising parameters which, following van de Ven and Creedy (2005), may be regarded as approximating those scales that are implicit in the tax structure.

Section 9.5 examines a wide range of equivalence scales designed for New Zealand, the United Kingdom, Australia and the OECD. To provide comparable estimates of parameters, the two-parameter equivalence scale function is fitted to the various scales used, and the results are applied to the New Zealand data. It is not the aim of this chapter to compare results with recent studies of inequality and poverty in New Zealand in recent years. Each of the studies uses a limited range of equivalence scales whereas the present chapter emphasises the importance of considering a wider range so that readers can view results using alternative value judgements rather than a set which is implicitly introduced by the investigator.

9.1 Alternative Concepts and Measures

This section describes the parametric equivalence scales, along with the inequality and poverty measures used in later sections. Subsection 9.1.1 defines the functional form of the equivalence scale; this form was used in Parts II and III above. This function, while essentially pragmatic, is highly flexible and depends on only two easily interpreted parameters. Subsection 9.1.2 compares the use of alternative units of analysis, and reviews the difficulty arising from the fact that for heterogeneous populations the basic equity principle involved in the 'principle of transfers' is inconsistent with an alternative principle of 'Pareto indifference' or anonymity.

9.1.1   Adult Equivalence Scales

Let y_i denote the income of the ith household, for $i = 1, ..., N$. The number of individuals in the household is n_i, while the household's demographic structure is denoted by the vector d_i, which provides the number of individuals in various demographic groups based on age and gender classifications. Using these definitions, the adult equivalent size of household may be expressed as:

$$m_i = m\left(n_i, d_i\right) \tag{9.1}$$

This size is normalised so that $m\left(n = 1, d = \text{adult}\right) = 1$. Household income is adjusted to obtain the equivalent income or 'living standard', defined by:

$$z_i = \frac{y_i}{m_i} \tag{9.2}$$

A household consisting of one adult with an income of y is therefore judged to have the same 'living standard' as an n-person household with an income of $ym\left(n, d\right)$. Further progress requires the form of $m\left(n_i, d_i\right)$ to be specified. The following analysis uses a flexible form, which distinguishes between the number of adults, $n_{a,i}$, and children, $n_{c,i}$, such that:

$$m_i = \left(n_{a,i} + \theta n_{c,i}\right)^\alpha \tag{9.3}$$

The parameter, θ, measures the size of children relative to adults, while α reflects economies of scale in consumption. This is an extension of the simple form, n_i^α, used by Buhmann *et al.* (1988) and Coulter *et al.* (1992), modified by Cutler and Katz (1992), and used by, for example, Banks and Johnson

(1994) and Jenkins and Cowell (1994). However, this extended form has not yet been widely adopted in empirical work so that its relation to other scales warrants further attention; section 9.5 below shows that it provides a good approximation to a wide range of scales.

9.1.2 Units of Analysis

In earlier empirical studies, it was not uncommon to use z_i as the living standard and simply to treat the income unit as the household. That is, no weights were used in computing inequality and poverty measures. However, recent work has demonstrated that the use of the household in combination with adult equivalent income has no welfare rationale, in terms of satisfying some basic value judgements. One approach to defining a unit of analysis, proposed by Ebert (1997), is to use the 'adult equivalent person'. This approach assigns to each of the adult equivalent persons in household i, an equivalent income of z_i. The income concept and the unit of analysis are treated consistently, ensuring that each individual's contribution to inequality and poverty depends on the demographic structure of the household to which they belong. An adult in a one-person household for example 'counts for one', whereas the same adult in a multi-adult household counts for 'less than one'.

An important feature of this approach is that it satisfies the basic equity principle, associated with the principle of transfers, which provides that a transfer of income from a poorer to a relatively richer household, that leaves the position of the richer household unchanged, causes inequality to rise. The fulfilment of this 'principle of transfers' enables Lorenz and Generalised Lorenz curve analyses to be conducted from the resulting distribution.

An alternative approach is to treat the individual as the basic unit of analysis. This approach assigns the adult equivalent income, z_i, of household i to each of the individuals. The value judgement inherent in this approach is that every person 'counts for one' irrespective of the demographic nature of the household to which they belong. This approach consequently has the property of anonymity, in that inequality and poverty measures remain unchanged when one individual in the population is replaced by another individual who has the same living standard but belongs to a different demographically structured household. This value judgement was called the 'compensation principle' by Shorrocks (2004) and the 'Pareto indifference principle' by Decoster and Ooghe (2002).

The individual unit of analysis does not in general satisfy the equity principle of transfers. As shown by Glewwe (1991, p.213) and Decoster and Ooghe (2002, pp.3-4), a transfer of income from a poor to a relatively rich (and larger) household may actually reduce inequality and raise social welfare. The presence of economies of scale causes a large household to be regarded as being 'more efficient' at generating welfare. An important implication is that in the context of heterogeneous populations, the basic equity principle inherent in the principle of transfers and the concept of Lorenz dominance (whereby one Lorenz curve lies unambiguously closer to the diagonal of equality) are no longer equivalent. This equivalence is a fundamental component of welfare analysis for homogeneous populations. Consequently, the choice between individuals and adult equivalents as the basic unit of analysis involves a choice between two incompatible value judgements. They can in principle lead to opposite conclusions about the effects on inequality of a tax policy change. Examples of such conflicts using tax microsimulation models are given by Decoster and Ooghe (2002) and Creedy and Scutella (2004).

9.2   Inequality Analysis for New Zealand

This section analyses the sensitivity of New Zealand's inequality and poverty measures to the equivalence scale parameters θ and α, and to the chosen unit of analysis. The analysis is conducted using data on the weekly expenditure levels of households, as opposed to incomes. The use of expenditure data may be thought to eliminate to some extent the effects of short term variations in income; on the use of expenditure rather than income data, see Blundell and Preston (1994, 1997) and Attanasio and Japelli (1997). The dataset is in fact the same as that used earlier. From the Household Economic Survey, household expenditure data for the years 1995, 1996, 1997, 1998 and 2001, were adjusted to 2001 prices using the Consumer Price Index (CPI). Surveys have been conducted only tri-annually since 1998. The surveys were then pooled to form one large database containing the weekly total expenditure level of each household along with information about the household's structure. This provided just over 13,500 households for analysis.

9.2.1 Inequality Measures

A range of inequality measures was examined, but similar results were obtained for all measures, so only those for the Atkinson inequality measure are reported here. Figures 9.1 and 9.2 show, for the two income units respectively, inequality plotted against the economies of scale parameter, α, for four values of the weight attached to children parameter, θ. These are 0.2, 0.4, 0.6 and 0.8. The lowest schedule in each diagram (the solid line) corresponds to the smallest value of θ, while the top schedule corresponds to the highest value of θ. The degree of constant relative inequality aversion used is 0.6. Although inequality increases as the degree of inequality aversion is raised, the general pattern remains unchanged.

These results replicate for New Zealand data the result, first shown using UK data, of Coulter *et al.* (1992), who found that increasing the value of α has two opposing effects on measures of inequality. The first is the concentration effect whereby α is inversely related to inequality. As the value of α is increased from low values, economies of scale are reduced and as a result equivalent income falls proportionately more for relatively larger households.

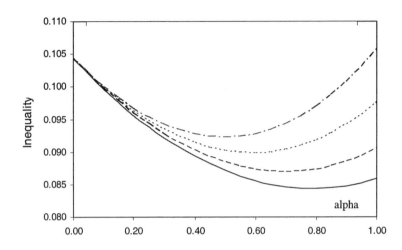

Figure 9.1: Inequality Sensitivity: Individuals

It is known that income and total expenditure are both positively correlated with household size. This implies that relatively richer households incur proportionately greater falls in equivalent income. The rise in α therefore has an equalising effect. Over low values of α, Figures 9.1 and 9.2 display the inverse relationship produced by the concentration effect.

However, over higher values of α, inequality is seen to rise with α, producing a U-shaped inequality profile. The proportionately larger fall in equivalent income for the larger households, as α increases from an already high value, eventually leads to the kind of reranking effect identified by Coulter *et al.* (1992), whereby the rank order of households (when ranked by equivalent income) changes. The examples show that over higher values of α, the reranking effect dominates the concentration effect, thereby causing inequality to rise. As observed by Jenkins and Cowell (1994), the reranking effect increases with the weight that is attached to children, θ, and hence the inequality profiles for higher values of θ show much greater curvature.

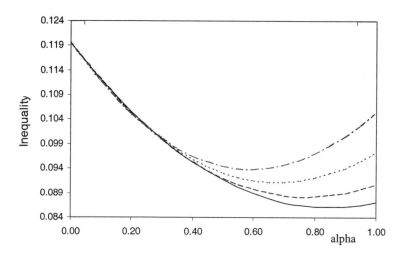

Figure 9.2: Inequality Sensitivity: Equivalent Adults

9.2.2 The Joint Distribution of z_i and n_i

The reranking discussed by Jenkins and Cowell can also be examined in terms of the covariance between z and n, if the income per equivalent adult is given by the simple form, $z_i = y_i/n_i^\theta$. Suppose that income and the number of persons in the income unit are jointly log-normally distributed as:

$$\Lambda\left(y_i, n_i\right) = \Lambda\left(y_i, n_i \mid \mu_y, \mu_n, \sigma_y^2, \sigma_n^2, \rho_{y,n}\right) \qquad (9.4)$$

First, for any lognormal distribution $\Lambda\left(x \mid \mu, \sigma^2\right)$, the following properties hold:

$$E\left(x\right) = \exp\left(\mu + \sigma^2/2\right) \qquad (9.5)$$

and:

$$x^\alpha \text{ is } \Lambda\left(x^\alpha \mid \alpha\mu, \alpha^2\sigma^2\right) \qquad (9.6)$$

For two variables jointly distributed as $\Lambda\left(x, y \mid \mu_x, \mu_y, \sigma_x^2, \sigma_y^2, \rho_{x,y}\right)$:

$$\frac{x}{y} \text{ is } \Lambda\left(\frac{x}{y} \,\middle|\, \mu_x - \mu_y, \sigma_x^2 + \sigma_y^2 - 2\rho_{x,y}\sigma_x\sigma_y\right) \qquad (9.7)$$

The covariance between z_i and n_i is by definition:

$$\mathrm{Cov}\,(zn) = E\left(\frac{y}{n^{\theta-1}}\right) - E\left(\frac{y}{n^\theta}\right)E\,(n) \tag{9.8}$$

Hence, using (9.6), (9.7) and (9.5) the average adult equivalent income is given by:

$$E\left(\frac{y}{n^\theta}\right) = \exp\left\{\mu_y - \theta\mu_n + \frac{1}{2}\left(\sigma_y^2 + \sigma_n^2 - 2\rho_{y,n}\theta\sigma_y\sigma_n\right)\right\} \tag{9.9}$$

A similar result holds for $E\left(y/n^{\theta-1}\right)$. It can be shown, after some manipulation, that $\mathrm{Cov}(zn)$ takes the form:

$$\mathrm{Cov}\,(zn) = (\exp A)\,(\exp B - 1) \tag{9.10}$$

where:

$$A = \mu_y + (\theta - 1)\,\mu_n + \frac{1}{2}\left\{\sigma_y^2 + \left(1+\theta^2\right)\sigma_n^2 - 2\rho_{y,n}\theta\sigma_y\sigma_n\right\} \tag{9.11}$$

and:

$$B = \rho_{y,n}\sigma_y\sigma_n - \theta\sigma_n^2 \tag{9.12}$$

Thus the covariance is positive if $\exp B - 1 > 0$, or if $B > 0$. Hence there is a positive correlation between adult equivalent income and the number of adults if:

$$\rho_{y,n}\frac{\sigma_y}{\sigma_n} > \theta \tag{9.13}$$

This condition is therefore simply interpreted in terms of the size of the regression coefficient in the linear regression relationship between logarithms of n and y. It is therefore precisely the elasticity condition mentioned by Coulter *et al.* (1992).

However, instead of using the simple form, $z_i = y_i/n_i^\theta$, the present empirical analysis also allows for variations in the weight attached to children, θ. Figure 9.3 shows the correlation coefficient, ρ, between z_i and n_i as α varies, for four values of θ, where the unit of analysis is the individual. The four values of θ are again 0.2, 0.4, 0.6 and 0.8; however, in this case the lowest

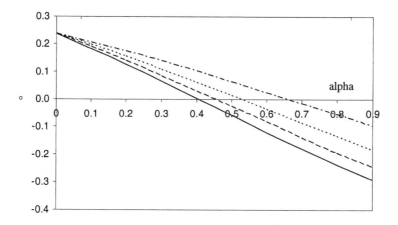

Figure 9.3: Correlation Between Equivalent Income and Household Size

(solid) line in the diagram corresponds to the highest value of $\theta = 0.8$, while the top line corresponds to $\theta = 0.2$. The correlation is initially positive, but falls as economies of scale are reduced and eventually becomes negative. Furthermore, the correlation falls faster for higher values of the parameter θ. This in turn causes the correlation to turn negative (introducing reranking) earlier, so that the profile of inequality turns up earlier (that is, for lower values of α) for higher values of θ. This is reflected in Figures 9.1 and 9.2.

The correlation also affects comparisons between the inequality profiles for different income units. For any given household, $m_i \leq n_i$, which leads the equivalent adult unit to give proportionately more weight to smaller households when compared with the individual unit. As α rises and the correlation between z_i and n_i falls, smaller households enjoy increasingly larger equivalent incomes relative to larger households. Consequently, as α rises, inequality measures based on the equivalent adult unit fall relative to those based on the individual unit. This is seen in Figure 9.4, which shows

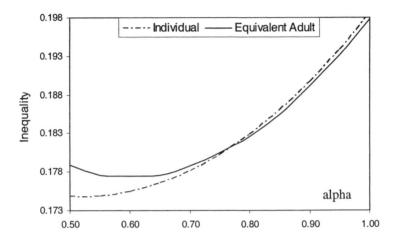

Figure 9.4: Inequality Measures: Theta = 0.8

the inequality measures for the equivalent adult and individual units in the case of a high inequality aversion coefficient of 1.2 when the weight attached to children is $\theta = 0.8$.

9.2.3   The Weight Attached to Children

Another finding from the sensitivity analysis is that, for all values of α and for a given unit of analysis, inequality is positively related to the weight attached to children, θ. This result is independent of inequality aversion and the unit of analysis. The feature was suggested by Banks and Johnson (1994), but Jenkins and Cowell (1994, pp. 892-893) argued that the relationship need not necessarily be monotonic, although it 'may be difficult to characterise precisely from theoretical analysis alone'. However, some insight may be obtained as follows. The adult equivalent size of a household may be written, where for convenience subscripts for the household have been omitted, as:

$$m = s^{\alpha} \tag{9.14}$$

where:

$$s = n_a + \theta n_c \qquad (9.15)$$

Assuming that the number of adults and the number of children are independent of each other, the variance of s is described by:

$$\sigma_s^2 = \sigma_{n_a}^2 + \theta \sigma_{n_c}^2 \qquad (9.16)$$

Hence σ_s^2 rises with θ. Taking logs of equation (9.14) gives $\log m = \alpha \log s$ and the variance of $\log m$ is thus:

$$\sigma_{\log m}^2 = \alpha^2 \sigma_{\log s}^2 \qquad (9.17)$$

Movements in σ_s^2 and $\sigma_{\log s}^2$ are monotonic, so the rise in σ_s^2 and hence in $\sigma_{\log s}^2$ as a result of an increase in θ leads $\sigma_{\log s}^2$ to increase. It is then necessary to consider the effect of such an increase on the dispersion of equivalent income, given by $z = y/m$. Taking logs gives $\log z = \log y - \log m$. The variance of logarithms of equivalent income is therefore:

$$\sigma_{\log z}^2 = \sigma_{\log y}^2 + \sigma_{\log m}^2 - 2cov_{\log s, \log m} \qquad (9.18)$$

Hence the dispersion, measured by the variance of logarithms of equivalent income, $\sigma_{\log z}^2$, rises with $\sigma_{\log m}^2$, which has been seen to rise with θ. But the covariance term is also affected positively by θ. Hence, although a positive effect has been found using the present data, it is possible in principle, over some range of parameter values, for the dispersion of equivalent income to fall as the weight attached to children increases.

9.3 Poverty Measures

This section considers the sensitivity of alternative poverty measures to the parameters of the adult equivalence scale. Results are reported here for two measures of poverty, although a wider range was considered. The poverty line beneath which individuals are judged to be in poverty is denoted z_p. The first measure, P_0, is the widely used headcount measure of poverty, which counts the proportion of individuals below the poverty line. The second measure, P_1, is equal to P_0 multiplied by $1 - \bar{z}_p/z_p$, where $\bar{z}_p$ is the average income of those below the poverty line. Hence P_1 depends on the average depth of poverty as well as the number of individuals below the poverty line. These are the first two measures in the class of poverty measures introduced by Foster *et al.* (1984).

Variations in the poverty measures are displayed in Figures 9.5 and 9.6, which show poverty against α (the economies of scale parameter) for four values of θ (the weight attached to children), again of 0.2, 0.4, 0.6 and 0.8. In these diagrams, as in the inequality diagrams, the lowest schedule is for the lowest value of θ. Figure 9.5 uses the individual as the unit of analysis, while Figure 9.6 uses the child as the unit of analysis; this unit was chosen in view of the interest in child poverty. A crucial role is obviously played by the choice of poverty line, again involving a value judgement. However, after experimenting with a range of poverty lines it was found that the type of variation in the measures found here does not depend on the precise poverty line. Results are therefore reported here, for each poverty measure and unit of analysis, for just one poverty line: in terms of equivalent expenditure, this is equal to \$195 per week. Clearly, poverty rises as a greater weight is attached to children and as the poverty line is increased.

The figures show that poverty strictly rises with α. This is a feature of the present data, as the relationship is not necessarily monotonic. Jointly considering the behaviour of the inequality and poverty measures, it may appear strange that inequality can fall at the same time as poverty rises, which is observed over low values of α. However, the two measures reflect separate effects on the distribution of equivalent income of changes in the scale parameter. Changes in poverty are dominated by shifts in the distribution of equivalent income, while inequality changes are dominated by changes in its dispersion. When α is increased over low values, the concentration ef-

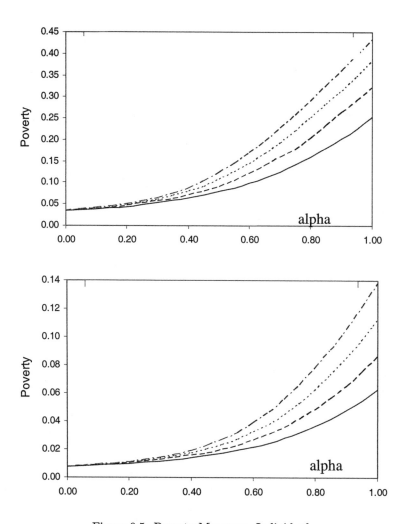

Figure 9.5: Poverty Measures: Individual

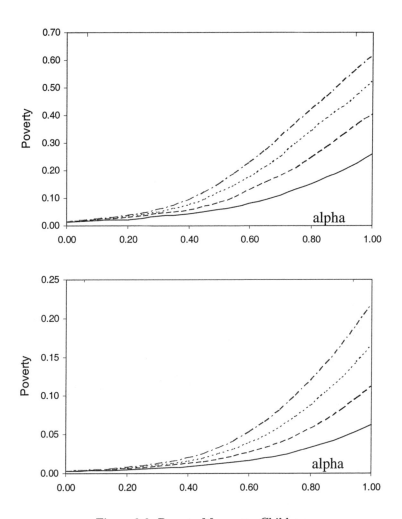

Figure 9.6: Poverty Measures: Children

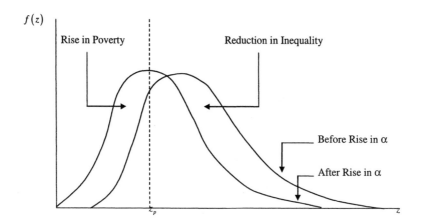

Figure 9.7: Increasing Alpha Over Low Ranges

fect causes the distribution of equivalent income to become less skewed as inequality falls. At the same time poverty rises, as a greater area of the distribution falls below the poverty line. The behaviour of the distribution of equivalent income over low values α of is shown in Figure 9.7.

Once reranking (associated with the negative correlation between equivalent income and household size, discussed above) takes effect, increases in α cause inequality to rise, and the distribution of equivalent income becomes increasingly skewed. Again, poverty rises as the distribution continues to shift to the left. Figure 9.8 shows how the distribution of equivalent income changes as α is increased over higher values.

It is also of interest to consider whether poverty is higher when the child, as opposed to the individual, is used as the unit of analysis. Much attention is indeed given to child poverty in public debates. From the diagrams above, it is clear that poverty is indeed higher over the higher ranges of α, where there is a negative correlation between the equivalent income and the household size. Therefore larger households, those with more children, are likely to

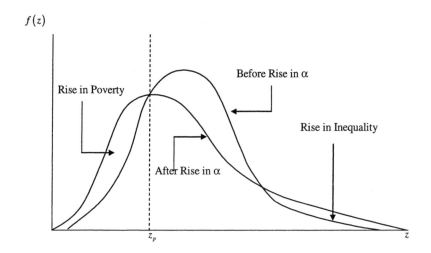

Figure 9.8: Increasing Alpha Over High Ranges

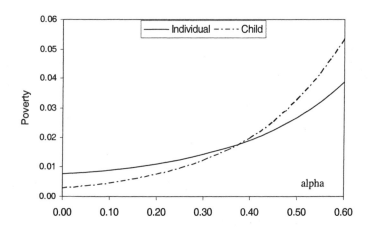

Figure 9.9: Poverty Measures P1: Poverty Line $= 195$ and Theta $= 0.8$

have lower equivalent incomes over the relevant range. A focus on children as the population group thus places relatively more units below any given poverty line. However, for lower values of α it has been seen above that there is a positive correlation between equivalent income and household size. Hence it is possible for poverty to be lower when the focus is on children only, compared with the use of all individuals. This is illustrated in Figure 9.9, which provides the P_1 poverty measure for both the individual and child units of analysis based on a poverty line of \$195 where the weight attached to children is $\theta = 0.8$. The child unit of analysis produces lower measures of poverty over low levels of α, but then increases at a greater rate as α is raised.

9.4 Equivalence Scales and Direct Taxation

This section turns from expenditure to income, and considers the role of equivalence scales and the unit of analysis in the context of the effects of direct taxation. One effect of taxation is to cause a change in the rankings of households when moving from the pre-tax to the post-tax income distribution. This type of reranking is quite different from that discussed earlier, which was interpreted in terms of a negative correlation between equivalent income and household size. The reranking of unadjusted incomes – that is, total household income without any adjustment for size and composition – is of course a deliberate aim of the tax system. This is because the size and composition of households are considered as relevant non-income characteristics. Value judgements about the desirable redistribution arising from taxes and transfers are closely linked with such differences. In considering the tax treatment of those considered to be pre-tax 'equals', the equivalence scales determine the meaning attached to 'equality'. Reranking in terms of equivalent incomes cannot be expected to be zero, given that some reranking can also arise as the result of government policy that is not directly related to equity objectives. For example, unemployment benefits may be designed to encourage labour market participation, or certain types of income may be treated differently on efficiency grounds.

The reranking of equivalent incomes opposes the vertical redistributive effect of taxation, since an additional dispersion of pre-tax equals is introduced. It is therefore of interest to consider how it varies with the choice of adult equivalence scale. Following Atkinson (1979) and Plotnick (1981), reranking is defined as:

$$R = G_y - C_y \qquad (9.19)$$

where G_y is the Gini inequality measure of post-tax income, and C_y is the concentration measure of post-tax income; this is obtained as a Gini-type measure, but with post-tax incomes ranked by pre-tax incomes.

In order to concentrate on direct taxes and transfers, the following results were obtained using information on the pre-tax annual incomes and disposable incomes of households in the 2001 Household Economic Survey. Hence the post-tax income measure is obtained from pre-tax income by deducting all direct taxes and adding all transfer payments. Figure 9.10 shows, for four values of θ, the variation in reranking expressed as a percentage of the redistributive effect, L, measured as the difference between the Gini inequality of pre- and post-tax incomes, when individuals are regarded as the basic unit of analysis (income per adult equivalent is weighted by the number of individuals in the household). Figure 9.11 shows a similar pattern of reranking in the case where the basic income unit is the 'equivalent adult' and thus the number of equivalent adults is used as the weight for each household. While the variations in reranking are similar to those found in Figure 9.10, the values, as a percentage of redistribution, are systematically slightly lower in Figure 9.11.

These results show that the degree of reranking is relatively low. The profiles of reranking with variations in α are U-shaped for the lower values of

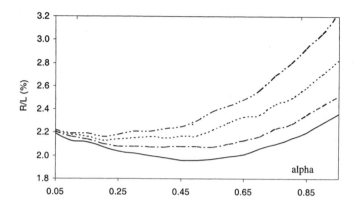

Figure 9.10: Reranking (Individuals)

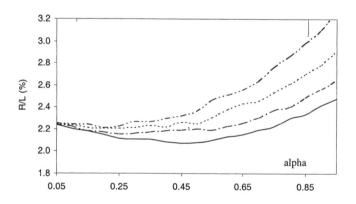

Figure 9.11: Reranking (Equivalent Adults)

θ and become J-shaped for higher values. For the range of values displayed here, reranking is lower for smaller values of θ, the difference increasing for the higher θ. However, as θ is reduced further, below the lowest profile shown, the degree of reranking begins to increase: hence a reranking-minimising set of equivalence scales exists. It was suggested by van de Ven and Creedy (2005) that a tax and transfer system can be identified with a set of implicit scales which are likely to be in the region of the reranking-minimising scales. It is not suggested that these necessarily reflect the value judgements of policy makers; indeed the analysis of such implicit scales can be useful in suggesting possible reforms to the tax structure, if they are found to deviate widely from actual value judgements. In the present context, where individuals are used as weights, minimum reranking was found for θ at around 0.05 and for α at around 0.45. These values are obviously very different from those generally used in empirical studies and, in particular, involve a negligible weight attached to children. This result perhaps suggests a need to reconsider the allowances in the tax and transfer system.

9.5   Alternative Equivalence Scales

This section examines the extent to which the parametric form of the equivalence scale used above approximates alternative equivalence scales that appear in the literature, and contrasts inequality and poverty measures which arise from those scales. Tables 9.1 to 9.3 describe 29 equivalence scales analysed. There is no suggestion that this is exhaustive as they consist of an arbitrary selection concentrating largely on New Zealand and Australia. The scales are grouped according to the regions for which they were designed and the sources from which they were obtained.

As the equivalence scales are based on a variety of different approaches and functional forms, they are not directly comparable. There is, for example, a wide variation in the extent to which children are distinguished by age and

Table 9.1: Equivalence Scales: Part 1

Scale No.	Title	R^2	θ	α
	New Zealand			
	Brashares, Edith and Aynsley, Maryanne (October 1990) Income Adequacy Standards for New Zealand			
1	Jensen's 1978 Equivalence Scale (Annex 5, p.1)	NA	0.781	0.737
2	Jensen's 1988 Equivalence Scale (Annex 5, p. 2)	NA	0.730	0.621
	Michelini, Claudio (April 1999) New Zealand Household Consumption Equivalence Scales from Quasi-Unit Record Data			
3	Commodity-specific and household-type equivalence scales: ELES model (p.14, Table 1 - Total Expenditure)	0.999	0.490	0.711
4	Estimates of the household Equivalence Scales for total consumption when the equivalence parameter m_o is commodity-invariant - PS-AID(θ_j) (p.17, Table 2 - PS-AID(θ_j)	0.987	0.620	0.949
5	Estimates of the household Equivalence Scales for total consumption when the equivalence parameter m_o is commodity-invariant - PS-QAID(θ_j) (p.17, Table 2 - PS-QAID(θ_j))	0.991	0.650	0.896
6	Estimates of the household Equivalence Scales for total consumption when the equivalence parameter m_o is commodity-invariant - PS-QAID(θ_j) - H (p.17, Table 2 - PS-QAID(θ_j) - H)	0.956	0.720	0.622
7	Estimates of the household Equivalence Scales for total consumption when the equivalence parameter m_o is commodity-invariant - EPS(α)-QAID(θ_j) (p.17, Table 2 - EPS(α)-QAID(θ_j))	0.999	0.670	0.782
8	Estimates of the household Equivalence Scales for total consumption when the equivalence parameter m_o is commodity-invariant - EPS(α)-QAID$(\theta_j)^d$ (p.17, Table 2 - EPS(α)-QAID$(\theta_j)^d$)	0.999	0.670	0.775
9	Estimates of the household Equivalence Scales for total consumption when the equivalence parameter m_o is commodity-invariant - EPS(β,λ)-QAID(θ_j) (p.17 Table 2 - EPS(β, λ)-QAID(θ_j))	1.000	0.580	0.799
10	Estimates of the household Equivalence Scales for total consumption when the equivalence parameter m_o is commodity-invariant - EPS(β,λ)-QAID$(\theta_j)^d$ (p.17 Table 2 - EPS(β, λ)-QAID$(\theta_j)^d$)	0.998	0.630	0.797

Table 9.2: Equivalence Scales: Part 2

Scale No.	Title	R^2	θ	α
11	Commodity-specific and household-type equivalence scales obtained from the PS-AID(θ_{ij}) model (p.18, Table 3 - PS-AID(θ_{ij}), Tot.Expenditure)	0.992	0.890	0.904
12	Commodity-specific and household-type equivalence scales obtained from the PS-QAID(θ_{ij}) model (p.18, Table 3 - PS-QAID(θ_{ij}), Tot.Expenditure)	0.963	0.890	0.825
13	Commodity-specific and household-type equivalence scales obtained from the EPS(α)-QAID(θ_{ij}) model (p.20, Table 4 - EPS(α)-QAID(θ_{ij}), Tot.Expenditure)	0.957	0.670	1.014
14	Commodity-specific and household-type equivalence scales obtained from the EPS(β,λ)-QAID(θ_{ij}) model (p.20, Table 4 - EPS(β, λ)-QAID(θ_{ij}), Tot.Expenditure)	0.986	0.890	0.395
15	Heuristic Household Equivalence Scales - Easton, 1980 (p.21, Table 6 - Easton, 1980)	NA	0.916	0.606
16	Heuristic Household Equivalence Scales - Smith, 1989 (p.21, Table 6 - Smith, 1989)	NA	0.713	0.972
	United Kingdom			
	Brashares, Edith and Aynsley, Maryanne (October 1990) Income Adequacy Standards for New Zealand			
17	Townsend's Equivalence Scale (Annex 5, p.49, Table 38 - Townsend)	0.995	0.890	0.551
18	The United Kingdom Supplementary Benefit Equivalence Scale 1968/69 (Annex 5, p.49, Table 38 - Supplementary Benefit)	0.997	0.650	0.658
	Van de Ven, Justin (November 18, 2003) Demand Based Equivalence Scale Estimates for Australia and the UK			
19	Equivalence Scales by Estimation Method for Engel Estimates for the UK (p.15, Table 3 - UK, Engel)	0.999	0.470	0.928
20	Equivalence Scales by Estimation Method for Rothbarth Estimates for the UK (p.15, Table 3 - UK, Rothbarth)	0.997	0.370	0.876

Table 9.3: Equivalence Scales: Part 3

Scale No.	Title	R^2	θ	α
21	Equivalence Scales by Estimation Method for DS(a) Estimates for the UK (p.15, Table 3 - UK, DS(a))	1.000	0.630	0.576
22	Equivalence Scales by Estimation Method for DS(b) Estimates for the UK (p.15, Table 3 - UK, DS(b))	1.000	0.640	0.501

Australia

Brashares, Edith and Aynsley, Maryanne (October 1990) Income Adequacy Standards for New Zealand

23	Henderson Equivalence Scale (Annex 5, p.40, Table 30 - Head Working - All Costs)	0.989	0.810	0.562

Van de Ven, Justin (November 18, 2003) Demand Based Equivalence Scale Estimates for Australia and the UK

24	Equivalence Scales by Estimation Method for Engel Estimates for Australia (p.15, Table 3 - Australia, Engel)	0.999	0.530	1.013
25	Equivalence Scales by Estimation Method for Rothbarth Estimates for Australia (p.15, Table 3 - Australia, Rothbarth)	0.994	0.300	0.886
26	Equivalence Scales by Estimation Method for DS(a) Estimates for Australia (p.15, Table 3 - Australia, DS(a))	1.000	0.600	0.676
27	Equivalence Scales by Estimation Method for DS(b) Estimates for Australia (p.15, Table 3 - Australia, DS(b))	0.999	0.470	0.639

OECD

28	The OECD scale (p.172)	0.998	0.700	0.884
29	The Modified OECD scale (p.172)	0.994	0.580	0.763

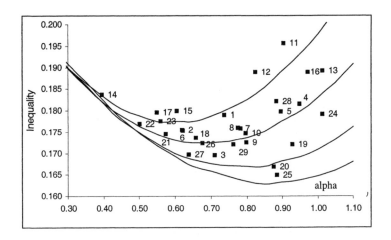

Figure 9.12: Inequality (Equivalent Adults, Epsilon $= 1.2$)

gender. However, it is possible to examine how closely they approximate the functional form used above by, for each scale, using the equivalent sizes, m, to fit the two-parameter form. This is achieved by carrying out regressions using the equation:

$$\log m_i = \beta + \alpha \log (n_{a,i} + \theta n_{c,i}) + \psi_i \qquad (9.20)$$

As this equation is nonlinear in the parameters, regressions were carried out for a range of θ values, and the value producing the highest R^2 was taken as the required estimate, along with the corresponding value of α. Tables 9.1 to 9.3 show the value of R^2 from these regressions together with the estimates of the parameters, θ and α. As shown by the high values of R^2, the two-parameter form of equivalence scale provides a very good fit for all scales analysed; the lowest value of R^2 is 0.956. Where NA is shown in the R^2 column (for scales 1, 2, 15 and 16), these scales were already based on the two-parameter form and therefore no estimation was required.

There are substantial variations in the estimated values of α and θ. The weight attached to children, θ, ranges from 0.300 (scale no. 25) to 0.916

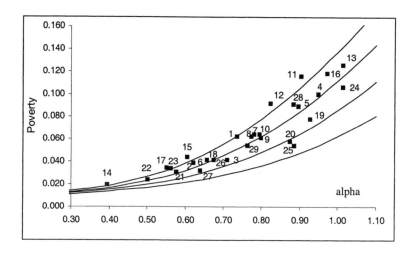

Figure 9.13: Poverty P1 (Individual; Poverty Line = 195)

(scale no. 15), while the parameter reflecting economies of scale, α, ranges from 0.395 (scale no. 14) to 1.014 (scale no. 13). Due to the nonlinear nature of the poverty and inequality profiles, observed variations in θ and α provide little indication as to the variation in inequality and poverty measures that would result from the different equivalence scales. For this reason, each scale was in turn applied to the New Zealand expenditure data, from which inequality and poverty measures were then calculated.

Figure 9.12 shows the inequality profiles produced using the equivalent adult unit of analysis and a high inequality aversion coefficient of 1.2, for four different values of θ. Plotted on this figure are the measures of inequality produced using parameter estimates for each of the 29 equivalence scales. There is clearly a considerable range of inequality measures resulting from these scales. The two extremes are provided by scales 25 and 11, where inequality for the latter is 18 per cent higher than for the former. Figure 9.12 shows that a number of the scales differ mainly in the size of α and lie roughly on the relatively flat section of the inequality profiles, where inequality is not particularly responsive to changes in α. The use of only those scales would give the misleading impression that the choice of scale is not important.

Consider scales 11, 12, 13 and 14 produced by Michelini (1999) for New Zealand. They all produce relatively high inequality measures. However, scale 14 is placed on the downward sloping segment of its inequality profile, while the others are on the upward sloping segment of their profiles. A comparison of those scales alone may also give the impression that inequality is not sensitive to a large variation in α, whereas intermediate values would give substantially lower measures of inequality.

Figure 9.13 shows the profiles of the poverty measure P_1, using the individual as the unit of analysis and a poverty line of \$195 per week. Plotted on this figure are the measures of poverty produced using each of the 29 equivalence scales. The variation in poverty is substantial. Further, the scales which produced inequality measures at either extreme of the distribution do not produce the extreme poverty measures. Instead, scales 14 and 13 provide the largest differential in poverty: when moving from the former to the latter, poverty increases by over 540 per cent. It can also be seen that, whereas the Michelini scales 13 and 14 produce similar inequality measures – being on different sides of the U-shaped profiles – they produce substantially different poverty measures. It is clear that considerable care needs to be taken in comparing results for alternative scales, and in particular much caution is required before declaring that analyses are not affected by the choice of scale.

9.6   Conclusions

This chapter has examined the sensitivity of several inequality and poverty measures to the choices of the adult equivalence scale and the unit of analysis. Use was made of a highly flexible two-parameter functional form of the adult equivalence scale, allowing for economies of scale in consumption and a separate weight added to children. Three units of analysis – the household, the equivalent adult and the individual – were examined. The use of individuals is consistent with an anonymity principle, while the use of the number of equivalent adults is consistent with the principle of transfers.

Profiles of inequality against the economies of scale parameter, for a given weight attached to children, were found to be U-shaped, consistent with other studies. The role of the correlation between the total expenditure per equivalent adult and the size of the household was found to be crucial in generating the U-shaped profile. A negative correlation (despite the positive correlation between total household expenditure and household size) is more likely, the lower is the weight attached to children and the higher are economies of scale. It was shown that a negative correlation is equivalent to the reranking, identified by Coulter *et al.* (1992), that arises as the scale parameter increases. The profiles of inequality and poverty for individuals and equivalent adults as the units of analysis were found to intersect over a range of parameter values. For poverty measures, the profiles of poverty with the economies of scale parameter were upward sloping, with a higher scale parameter increasing poverty over the whole range in all cases.

The effect of alternative equivalence scales and income units on the reranking arising from the direct tax system was also examined. Profiles of reranking for an increasing scale parameter were found to be J-shaped. A reranking-minimising set of parameters were investigated, and were found to be substantially lower than scales commonly used in New Zealand. Finally, a wide range of equivalence scales designed for New Zealand, the United Kingdom, Australia and the OECD were examined. The two-parameter form provided a very good fit to these scales. The scales were applied to the New Zealand data and the resulting inequality and poverty measures were contrasted.

The results demonstrate that considerable care needs to be taken in the choice of adult equivalence scales and the income unit. Applied studies of inequality and poverty often use only a single set of scales, claiming that results are not affected. However, given the different patterns of variation in summary measures found, the results reinforce the suggestion of Coulter *et al.* (1992) that much caution is required before declaring that analyses are not affected by the choice of scale. Some authors argue that, in making comparisons over time or between alternative tax structures, only the absolute values of inequality and poverty measures are affected, not the relative values. However, extensive analyses have shown that this comforting situation cannot be taken for granted. It is therefore useful to examine results for a range of scales and units of analysis, just as it has become common to use a range of inequality aversion parameters and summary measures.

Part VI

Conclusions

Chapter 10

Conclusions

This book has reported a number of empirical analyses of the effects on households' welfare, measures of inequality and revenue of indirect taxes in New Zealand. The effects of existing taxes, along with a range of potential policy reforms, were examined. Welfare changes were measured in terms of equivalent variations, and inequality measures were based on the distribution of a money metric measure of utility. In examining the efficiency effects of tax changes, much use was made of the important concept of the excess burden, and marginal excess burden. The approach differs from studies based entirely on measures of tax paid, and net-of-tax consumption, but requires strong assumptions regarding preferences. Household demands were modelled using the Linear Expenditure System, but the parameters of utility functions were allowed to vary, depending on household total expenditure as well as demographic composition. This approach therefore allowed for considerable preference heterogeneity.

The empirical analyses of indirect taxes began in Part II, which concentrated on the present structure of indirect taxes and potential reforms. Recent debates relating to indirect taxes in New Zealand have been concerned largely with the various excise taxes on alcohol, tobacco and petrol. Indeed some commentators have recommended the revenue-neutral removal of all excise taxes in New Zealand and argued that their abolition would reduce inequality and increase the efficiency of the tax system by reducing excess burdens. After describing, in chapter 2, the effective tax rates and the data used, chapter 3 concentrated on the effects of excise taxes. New Zealand's current system of indirect taxes was found to be relatively efficient at raising tax revenue, having generally low marginal welfare costs per dollar of revenue raised. However, smoking household groups incur larger welfare costs on average than their non-smoking counterparts, reflecting the high effective tax rate on tobacco.

The standard Goods and Services Tax (GST) rate required to support the revenue-neutral removal of the alcohol and tobacco excise taxes was found to be 14.4 per cent. If in addition the petrol excise tax is removed, the required GST rate rises to 15.9 per cent. The direction and magnitude of the welfare and redistributive effects of the reforms were found to vary substantially among household groups. Smoking households experienced relatively larger efficiency gains and greater reductions in inequality than non-smoking households. The increases in the standard GST rate required to achieve revenue neutrality enlarged the distortions between the prices of the commodity groups which attract GST relative to the two commodity groups which do not attract GST. These countered the efficiency gains generated by the removal of the excise taxes and led some non-smoking household groups to incur efficiency losses from the reforms. For both reforms, the large reductions in tax paid that were acquired by smoking household groups were found to be primarily funded by those non-smoking household groups who already pay the largest amounts of indirect tax under the current schedule.

Chapter 3 found marginal welfare gains for such a reform to be of the order of approximately 40 cents per dollar of (reduced) tax revenue for smoking households, and only 5 cents per dollar of (extra) tax revenue for non-smoking households. Comparable estimates for other taxes are not available, and it would be interesting to compare these welfare effects, particularly for smoking households, with those arising from income taxation. In terms of equity, the overall reduction in inequality (of money metric utility per adult equivalent) resulting from the proposed reform was found to be around the range of 1.5 to 2.5 per cent, depending on the degree of inequality aversion and the parameters used in the adult equivalence scale. Overall measures of social welfare over all households, allowing for the combined effect of equity and efficiency, were found to increase by only one half of one per cent when all excises are removed. The results therefore offer little support for the view that excises are highly regressive and inefficient. Any policy decision in this context must of course also combine these findings with perceived or measured effects of excises on the environment and health levels.

Chapter 4 concentrated on the potential implications for New Zealand households of a hypothetical increase in the petrol excise tax. Two cases were considered, of a 5 cents and 15 cents increase per litre. The welfare effects of the petrol excise tax increase were found to vary considerably among demographic groups, reflecting the different variations in budget shares with total expenditure. Importantly the marginal excess burdens also varied substantially, though most cases ranged between about 35 and 55 cents per dollar of extra revenue. Any public expenditure financed from such a tax increase would therefore need to establish significant external benefits. Inequality comparisons, based on money metric utility per adult equivalent, were also made based on the distribution of individual values. The majority of household types, along with the overall comparison, showed very small increases in inequality. The results suggest that the most important consideration from such a selective tax increase arises from the marginal welfare costs generated.

Part III concentrated on issues relating to the desire to reduce carbon dioxide emissions. Chapter 5 turned to the potential effects on consumer prices in New Zealand arising from the imposition of a carbon tax rate of $25 per tonne of carbon dioxide. The resulting effects of the price changes on households' welfare and inequality were examined. The price changes were computed using information about inter-industry transactions and fuel use by industries. It was found that households with relatively low total expenditure levels spend a proportionately greater amount of their budget on carbon-intensive commodities such as petrol and domestic fuel and power. Despite this, the distributional effect of the carbon tax was not unambiguous, in view of the substantial price increases for several commodity groups on which households with relatively higher total expenditure spend proportionately more. The ambiguity of the distributional effect of the carbon tax was confirmed by the welfare measures which show that for the majority of household types, the relative burden of the carbon tax (the equivalent variation divided by total expenditure) does not vary monotonically with total expenditure; over some ranges it is regressive while for other ranges of total expenditure it was found to be progressive.

The marginal excess burdens arising from the carbon tax were generally small. Even for very high inequality aversion, the carbon tax was found to give rise to a very small redistributive effect. The marginal welfare cost, reflecting the efficiency of the carbon tax, was found to be around 15 cents per dollar of additional tax revenue. These relatively small burdens and distributional effects can therefore be compensated by an appropriately designed policy of revenue recycling.

Moving from the effects of a carbon tax designed to reduce emissions by raising the relative price of carbon-intensive goods, chapter 6 examined the nature of the least disruptive changes in the New Zealand economy that are necessary to achieve a target annual rate of reduction in carbon dioxide emissions. Disruption was measured in terms of a cost function that depends on the sum of the squares of the proportionate changes in final demands. The chapter concentrated on changes in final consumer demands and changes in the quantities and mixture of fossil fuels used by industries. A situation in which target emission levels are achieved by reducing all final demands would imply an increase in aggregate unemployment and a negative growth rate of GDP. To overcome this problem, constraints on GDP and employment growth were imposed, implying that the final demands of some industries need to increase while other industries decline.

Chapter 6 found that the magnitude of an industry's required change in final demand was determined by the relative efficiency with which they could achieve the stated constraints. The carbon intensity of an industry's output was balanced against its employment weight and value of final demand. The small orders of magnitude which resulted from these calculations suggest that reducing carbon dioxide emissions is economically feasible. That is, reductions can be achieved while maintaining acceptable levels of key macroeconomic variables if structural change can be encouraged in the areas indicated by this study. Further employment was found to be essential in achieving the growth constraint. Consequently, the addition of an employment constraint was found to make a negligible difference to the changes in final demand. Raising the magnitudes of the constraints was found to increase the spread of the distribution, thereby increasing the costs of adjustment. An increase in the carbon constraint of 1 percentage point was found to increase this cost more than increasing each of the growth constraints by 0.5 percentage points.

The required changes in the fuel-use coefficients were also small, with only two industries required to reduce specific fuel demands by more than 1 per cent to achieve a 1 per cent reduction in carbon dioxide emissions. Again, this supports the conclusion that such reductions in carbon dioxide emissions are feasible. The chapter also compared the nature of reductions obtained using a carbon tax with minimum disruption changes, and showed that, in principle, the required changes could be achieved using a differential set of carbon taxes.

Chapter 7 turned to the question of the revenue responsiveness properties of New Zealand's indirect taxes, that is the extent to which tax revenue increases when aggregate income increases. As consumption is financed from disposable income, it was therefore necessary to consider also the revenue responsiveness of income taxes. Using analytical expressions for revenue elasticities at the individual and aggregate levels, together with a simulated income distribution, numerical values for New Zealand were obtained. Treating income growth as equiproportionate, these suggest that the aggregate income and consumption tax revenue elasticities are both fairly constant as mean income increases, at around 1.3 and 1.0 respectively. This latter estimate assumes that increases in disposable income are accompanied by approximately proportional increases in total expenditure. Allowing for the more realistic case of non-equiproportionate income growth reduces revenue elasticities to around 1.1 (income tax) and 0.93 (consumption taxes). If there is a tendency for the savings proportion to increase as disposable income increases, a somewhat lower total consumption tax revenue elasticity, of around 0.85–0.90, is obtained at mean income levels which approximate current levels in New Zealand. Examination of the tax-share weighted expenditure elasticities for various goods also revealed that, despite the adoption of a broad-based GST at a uniform rate in New Zealand, the persistence of various excises has an important effect on the overall consumption tax revenue elasticity, especially for individuals at relatively low income levels.

Part V of the book concentrated on measurement issues. Chapter 8 examined a question arising from the desire to measure the disproportional effects of indirect taxation, first considered in chapter 3 using the equivalent variation. Many studies rely instead on the use of tax payments by households. It is therefore important to know if the two alternative local measures, tax-progressivity and welfare-progressivity, are likely to coincide. If the simpler use of tax revenue, compared with that of equivalent variations, were found to give similar conclusions regarding progressivity, it would be most convenient. In the context of an indirect tax imposed on a single good, welfare-progressivity requires the welfare loss from the tax as a fraction of total expenditure to rise with total expenditure. When the parameters of the direct utility function are held constant over all levels of total expenditure, chapter 8 showed for the Linear Expenditure System that the condition for welfare-progressivity is the same as that required for tax-progressivity, namely that the taxed good is a luxury.

This constancy (or preference homogeneity) implies a particular pattern for the variation in budget shares with total expenditure, which does not reflect the complex variations found in practice. When, instead, parameters are allowed to vary, enabling heterogeneous preferences amongst households, it was found that tax-progressivity and welfare-progressivity can conflict. The empirical application of these conditions to New Zealand data showed that many such cases can arise. Furthermore, conflicting results were obtained when examining the disproportionality of the effective indirect tax structure in NZ (allowing for GST and excise taxes). The majority of conflicts were found to arise where tax-regressivity existed at the same time as welfare-progressivity. The results show the importance of allowing for heterogeneous preferences in welfare analysis and further suggest that care should be taken when judging the effects of indirect taxes on the basis of tax revenue alone.

Several chapters evaluated tax reforms on the basis of distributional changes. The existence of households of differing size and composition necessitated the use of adult equivalence scales. It was also necessary to make a decision regarding the unit of analysis to examine. A convenient parametric form of scales was used, along with the choice of the individual as the unit (rather than the use of equivalent adults or households). Chapter 9 examined these issues in detail, considering the sensitivity of several inequality and poverty measures to the choices of the adult equivalence scale and the unit of analysis. The highly flexible two-parameter functional form of adult equivalence scales was used, as in earlier chapters. This allows for economies of scale in consumption and has a separate weight added to children. Three units of analysis – the household, the equivalent adult and the individual – were considered. The use of individuals is consistent with an anonymity principle, while the use of the number of equivalent adults is consistent with the principle of transfers.

Chapter 9 reported profiles of inequality against the economies of scale parameter, for a given weight attached to children. They were found to be U-shaped, which is consistent with other studies. The role of the correlation between the total expenditure per equivalent adult and the size of the household was found to be crucial in generating the U-shaped profile. A negative correlation (despite the positive correlation between total household expenditure and household size) is more likely, the lower is the weight attached to children and the higher is the economies of scale parameter. The profiles of inequality and poverty for individuals and equivalent adults as the units of analysis (or weights) were found to intersect over a range of parameter values. For poverty measures, the profiles of poverty with the economies of scale parameter were upward sloping, with a higher scale parameter increasing poverty over the whole range in all cases.

The effect of alternative equivalence scales and income units on the reranking arising from the direct tax system was also examined in chapter 9. Reranking relates to the changes in the rank order of households when moving from the pre-tax to the post-tax distribution of income. Profiles of reranking for an increasing adult equivalence scale parameter were found to be J-shaped. A reranking-minimising set of parameters were investigated, and were found to be substantially lower than scales commonly used in New Zealand. Finally, a wide range of equivalence scales designed for New Zealand, the United Kingdom, Australia and the OECD were examined. The two-parameter form provided a very good fit to these scales. The scales were applied to the New Zealand data and the resulting inequality and poverty measures were contrasted.

The results in chapter 9 demonstrated that considerable care needs to be taken in the choice of adult equivalence scales and the income unit. Applied studies of inequality and poverty often use only a single set of scales, claiming that results are not affected. However, given the different patterns of variation in summary measures found, the results suggest that much caution is required before declaring that analyses are not affected by the choice of scale. Some authors argue that, in making comparisons over time or between alternative tax structures, only the absolute values of inequality and poverty measures are affected, not the relative values. However, extensive analyses have shown that this comforting situation cannot be taken for granted. It is therefore useful to examine results for a range of scales and units of analysis, just as it has become common to use a range of inequality aversion parameters and summary measures.

The book did not set out to make policy recommendations, since these inevitably involve value judgements. Rather, the aim was to contribute to rational policy analysis by providing information about potential orders of magnitude involved, and examining the implications of adopting specified value judgements, for example regarding inequality aversion.

Appendix A

Income and Consumption Taxes

This appendix uses simple tax models to examine the interaction between income and consumption taxes. It suggests that in examining tax progressivity, it is preferable to consider the overall impact of all taxes and transfer payments rather than relating payments of a single tax to gross income. If it is desired to consider a consumption tax in isolation in a cross-sectional context, it is argued that the distributional impact is best measured in terms of total household expenditure, rather than gross income. Section A.1 examines the simplest possible model containing a progressive income tax and a general consumption tax in which all expenditure is taxed at a fixed rate, and there is no saving. Misleading results regarding progressivity can arise when using ratios of consumption tax to household gross income. Section A.2 introduces saving behaviour into the model, which is extended from a single-period to a two-period framework.

A.1   The Simplest Case

Suppose that m represents the total expenditure of a household. Suppose that there is a general consumption tax, such as a retail sales tax (or an equivalent value-added tax), in which a common *ad valorem* rate of tax, v, is imposed on the tax-exclusive price of every good. The tax-inclusive rate corresponding to v is equal to $v/\left(1+v\right)$, since this generates the same revenue when applied to gross expenditure, m. If $V\left(m\right)$ denotes the consumption tax paid by the household, then:

$$V\left(m\right) = \frac{v}{1+v}m \qquad (A.1)$$

Let y denote the corresponding household income, and suppose that income tax of $T\left(y\right)$ is paid. If there is neither saving nor expenditure arising from borrowing or the use of other assets, then the total tax paid by the household, $R\left(y\right)$, is given by:

$$R\left(y\right) = T\left(y\right) + \frac{v}{1+v}\left\{y - T\left(y\right)\right\} \qquad (A.2)$$

The simplest case of a progressive income tax is one in which a constant marginal tax rate, t, is applied to income measured above a tax-free threshold, a, so that, for $y > a$, the tax is $t\left(y - a\right)$ or:

$$T\left(y\right) = -at + ty \qquad (A.3)$$

The income tax is therefore equivalent, for those who pay tax, to a combined tax and transfer scheme in which there is an unconditional transfer or social dividend of at and a proportional tax applied to all income. The average income tax rate, given by $T\left(y\right)/y = t(1 - a/y)$, rises as y increases, so the tax is progressive.

Substituting (A.3) into (A.2) gives:

$$R\left(y\right) = -\frac{at}{1+v} + y\left(\frac{t+v}{1+v}\right) \qquad (A.4)$$

and comparison with (A.3) shows that the combined effect of the income and consumption tax can be made, with suitable choice of parameters, equivalent to the income tax in every way (for those above a).

It was mentioned earlier that many commentators, when concentrating only on the consumption tax, wish to examine the ratio of the consumption tax to gross income, y, rather than taking the value of total household expenditure, m, which is the relevant tax base, as denominator. In the present case, the former ratio is found to be:

$$\frac{V(m)}{y} = \frac{v}{1+v}\left\{(1-t) + \frac{at}{y}\right\} \tag{A.5}$$

and $V(m)/y$ decreases as y increases, with:

$$\frac{\partial}{\partial y}\left(\frac{V(m)}{y}\right) = -\frac{at}{y^2}\left(\frac{v}{1+v}\right) \tag{A.6}$$

People who take this view would therefore describe the consumption tax, which is a fixed proportion of total expenditure, as a regressive tax. It is not clear that, even in this very simple framework, such an approach, in which a single tax is assessed in relation to a different tax base, is useful.

Suppose that the marginal rate of income tax is increased and at the same time the general consumption tax rate is reduced in order to keep aggregate revenue over all households, R, constant, while also holding a constant. In the case where all households have $y > a$, it can be shown that the required changes in t and v are given by:

$$\left.\frac{dt}{dv}\right|_R = -\frac{1}{1+v}\left(\frac{1}{1-a/\bar{y}} - t\right) \tag{A.7}$$

where $\bar{y}$ is arithmetic mean income. It is therefore possible for t to increase by more than the fall in v, so that the ratio, $V(m)/y$, can fall at a faster rate than before, suggesting that the consumption tax becomes more regressive. The paradoxical result can therefore arise whereby a reduction in the proportional tax rate and revenue from a so-called regressive tax is associated with an increase in its degree of regressivity, simply because another tax, in this case the income tax, has become more progressive. The lesson from this type of analysis is that in analysing tax systems in which there are several taxes, what really matters is the overall effect of all taxes and transfers. However, if it is desired to give attention to a single tax in isolation, there is something to be said for looking at that tax in relation to its own base.

The above framework is the simplest model that could be used to examine the interaction between direct and indirect taxation in a system which is, from an overall point of view, progressive. The following section extends the model to allow for savings.

A.2   Allowing for Savings

When commentators argue that a general consumption tax is necessarily regressive, they are not only using an approach in which a single tax is examined in relation to gross income rather than its own base, but usually have in mind the idea that high-income households save a larger proportion of their disposable income than low-income households. Total expenditure is thus given by:

$$m = c\{y - T(y)\} \tag{A.8}$$

where c denotes the proportion of disposable income that is consumed, and this is thought to decrease with y. Hence the ratio of the amount paid under the consumption tax to gross income falls more rapidly than in the previous section.

The introduction of savings necessarily introduces the need for a multi-period analysis, though this is nearly always ignored in popular debate. The accumulated savings are inevitably used for consumption at some future date, when they will attract the appropriate consumption tax. The precise time profile of tax payments depends on the extent to which disposable income is shifted between periods. However, in a multi-period framework the progressivity of the overall tax system needs to be judged in terms of the present value of tax payments in relation to the present value of income.

Whether or not the overall progressivity of the tax system, viewed in present value terms, is affected by differential saving patterns depends on the tax treatment of the income derived from savings. In practice this can take several forms and each form of income typically attracts a different tax rate. It does not seem helpful to describe the progressivity or regressivity of a consumption tax as being affected by saving behaviour, when it is the tax treatment of the income derived from savings that is the crucial influence on the overall tax system and is independent of the consumption tax structure.

The multi-period case can be illustrated as follows. For convenience, suppose that just two periods are relevant and income, y, is the same in each period, while saving takes place in only the first period. The tax rates and tax-free threshold are assumed to be constant over the two periods. If savings attract an interest rate of r (irrespective of their form), and if there is no interest-income tax, then consumption in the first period is $c \{y - T(y)\}$ while in the second period it is equal to:

$$\{y - T(y)\} + (1 + r)(1 - c)\{y - T(y)\} \tag{A.9}$$

If tax and income streams are discounted at the same rate, r, then it can be shown that the present value of tax payments, R_{pv}, is equal to:

$$R_{pv} = \left(1 + \frac{1}{1+r}\right) R(y) \tag{A.10}$$

where $R(y)$ is the same as in (A.2). This is independent of c, so that the ratio of the present value of tax payments to the present value of income is precisely as in the single-period framework of the previous section. In this case, savings are therefore irrelevant in evaluating the tax system. This simple result no longer holds if there is an interest-income tax; indeed, if the higher-income groups save relatively more than the poorer groups, the overall progressivity of the system is increased. In practice, those who save more typically have access to savings vehicles which generate relatively higher after-tax rates of return, and this reduces progressivity.

It can therefore be argued that it is a misleading use of language to describe a consumption tax as being regressive because of differential saving patterns, when the real influence on the progressivity of the system as a whole is the income tax treatment of the income derived from savings. Those

who wish to draw attention to differential saving rates as an influence on
the redistributive effect of the tax system should concentrate attention on
the differential tax treatment of saving vehicles. As argued in the previous
section, if attention is to be given only to a consumption tax using a single-
period framework, it is appropriate to consider the tax paid in relation to
household total expenditure.

These comparisons are of course comparative-static comparisons between
structures; they do not relate to a transition towards a consumption tax,
which involves intergenerational issues that are not considered here. Intergenerational redistribution arises because of the difference in the time profiles
of consumption and income.

Appendix B

Welfare Changes and Tax Burdens

This appendix defines the concepts of welfare change and excess burden used in several chapters of this book. The discussion relies on diagrams.[1] It concentrates on the welfare loss imposed on a single individual arising from a tax on a single good. Importantly, general equilibrium effects are ignored.

B.1 A Money Measure of Welfare Change

This section explains the concept of welfare change used to examine tax burdens. These concepts apply to welfare changes arising from any set of price changes, but here the price change is assumed to arise purely from a tax change, so that the excess burden concept is relevant. This section defines the equivalent and compensating variations, and the excess burden for the case of a tax on a single good.

Consider a single individual who is maximising utility subject to a fixed budget. There are just two goods, X and Y. Good Y may be considered as a composite of all other goods, with the price set equal to unity. Hence units of Y are equivalent to money units. In the initial situation, the budget line, with a slope equal to the relative price of X to that of Y, is shown as AB in

---

[1]For a more technical treatment and discussion of the literature, see Creedy (1998b).

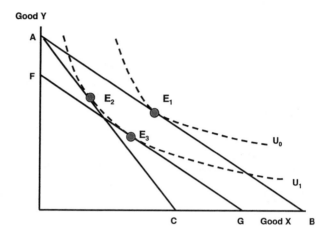

Figure B.1: A Tax on Good X

Figure B.1. The optimal position is E_1, a tangency position on indifference curve U_0. Suppose a selective tax is imposed on good X. This causes the price of X to increase so that the budget line pivots to AC. The new optimal position is E_2 on indifference curve U_1.

There is a reduction in the individual's welfare as a result of the tax, as indicated by the move from U_0 to the lower indifference curve U_1. However, the difference $U_0 - U_1$ does not provide a useful measure of welfare change because utility is an ordinal concept. The utility levels themselves are arbitrary and the utility function provides simply a preference ordering of alternative bundles. The ordering is only assumed to have some standard properties, such as transitivity and decreasing marginal rates of substitution.

Welfare changes are instead based on the change in the cost of reaching a particular indifference curve as relative prices change. This cost is not affected by the arbitrary utility number assigned to the indifference curves. Figure B.1 shows that utility level U_1 can be attained at the pre-tax prices if the individual faces budget line FG, which is parallel to AB. The optimal position along this hypothetical constraint is E_3. Hence, a variation in the individual's budget is equivalent to the tax imposed on X, in the sense that the individual would be indifferent between that budget variation (at the old prices) and the tax. This equivalent variation, denoted EV, is measured in terms of a quantity of good Y by AF, the vertical distance between the two budget lines AB and FG. Another way of describing the EV is that it represents the maximum amount the individual would be prepared to pay to avoid the tax and associated price change.

The utility function can in principle be converted into another function that describes the minimum total expenditure needed to reach a specified indifference curve at a given set of prices. Such a function is called the expenditure function, $E(P,U)$, and has as its arguments, not the amounts of the goods consumed, as with $U(x,y)$, but prices and utility. Given this function, the equivalent variation is:

$$EV = E(P_1, U_1) - E(P_0, U_1) \qquad \text{(B.1)}$$

where P_0 and P_1 are the vectors of pre-tax and post-tax prices respectively. This is the distance AF in Figure B.1. The first term, $E(P_1, U_1)$, is the individual's budget, m_1, which in this case is assumed to be fixed, so that $m_1 = m_0 = E(P_0, U_0)$.

For welfare changes involving price changes of several goods, $i = 1, ..., n$, so the vector P now has n elements, the equivalent variation is:

$$EV = E(P_1, U_1) - E(P_0, U_1) = \sum_{i=1}^{n} \int_{P_{0,i}}^{P_{1,i}} x_i^H (P, U_1) \, dP_i \qquad \text{(B.2)}$$

The summation over goods raises no problems for equivalent variations, but introduces the 'path dependency' problem for Marshallian consumer's surplus measures, whereby the order in which price changes are taken affects the result.

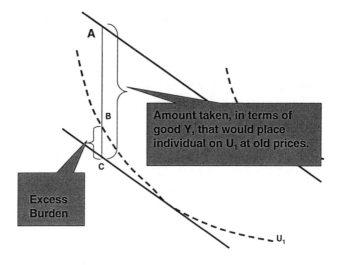

Figure B.2: Welfare Change and Excess Burden

B.2   The Excess Burden

It is useful to concentrate on the area in Figure B.1 around the two points E_2 and E_3, which lie on indifference curve U_1. This expanded area is shown in Figure B.2. Since point B represents the position actually reached by the individual after the imposition of the tax on X, the vertical distance AB shows the tax paid, expressed in terms of good Y. This is less than the equivalent variation in income that also places the individual on U_1 at pre-tax prices. The difference between the equivalent variation and the tax paid, T, represents the excess burden, EB_{EV}, of the tax. This is the distance BC in Figure B.2.

The tax revenue can be used to finance government projects or for re-distribution to other individuals. However, the excess burden $EV - T$ is not available for anyone to spend. It represents a pure efficiency loss arising from the tax. The size of this excess burden depends partly on the degree of con-vexity of the indifference curve, which reflects the degree of substitutability between the two goods.

As shown above, the excess burden is the vertical distance traced out by moving along the post-tax indifference curve from E_2 to E_3 as the relative price changes from the post-tax to the pre-tax ratio. This movement actually traces out part of a demand curve, in this case a Hicksian demand curve for good X: demand changes as the price varies, while utility is constant.[2] This contrasts with the Marshallian demand curve for X, which relates to the movement between E_1 and E_2. These two demand curves are shown in the lower part of Figure B.3, for variations between P_0 and P_1.

For a small change in the price, the area to the left of the Hicksian demand curve between the prices represents an expenditure level (since it is a money price per unit multiplied by a quantity). In just the same way that the Hicksian demand is produced by *gradually* moving along U_1 as the relative price varies, it is necessary to add up all the areas for each small price change. The total area – obtained by adding all horizontal strips – gives the expenditure required to obtain the equivalent variation. Hence EV is the area $P_1E_2E_3P_0$ in Figure B.3.

The distance between the two price lines, $P_1 - P_0$, represents the tax per unit imposed on the good, so that multiplying this by the quantity of the good purchased after the imposition of the tax gives the tax revenue. Hence revenue is represented by the area indicated in Figure B.4. The difference between these two areas is the excess burden, BDC in Figure B.4.

The above analysis relates to the burden of the tax compared with the no-tax situation. It is often useful to measure the marginal excess burden, MEB, which relates to changes in the tax rate. In terms of the equivalent variation, this simply involves changes in EV and T, so that $MEB = \Delta EV - \Delta T$. This gives rise to two related concepts. First, the marginal welfare cost is given by $MWC = MEB/\Delta T = \Delta EV/\Delta T - 1$ and the marginal cost of funds,

---

[2] Another Hicksian demand curve could be traced, relating to movements along U_0; this is examined in the following subsection.

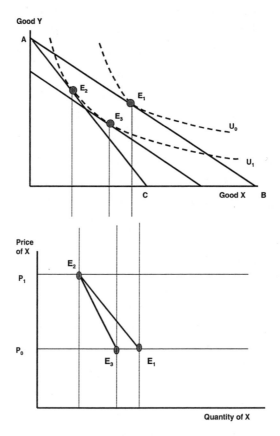

Figure B.3: Demand Curves for Good X

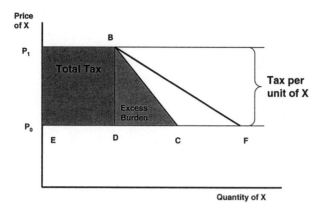

Figure B.4: The Excess Burden as an Area

$MCF = \Delta EV / \Delta T$. Combining the two measures gives $MCF = MWC + 1$. When considering a policy of increasing a tax rate in order to finance a public project, it is the MCF that is relevant.

B.3 The Compensating Variation

It is also possible to consider the amount of money that, if given to the individual, would allow the initial indifference curve, U_0, to be reached at the new prices. This is the compensating variation. The comparisons are illustrated in Figure B.6. The hypothetical budget line FG is parallel to the post-tax budget line AC but places the individual at E_3 on indifference curve U_0. The compensating variation is AF, the vertical difference between the two budget lines at the new prices. Dropping a vertical line from E_3, the tax paid is the distance between the budget lines AB and AC, and the excess burden, based on the compensating variation, is the vertical distance between lines AB and FG at E_3. A feature of this measure of excess burden is that it is not based on the amount of tax actually paid. It allows for the tax that would be paid if the individual were in fact compensated. Another way of looking

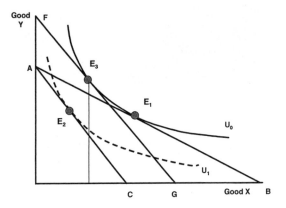

Figure B.5: The Compensating Variation

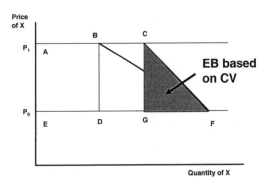

Figure B.6: Excess Burden Based on Compensating Variation

at the compensating variation is to recognise that it is the negative of the equivalent variation arising from a price change in the opposite direction. As with the equivalent variation, the concepts can also be illustrated in a diagram containing demand curves. In this case, the Hicksian demand curve relates to movements along U_0, so it starts from point F in Figure B.4. The excess burden based on the compensating variation is shown in Figure B.5. The tax deducted from the compensating variation (the area to the left of CF) is the rectangle ACGE.

Appendix C

The Simulation Model

This appendix shows how parameters of the Linear Expenditure System (LES) can be obtained, for each of a variety of total expenditure groups, using only cross-sectional budget data. The strong *a priori* restrictions underlying this parametric approach represent the cost of obtaining a large number of demand elasticities where cross-sectional data only are available.

C.1 The Linear Expenditure System

One serious limitation of the LES, when a single set of parameters is used, is that its implications for optimal indirect taxes are very strong, since it gives rise to uniform indirect taxes. However, the approach presented here explicitly allows for heterogeneity. Instead of using a single set of parameters, the welfare measures are based on estimates of the LES for each of a range of total expenditure groups. Households within each group are assumed to have the same preferences, but these are allowed to vary with total expenditure. The uniformity of optimal indirect taxes does not arise with taste heterogeneity.

The LES has additive direct utility functions of the form:

$$U = \prod_{i=1}^{n} (x_i - \gamma_i)^{\beta_i} \qquad (C.1)$$

213

where x_i denotes the consumption of the ith good and γ_i is the committed consumption, with $x_i > \gamma_i, 0 \leq \beta_i \leq 1$. The normalisation $\sum_i \beta_i = 1$ is also imposed. The maximisation of utility subject to the budget constraint $m = \sum_i p_i x_i$ gives rise to the linear expenditure function for each good, i, of the form:

$$p_i x_i = \gamma_i p_i + \beta_i \left(m - \sum_j p_j \gamma_j \right) \qquad (C.2)$$

This can be rewritten in the more succinct form:

$$x_i^* = \frac{\beta_i m^*}{p_i} \qquad (C.3)$$

where $m^* = m - \sum_j p_j \gamma_j$ is called supernumerary income, and $x_i^* = x_i - \gamma_i$ is called the supernumerary consumption of good i.

From differentiation of each expenditure function, given in equation (C.2), the own-price elasticity of demand for the ith good, η_{ii}, is given by:

$$\eta_{ii} = -\frac{\beta_i}{p_i x_i} \left(m - \sum_{j \neq i} p_j \gamma_j \right)$$

After some rearrangement this can be written more simply as:

$$\eta_{ii} = \frac{\gamma_i (1 - \beta_i)}{x_i} - 1 \qquad (C.4)$$

The cross-price elasticity, η_{ij}, that is the elasticity of demand for good i in response to a change in the price of good j, for all i, j pairs, is expressed as:

$$\eta_{ij} = \frac{\beta_i \gamma_j p_j}{p_i x_i}$$

This can usefully be written in the form:

$$\eta_{ij} = -\frac{\beta_i \gamma_j}{x_j} \left(\frac{w_j}{w_i} \right) \qquad (C.5)$$

where the term $w_i = p_i x_i / m$ is the expenditure or budget share of the ith good. The total expenditure elasticity of good i, e_i, is given by:

$$e_i = \frac{\beta_i m}{p_i x_i}$$

Using the definition of w_i, this becomes:

$$e_i = \frac{\beta_i}{w_i} \qquad (C.6)$$

C.2 Estimation for Each Total Expenditure Group

The approach suggested here is to examine tax and distributional issues by making allowance for variations in the βs and γs as total expenditure varies. Suppose that household budget data are available giving, for each of a range of total expenditure groups, the expenditure weights or budget shares, w_i, for each commodity group. These weights can be used to find, for each total expenditure group, the set of total expenditure elasticities, e_i, as explained below. Having calculated the e_is, the corresponding values of β_i can be obtained using the relationship given in equation (C.6), so that:

$$\beta_i = e_i w_i \qquad (C.7)$$

Consider the calculation of committed expenditure, $p_i \gamma_i$, for each commodity group and total expenditure or income group. If a value of the own-price elasticity of demand is available using extraneous information for each good at each income level, then equation (C.4) can be used, after rearrangement, since:

$$p_i \gamma_i = \frac{m w_i \left(1 + \eta_{ii}\right)}{1 - \beta_i} \qquad (C.8)$$

The required set of own-price elasticities, η_{ii}, may be obtained using a result established by Frisch (1959) for directly additive utility functions. Frisch showed that the price elasticities can be expressed as:

$$\eta_{ij} = -e_i w_j \left(1 + \frac{e_j}{\xi}\right) + \frac{e_i \delta_{ij}}{\xi} \qquad (C.9)$$

where ξ denotes the elasticity of the marginal utility of total expenditure with respect to total expenditure; this is called the Frisch parameter. These elasticity expressions automatically satisfy the homogeneity and additivity restrictions. The own-price elasticities are:

$$\eta_{ii} = e_i \left\{\frac{1}{\xi} - w_i \left(1 + \frac{e_i}{\xi}\right)\right\} \qquad (C.10)$$

With ξ and set of budget shares for a variety of total expenditure groups, the values of β_i and $p_i\gamma_i$ for each of a range of total expenditure groups can be calculated. These results, along with proportionate price changes, are sufficient to calculate the welfare effects of any specified change in the tax structure, as shown in the following section.

C.3 Welfare Measures

Given estimates of β_i and $p_i\gamma_i$ for each commodity and total expenditure group, it is required to obtain welfare effects for specified proportionate price changes, assuming all consumers face the same prices. This section shows how compensating and equivalent variations, and equivalent incomes, can be calculated.

The first stage in obtaining the expenditure function is to derive the indirect utility function, $V(p, m)$, which expresses utility as a function of prices and income and is obtained by substituting the solution for the demands, given in equation (C.3), into the utility function of equation (C.1). Hence, as shown in chapter 3:

$$V(p, U) = (m - A)/B \qquad \text{(C.11)}$$

where the terms A and B are given by:

$$A = \sum_i p_i\gamma_i \qquad \text{(C.12)}$$

$$B = \prod_i \left(\frac{p_i}{\beta_i}\right)^{\beta_i} \qquad \text{(C.13)}$$

The expenditure function is the minimum expenditure required to achieve utility U at prices p, written as $E(p, U)$. It is given by rearranging equation (C.11), that is inverting the indirect utility function, to give:

$$E(p, U) = A + BU \qquad \text{(C.14)}$$

C.3.1 Compensating and Equivalent Variations

Suppose that prices change from p_0 to p_1 as a result of the imposition of indirect taxes. The compensating variation, CV, is the difference between the minimum expenditure required to achieve the original utility level, at the new prices, and the initial total expenditure. Hence in the context of a price rise it is the amount that needs to be given to an individual in order to restore the original utility level, at the new prices. Hence:

$$CV = E\left(p_1, U_0\right) - E\left(p_0, U_0\right) \tag{C.15}$$

Using equation (C.14) and adding subscripts to indicate the relevant set of prices, this becomes:

$$CV = A_1 + B_1 U_0 - m_0 \tag{C.16}$$

After substituting for $U_0 = \left(m_0 - A_0\right)/B_0$, this can be rearranged to give:

$$CV = A_0 \left[\frac{A_1}{A_0} + \frac{B_1}{B_0}\left(\frac{m_0}{A_0} - 1\right)\right] - m_0 \tag{C.17}$$

The term A_1/A_0 is equal to $\sum_i p_{1i}\gamma_i / \sum_i p_{0i}\gamma_i$ and is therefore a Laspeyres type of price index, using the committed consumption of each good as the weight. For this reason it is sometimes referred to as a price index of necessities.

Since actual prices are not usually available, it is necessary to convert this form of the price index into one involving only proportional changes in prices. If $\dot{p}_i$ denotes the proportionate change in the price of the ith good, then $p_{1i} = p_{0i}\left(1 + \dot{p}_i\right)$ and:

$$\frac{A_1}{A_0} = 1 + \sum_i s_i \dot{p}_i \tag{C.18}$$

where the term s_i is defined as:

$$s_i = \frac{p_{0i}\gamma_i}{\sum_i p_{0i}\gamma_i} \tag{C.19}$$

The term B_1/B_0 in (C.17) simplifies to:

$$\frac{B_1}{B_0} = \prod_i \left(\frac{p_{1i}}{p_{0i}}\right)^{\beta_i} \tag{C.20}$$

which is interpreted as a weighted geometric mean of price relatives. It is sometimes referred to as reflecting the price of 'luxuries'. Again it is necessary to express this in terms of the proportionate changes, so that:

$$\frac{B_1}{B_0} = \prod_i (1 + \dot{p}_i)^{\beta_i} \tag{C.21}$$

Equation (C.17) is used, with equations (C.18) and (C.21), to calculate the compensating variation, given a set of proportionate price changes and the coefficients β_i, along with the initial cost of committed expenditure for each good, $p_i \gamma_i$. An important feature of the results is that the precise values of γ_i and p_i are not required.

The equivalent variation is the difference between the post-change total expenditure and the minimum expenditure required to achieve post-change utility at the pre-change prices. It is the compensating variation corresponding to a price change in the opposite direction. Hence:

$$EV = E\left(p_1, U_1\right) - E\left(p_0, U_1\right) \tag{C.22}$$

This can be written as:

$$EV = m_1 - (A_0 + B_0 U_1) \tag{C.23}$$

Substituting for $U_1 = (m_1 - A_1)/B_1$ into equation (C.23) and rearranging gives:

$$EV = m_1 - A_0 \left[1 + \frac{B_0}{B_1}\left(\frac{m_1}{A_0} - \frac{A_1}{A_0}\right)\right] \tag{C.24}$$

This expression may be compared with the compensating variation given in equation (C.17). The two price indices A_1/A_0 and B_1/B_0 may again be obtained using equations (C.18) to (C.21).

C.3.2 Money Metric Welfare Measures

The distributional effects of price changes can be measured using the distribution of a money metric welfare measure, defined as the value of total expenditure, m_e, which, at some reference set of prices, p_r, gives the same utility as the actual level. In terms of the indirect utility function, m_e is defined by the equation:

$$V(p_r, m_e) = V(p, m) \qquad (C.25)$$

Using the expenditure function gives:

$$m_e = E(p_r, V(p, m)) \qquad (C.26)$$

which may be written as:

$$m_e = F(p_r, p, m) \qquad (C.27)$$

For the linear expenditure system, this can be obtained using equations (C.14) and (C.11). The actual utility, U, can be expressed from the indirect utility function as $(m - A)/B$. The minimum expenditure required to achieve this utility level, at the reference set of prices, is given by:

$$m_e = A_r + \frac{B_r(m - A)}{B} \qquad (C.28)$$

Expanding the terms in A and B gives:

$$m_e = \sum_i p_{ri}\gamma_i + \left\{ \prod_i \left(\frac{p_{ri}}{p_i}\right)^{\beta_i} \right\} \left\{ m - \sum_j p_j\gamma_j \right\} \qquad (C.29)$$

The effect on welfare of a change in prices and income can then be measured in terms of a change in the money metric from m_{0e} to m_{1e}, where, as before, the indices 0 and 1 refer to pre-change and post-change values respectively. From this, changes in welfare at different income levels can be compared. Furthermore, values of a social welfare function can be obtained for a population group using values of m_{0e} and m_{1e} so that, according to the value judgements implicit in the welfare function, a change can be judged in terms of its overall effect.

An important feature of the money metric is that it ensures that alternative tax policies are evaluated using a common set of reference prices. Consider the use of pre-change prices as reference prices, so that $p_{ri} = p_{0i}$ for all i. Substitution into equation (C.29) shows immediately that pre-change equivalent incomes are simply the actual incomes, and thus $m_{0e} = m_0$. After the change in the tax structure:

$$m_{1e} = \sum_i p_{0i}\gamma_i + \left\{ \prod_i \left(\frac{p_{0i}}{p_{1i}}\right)^{\beta_i} \right\} \left\{ m_1 - \sum_j p_{1j}\gamma_j \right\} \qquad (C.30)$$

This can be written as:

$$m_{1e} = A_0 \left[1 + \frac{B_0}{B_1}\left(\frac{m_1}{A_0} - \frac{A_1}{A_0}\right) \right] \qquad (C.31)$$

Comparison of equations (C.24) and (C.31) shows that when the reference prices are equal to the pre-change prices, the post-change money metric is the value of actual income after the change less the value of the equivalent variation; that is, $m_{1e} = m_1 - EV$.

C.4   Budget Shares and Expenditure Elasticities

Given cross-sectional budget data, the total expenditure elasticities, for different household types, can be obtained by first estimating the relationship, for each commodity group, between the budget shares and total household expenditure. If $w_i = p_i x_i / \sum_{i=1}^n p_i x_i = p_i x_i / y$ is the budget share of the ith good, a flexible specification that has been found to provide a good fit is (omitting subscripts):

$$w = \delta_1 + \delta_2 \log y + \frac{\delta_3}{y} \qquad (C.32)$$

This form has the convenient property that, if parameters are estimated using ordinary least squares, the adding-up condition, $\sum_{i=1}^{n} w_i = 1$, holds for predicted shares, at all total expenditure levels, y. For any given household, the parameters of their direct utility function (β and γ) are unique to both the household's total expenditure level as well as their demographic make-up. This approach enables considerable preference heterogeneity that is not found in representative agent frameworks.

At any given level of y, the expenditure elasticity is given by:

$$e = 1 + \frac{dw}{dy} \frac{y}{w} \qquad (C.33)$$

which can be expressed as:

$$e = 1 + \frac{(y/\delta_3)\,\delta_2 - 1}{(y/\delta_3)\,(\delta_1 + \delta_2 \log y) + 1} \qquad (C.34)$$

so that $e = 0$ for $y = 0$, and converges to 1 as $y \to \infty$ (though of course it may exceed unity over certain ranges of y).

The Frisch parameter cannot be calculated within the model and instead must be determined from extraneous information. The analysis was conducted using a fixed Frisch parameter of -1.9. Experiments with varying Frisch parameters, allowing the absolute Frisch to fall as total expenditure rises, showed that the results were not sensitive. Hence only the constant case is reported here. Tulpule and Powell (1978) used a value of $\xi = -1.82$ when calculating elasticities at average income for Australia, based on the work of Williams (1978), and this value was adopted by Dixon et al. (1982) in calibrating a general equilibrium model. The slightly higher absolute value was used here to avoid some negative committed expenditures.

Appendix D

Revenue Elasticity Computations

D.1   Expenditure Elasticities

Instead of using the database used in Parts II, III and V to examine the welfare effects of taxes for different household types, the aim of chapter 7 was to model tax revenue using a high level of aggregation, thereby minimising data requirements. Expenditure elasticities were obtained using the published summary table of average expenditures over a range of income groups in the 2001 New Zealand Household Economic Survey (HES), obtained from http://www.stats.govt.nz/. This table divides all households in the sample into $K = 11$ income groups. Within each group the budget shares for each of $n = 58$ commodity groups were obtained (by dividing average expenditure in each category by average total expenditure).[1] The ratio of averages is not the same as the average budget share, though earlier experiments using data for individual households showed that the differences were minor. Thus more commodity groups are used than with the welfare modelling, which consolidated commodities into 22 groups. Denote the arithmetic mean total expenditure of the kth group by m_k $(k = 1, ..., K)$ and the budget share of the

---

[1]Several commodity groups were excluded on the grounds that they more closely represented savings rather than expenditure.

ith commodity group and kth total expenditure group by w_{ki} $(i = 1, ..., n)$.

The calculation of elasticities was based on the same budget share relationship used elsewhere. That is, regressions were carried out of the form:

$$w_{ki} = a_{ik} + b_{ik} \log(m_k) + \frac{c_{ik}}{m_k} \tag{D.1}$$

for each commodity group, i. In addition to generally providing a good fit, this specification has the advantage that weights based on the estimated parameters add to unity. The required expenditure elasticities were obtained using:

$$e_{ki} = 1 + \frac{dw_{ki}}{dm_k} \frac{m_k}{w_{ki}} \tag{D.2}$$

with dw/dm taken from differentiation of (D.1).

The coefficient estimates are reported in Tables D.1 and D.2. It can be seen that the specification generally provides a good fit, being highly flexible despite its relative simplicity. The estimates here are based, as explained above, on average budget shares and average total expenditures within a range of income groups. This again contrasts with the welfare modelling, where data are available at the household level.

D.2 Income Distribution

The grouped frequency distribution of taxable income in New Zealand for 2000–2001 is given in Table D.3. This distribution is for income from all sources, and covers employed and self-employed individuals 15 years and older. A histogram of this distribution is shown in Figure D.1, where a second mode right at the bottom of the distribution (below $2000 per year) is evident. These very low annual incomes are likely to be associated with part time casual work by teenagers, or small amounts of interest income accruing to non-beneficiaries. Their (tax-share) contribution to the aggregate revenue elasticity is obviously negligible and there is nothing to be gained by modelling this mode in the present context. For this reason, the pragmatic

Table D.1: Budget Share Regressions

	a	b	c	R^2
Fruit	-0.00829	0.002749	2.087083	0.26022
Vegetables	0.054475	-0.00579	-1.37903	0.794889
Meat	0.225018	-0.02806	-13.3021	0.732829
Poultry	0.052294	-0.00617	-3.62406	0.302579
Fish	0.001745	0.000182	0.429412	0.195002
Farm products, fats, oils	0.126825	-0.0152	-4.4229	0.869153
Cereals, cereal products	0.135981	-0.01589	-5.7208	0.887933
Sweet products, beverages	0.139186	-0.01627	-7.28867	0.713447
Other foodstuffs	0.152218	-0.01774	-8.35408	0.381223
Meals away from home	-0.16374	0.03029	4.718327	0.971466
Rent	0.622274	-0.08312	-1.83007	0.928584
Payments to local authorities	-0.0882	0.013836	15.20095	0.950052
Property maintenance goods	0.081228	-0.0069	-8.63439	0.718421
Property maintenance	-0.68323	0.100973	43.35151	0.787053
Housing expenses n.e.c.	-0.03517	0.004634	3.377435	0.741892
Domestic fuel and power	0.196174	-0.02413	-0.94521	0.976625
Home appliances	-0.00112	0.003079	2.134009	0.024083
Household equipment	-0.00563	0.001527	0.727346	0.041477
Furniture	-0.10488	0.017014	6.453542	0.741345
Furnishings	-0.00076	0.000831	-0.64299	0.451658
Floor coverings	-0.06074	0.008517	4.952152	0.461902
Household textiles	-0.01107	0.002411	0.852601	0.124718
Household supplies	0.078421	-0.00923	-4.4682	0.502538
Household services	-0.08467	0.015257	16.66589	0.919618
Men's clothing	-0.0772	0.01134	5.588882	0.523455
Women's clothing	-0.17633	0.025524	13.84376	0.742386
Children's clothing	-0.00054	0.000862	0.267848	0.027241
Other clothing	0.029442	-0.00308	-3.3534	0.867552
Clothing supplies & services	-0.00295	0.000601	0.434927	0.015415
Men's footwear	-0.02062	0.003132	1.23944	0.597497
Women's footwear	-0.06346	0.008629	5.976196	0.878226
Children's footwear	0.002005	-8.35E-05	-0.35364	0.250285
Other footwear	0.010164	-1.05E-03	-1.32814	0.780407
Footwear supplies & services	0.003267	-3.81E-04	-0.3558	0.337931
Public transport within NZ	-0.06172	0.009624	5.100902	0.503206

Table D.2: Budget Share Regressions

	a	b	c	R^2
Overseas travel	-0.47099	0.07091	28.55522	0.787953
Road vehicles	0.291782	-0.02883	-31.0849	0.652508
Vehicle ownership expenses	0.625611	-0.0743	-42.9299	0.569541
Private transport costs n.e.c	-0.01354	0.002442	1.589636	0.058705
Tobacco products	0.166991	-0.0214	-8.79842	0.620878
Alcohol	-0.12924	0.021882	7.49086	0.629366
Medical goods	-0.02832	0.004974	3.036628	0.105698
Toiletries and cosmetics	0.00956	0.000191	-0.92042	0.395319
Personal goods	0.032463	-0.00257	-3.42718	0.58933
Pets, racehorses and livestock	0.120291	-0.01498	-7.75913	0.470165
Stationery and office equip.	0.070482	-0.00593	-5.10796	0.308231
Leisure goods	0.019047	0.000662	-4.02311	0.757771
Recreational vehicles	0.011469	-0.00076	-2.11383	0.635397
Goods n.e.c.	-0.0119	0.002321	0.9711	0.140835
Health services	-0.12371	0.020146	11.10986	0.545345
Personal services	-0.10878	0.015507	9.209476	0.352852
Educational and tuition	0.026106	-0.00101	1.068944	0.17518
Accommodation services	-0.07752	0.011855	4.266511	0.679455
Finance, ins. and legal	0.097855	-0.00857	-2.83561	0.185043
Vocational services	-0.00239	0.000818	-0.75566	0.896757
Leisure services	-0.03519	0.009307	0.15564	0.86498
Services n.e.c.	0.061889	-0.00639	-7.72831	0.46135
Outgoings n.e.c.	0.207629	-0.02421	-17.3681	0.078868

Table D.3: Grouped Distribution of Taxable Income: New Zealand

Range (000s)	No.	Average Income	Range (000s)	No.	Average Income
- 1	93,213	409.83	30 - 31	41,890	30,414.00
1 - 2	61,912	1,452.57	31 - 32	34,770	31,507.18
2 - 3	41,329	2,521.56	32 - 33	44,251	32,477.18
3 - 4	44,486	3,544.49	33 - 34	38,084	33,533.93
4 - 5	36,385	4,552.98	34 - 35	33,849	34,534.91
5 - 6	43,644	5,437.80	35 - 36	30,837	35,526.43
6 - 7	32,442	6,580.17	36 - 37	27,936	36,512.18
7 - 8	55,677	7,495.72	37 - 38	34,878	37,548.02
8 - 9	67,115	8,371.65	38 - 39	31,082	38,498.93
9 - 9.5	66,408	9,267.31	39 - 40	25,273	39,483.37
9.5 - 10	42,052	9,707.22	40 - 41	27,987	40,563.92
10 - 11	143,426	10,669.95	41 - 42	30,355	41,480.31
11 - 12	89,621	11,513.70	42 - 43	17,037	42,551.03
12 - 13	74,977	12,571.58	43 - 44	19,855	43,478.16
13 - 14	80,137	13,429.31	44 - 45	20,373	44,647.87
14 - 15	163,260	14,396.08	45 - 46	15,506	45,453.50
15 - 16	53,649	15,422.00	46 - 47	15,027	46,560.53
16 - 17	52,664	16,568.82	47 - 48	15,720	47,510.66
17 - 18	38,984	17,472.11	48 - 49	17,132	48,471.26
18 - 19	48,558	18,469.33	49 - 50	12,519	49,700.59
19 - 20	46,773	19,566.15	50 - 52	28,862	51,011.51
20 - 21	47,134	20,556.02	52 - 54	26,642	52,891.96
21 - 22	37,598	21,524.06	54 - 56	19,947	54,980.98
22 - 23	37,181	22,572.31	56 - 58	24,379	56,876.89
23 - 24	35,388	23,539.56	58 - 60	19,203	59,208.08
24 - 25	32,699	24,518.45	60 - 65	52,194	62,407.42
25 - 26	31,564	25,449.60	65 - 70	24,748	67,319.34
26 - 27	30,796	26,333.18	70 - 80	43,913	74,481.48
27 - 28	37,842	27,465.45	80 - 90	22,783	85,128.34
28 - 29	35,810	28,586.43	90 100	19,963	94,708.39
29 - 30	35,872	29,622.28	Over 100	47,218	182,074.25

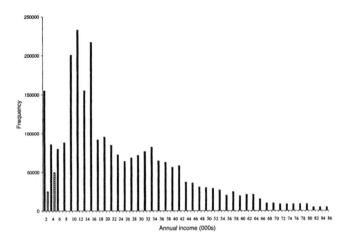

Figure D.1: Income Distribution

solution was adopted of adjusting the frequencies in the bottom two groups of the distribution, as shown by smaller marked blocks for those income classes. Such bimodal distributions can in fact be modelled using a mixture distribution comprising a weighted average of lognormal and exponential distributions; see Bakker and Creedy (1999).

The resulting distribution can then be modelled using a unimodal lognormal distribution, as discussed above, whose two parameters can be obtained directly as sample values of the mean and variance of logarithms. Further support for the lognormal is provided by the fact that the implied arithmetic mean value (using the properties of the lognormal mentioned earlier) was found to be close to the arithmetic mean calculated directly from the distribution.

Appendix E

Progressivity and the LES

This appendix provides some further details regarding the derivation of the conditions for welfare-progressivity. Committed expenditure for good i can be written in the form:

$$c_i = p_i \gamma_i = \frac{m w_i (1 + \eta_{ii})}{1 - \beta_i} \tag{E.1}$$

where η_{ii} is the own-price elasticity of demand for good i. The own-price elasticities are:

$$\eta_{ii} = e_i \left(\frac{1}{\xi} - w_i \left(1 + \frac{e_i}{\xi} \right) \right) \tag{E.2}$$

where ξ denotes the Frisch parameter. Using equation (E.2), committed expenditure on good i becomes:

$$c_i = m w_i \left(1 + \frac{e_i}{\xi} \right) \tag{E.3}$$

Total committed expenditure takes the form:

$$C = \sum_{i=1}^{n} p_i \gamma_i = m \sum_{i=1}^{n} \left(w_i + \frac{1}{\xi} w_i e_i \right) \tag{E.4}$$

As ξ is not commodity dependent, the 'adding-up' conditions, $\sum_{i=1}^{n} w_i = \sum_{i=1}^{n} e_i w_i = 1$, hold to give:

$$C = m \left(1 + \frac{1}{\xi} \right) \tag{E.5}$$

Differentiating equation (E.4) with respect to total expenditure, while holding the parameters of the direct utility function, β_k and γ_k, constant, gives:

$$\frac{d}{dm}\left(\frac{EV}{m}\right) = \frac{1}{m^2}\left(C^0 - (1+\dot{p}_k)^{-\beta_k}\left(C^0 + c_k\dot{p}_k\right)\right) \qquad \text{(E.6)}$$

The tax imposed on good k is welfare-progressive when this change is strictly positive, which occurs when:

$$(1+\dot{p}_k)^{\beta_k} > 1 + \frac{c_k}{C^0}\dot{p}_k \qquad \text{(E.7)}$$

Using the above results, and assuming the Frisch parameter, ξ, to be constant, gives the condition for welfare-progressivity as:

$$(1+\dot{p}_k)^{w_k e_k} > 1 + \frac{w_k(\xi + e_k)}{(\xi + 1)}\dot{p}_k \qquad \text{(E.8)}$$

Taking logs of both sides, applying the approximation $\log(1+x) = x$, and simplifying further gives the condition that welfare-progressivity requires $e_k > 1$, the same condition required for local tax-progressivity.

For the variable parameter case, the ratio of the equivalent variation to total expenditure becomes:

$$\frac{EV}{m} = \frac{1}{\xi}\left[(1+\dot{p}_k)^{-\Phi}(1+\dot{p}_k\Psi) - 1\right] \qquad \text{(E.9)}$$

where:

$$\Phi = \delta_{1k} + \delta_{2k}(\log m + 1) \qquad \text{(E.10)}$$

and:

$$\Psi = \xi\left(\delta_{1k} + \delta_{2k}\log m + \frac{\delta_{3k}}{m}\right) + (\delta_{1k} + \delta_{2k}(\log m + 1)) \qquad \text{(E.11)}$$

Differentiating with respect to m, and applying the approximation $\log(1+x) = x$, gives:

$$\frac{d}{dm}\left(\frac{EV}{m}\right) = \frac{\dot{p}_k}{m}(1+\dot{p}_k)^{-\beta_k}\left[\left(\delta_{2k} - \frac{\delta_{3k}}{m}\right) - \delta_{2k}w_k\dot{p}_k\left(1 + \frac{e_k}{\xi}\right)\right] \qquad \text{(E.12)}$$

Welfare-progressivity is implied when the term in square brackets is strictly positive. Using $\delta_{2k} - (\delta_{3k}/m) = m(dw_k/dm)$ and then dividing by w_k leads the first term in square brackets to become $(e_k - 1)$. Thus, welfare-progressivity occurs when:

$$e_k > 1 + \delta_{2k}\dot{p}_k \left(1 + \frac{e_k}{\xi} \right) \tag{E.13}$$

From which the inequality in chapter 8 is obtained.

Appendix F

The Almost Ideal Demand System

This appendix examines local tax- and welfare-progressivity using, instead of the Linear Expenditure System of chapter 8, the Almost Ideal Demand System (AIDS), devised by Deaton and Muellbauer (1980). This is based on the expenditure function:

$$\log E\,(p, U) = a\,(p) + b\,(p)\,U \tag{F.1}$$

where the two price indices $a\,(p)$ and $b\,(p)$ are defined as:[1]

$$a\,(p) = \alpha_0 + \sum_{i=1}^{n} \alpha_i \log p_i + \frac{1}{2} \sum_{i=1}^{n} \sum_{\ell=1}^{n} \gamma_{i\ell}^* \log p_i \log p_\ell \tag{F.2}$$

$$b\,(p) = \beta_0 \prod_{i=1}^{n} p_i^{\beta_i} \tag{F.3}$$

Letting m denote total expenditure, so that $m = \sum_{i=1}^{n} p_i x_i = E\,(p, U)$, the direct utility function takes the form:

$$U = \frac{\log m - a}{b} \tag{F.4}$$

It can be shown that when prices change from p^0 to p^1, the equivalent variation is:

$$EV = m - \exp\left(a\,(p^0) + b\,(p^0)\,U^1\right) \tag{F.5}$$

---

[1] The parameter β must be distinguished from its use in defining the LES above.

Defining the price index $P = \exp a\,(p)$, this becomes:

$$EV = m - P^0 \exp\left(\frac{b\,(p^0)}{b\,(p^1)}\log\left(\frac{m}{P^1}\right)\right) \qquad (F.6)$$

Consider imposing a tax on only good k, as before. The term $\frac{b(p^0)}{b(p^1)}$ simplifies to:

$$\frac{b\,(p^0)}{b\,(p^1)} = (1 + \dot{p}_k)^{\beta_k} \qquad (F.7)$$

and the equivalent variation as a fraction of total expenditure is:

$$\frac{EV}{m} = 1 - \exp\left\{(1 + \dot{p}_k)^{\beta_k}\log\left(\frac{m}{P^1}\right) - \log\left(\frac{m}{P^0}\right)\right\} \qquad (F.8)$$

Applying the approximation $-x = 1 - \exp x$ gives:

$$\frac{EV}{m} = \log\left(\frac{m}{P^0}\right) - (1 + \dot{p}_k)^{\beta_k}\log\left(\frac{m}{P^1}\right) \qquad (F.9)$$

From Shephard's lemma, the budget share for good i takes the form:

$$w_i = \frac{\partial \log E\,(p, U)}{\partial \log p} \qquad (F.10)$$

Hence, using the expenditure function the budget share in the AIDS is defined by:

$$w_i = p_i\frac{\partial a\,(p)}{\partial p_i} + Up_i\frac{\partial b\,(p)}{\partial p_i} \qquad (F.11)$$

It follows that:

$$w_i = \alpha_i + \sum_k \gamma_{ik}\log p_k + \beta_i \log\left(\frac{m}{P}\right) \qquad (F.12)$$

The total expenditure elasticity, e_i, for good i is thus:

$$e_i = \frac{dw_i}{dm}\frac{m}{w_i} \qquad (F.13)$$

$$= \frac{\beta_i + w_i}{w_i} \qquad (F.14)$$

which enables the parameter β_i to be expressed as:

$$\beta_i = w_i\,(e_i - 1) \qquad (F.15)$$

Differentiating equation (F.9) with respect to total expenditure, holding the parameter of the direct utility function, β_k, constant, gives:

$$\frac{d}{dm}\left(\frac{EV}{m}\right) = \frac{1}{m}\left(1 - (1 + \dot{p}_k)^{-\beta_k}\right) \qquad \text{(F.16)}$$

Hence welfare-progressivity is implied when $1 > (1 + \dot{p}_k)^{-\beta_k}$. Taking logs of both sides and applying the approximation, $\log(1 + x) = x$, gives the condition:

$$\beta_k \dot{p}_k > 0 \qquad \text{(F.17)}$$

Using $\beta_k = w_k (e_k - 1)$ and substituting in equation (F.17) gives the condition that $e_k > 1$ is required for a tax placed on the good to be locally welfare-progressive.

When parameters are allowed to vary, it has been shown above that $\beta_i = w_i (e_i - 1)$. This gives:

$$\beta_i = w_i \dot{w}_i = m\,(dw_i/dm) \qquad \text{(F.18)}$$

so that $(dw_i/dm) = \beta_i/m$. Integration therefore leads to:

$$w_i = h_i + \beta_i \log m \qquad \text{(F.19)}$$

where h_i is a constant of integration.[2]

As discussed above, empirical studies of budget data have found a more general form to be useful, which combines both the elements of the LES and AIDS models, whereby for good i:

$$w_i = \delta_{1i} + \delta_{2i} \log m + \frac{\delta_{3i}}{m} \qquad \text{(F.20)}$$

In practice, the parameters, δ_{1i}, δ_{2i} and δ_{3i} can be estimated by regressing budget shares for good i, obtained from sample surveys, on households' total

---

[2]This form was explicitly discussed by Deaton and Muellbauer (1980), who also referred briefly to the more general form discussed here.

expenditure levels. Using this specification, the total expenditure elasticity for the good, $e_i = 1 + \dot{w}_i$, is expressed as:

$$e_i = \frac{(\delta_{1i} + \delta_{2i}(1 + \log m))}{(\delta_{1i} + \delta_{2i}\log m + \frac{\delta_{3i}}{m})} \tag{F.21}$$

The implied variation in β_i is therefore:

$$\beta_i = w_i(e_i - 1) \tag{F.22}$$

$$= \delta_{2i} - \frac{\delta_{3i}}{m} \tag{F.23}$$

This more general budget share relationship leads the parameters of the AIDS model to be functions of total expenditure, m, which in turn allows for heterogeneous preferences among households. The consequence of this allowance for welfare-progressivity is explored as follows.

Substituting for β_k into the expression for EV/m, gives:

$$\frac{EV}{m} = \log\left(\frac{m}{P^0}\right) - (1 + \dot{p}_k)^{-\left[\delta_{2k} - \frac{\delta_{3k}}{m}\right]}\log\left(\frac{m}{P^1}\right) \tag{F.24}$$

Differentiating with respect to total expenditure, m, gives:

$$\frac{d}{dm}\left(\frac{EV}{m}\right) = \frac{1}{m}\left(1 + (1 + \dot{p}_k)^{-\beta_k}\log(1 + \dot{p}_k)\frac{\delta_{3k}}{m}\log\left(\frac{m}{P^1}\right) - (1 + \dot{p}_k)^{-\beta_k}\right) \tag{F.25}$$

Constraining the derivative to be strictly positive, welfare-progressivity is implied when:

$$1 > (1 + \dot{p}_k)^{-\beta_k}\left(1 - \log(1 + \dot{p}_k)\frac{\delta_{3k}}{m}\log\left(\frac{m}{P^1}\right)\right) \tag{F.26}$$

Taking logarithms of this expression:

$$0 > -\beta_k\log(1 + \dot{p}_k) + \log\left(1 - \log(1 + \dot{p}_k)\frac{\delta_{3k}}{m}\log\left(\frac{m}{P^1}\right)\right) \tag{F.27}$$

Applying the approximation $\log(1 + x) = x$ gives:

$$0 > -\beta_k\dot{p}_k - \dot{p}_k\frac{\delta_{3k}}{m}\log\left(\frac{m}{P^1}\right) \tag{F.28}$$

Substituting for β_k, welfare-progressivity is found to occur when:

$$e_k > 1 - \frac{\delta_{3k}}{mw_k} \log\left(\frac{m}{P^1}\right) \qquad \text{(F.29)}$$

Hence, as with the LES, identifying good k as a luxury may no longer be sufficient to establish the welfare-progressivity of the tax. The conditions are given below for necessities and luxuries in turn. These conditions are based on the assumption that $m > P^1$.

For necessities, $\delta_{3k} > 0$ is a necessary condition for welfare-progressivity. The sufficient condition is:

$$\delta_{3k} > \frac{mw_k \left(1 - e_k\right)}{\log\left(\frac{m}{P^1}\right)} > 0 \qquad \text{(F.30)}$$

The condition $\delta_{3k} < 0$ is sufficient for welfare-regressivity.

For luxuries, $\delta_{3k} > 0$ is a sufficient condition for welfare-progressivity. The condition $\delta_{3k} < 0$ is necessary for welfare-regressivity, and the sufficient condition is:

$$\delta_{3k} < \frac{mw_k \left(1 - e_k\right)}{\log\left(\frac{m}{P^1}\right)} < 0 \qquad \text{(F.31)}$$

These conditions depend crucially on the parameter, δ_{3k}, as this is the additional term introduced by the more general budget share relationship. The conditions for tax and welfare disproportionality for the extended AIDS are summarised in Figure F.1.

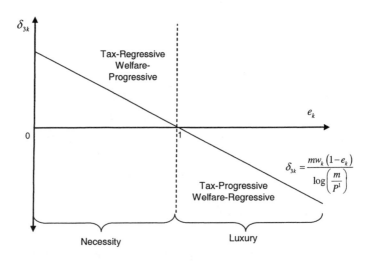

Figure F.1: Conditions for the AIDS Model

Appendix G

Carbon Tax Tables

This appendix provides details relating to the computation of the effects of carbon taxes and minimum disruption changes, examined in Part III. Tables G.1 and G.2 show the translation between the Energy Account Industry Classification (EAIC) and the 49 Industry Group Classification (IGC). Table G.3 gives the fuel demands, the F matrix, by industry, again for the year ended March 1996.

Table G.1: Translation Between the Energy Account Industry Classification
(EAIC) And The 49 Industry Group Classification (IGC)

EAIC Code	EAIC Description	IGC Code	IGC Description
A01	Agriculture	1	Horticulture and Fruit Growing
		2	Livestock and Cropping Farming
		3	Dairy Cattle Farming
		4	Other Farming
		5	Services to Agriculture, Hunting and Trapping
A02	Fishing and Hunting	5	Services to Agriculture, Hunting and Trapping
		7	Fishing
A03	Forestry and Logging	6	Forestry and Logging
A04	Extraction, Mining, Quarrying and Exploration - including gas distribution and supply	8	Mining and Quarrying
		9	Oil and Gas Exploration and Extraction
		27	Gas Supply
B01	Petroleum Product Refining, Distribution and Supply	18	Petroleum and Industrial Chemical Manufacturing
B02	Electricity Generation, Distribution and Supply	26	Electricity Generation and Supply
C01	Slaughtering and Meat Processing	10	Meat and Meat Product Manufacturing
C02	Dairy Products	11	Dairy Product Manufacturing
C03	Beverages, Tobacco, confectionery and sugar, and other food	12	Other Food Manufacturing
		13	Beverage, Malt and Tobacco Manufacturing
C04	Textile, Apparel and Leather goods	14	Textile and Apparel Manufacturing
C05	Wood Processing and Wood Products	15	Wood Product Manufacturing
C06	Paper and Paper Products, Printing and Publishing	16	Paper and Paper Product Manufacturing
		17	Printing, Publishing and Recorded Media
C07	Chemicals, Related Products and Plastics	19	Rubber, Plastic and Other Chemical Product Manufacturing
C08	Concrete, Clay, Glass and Related Minerals Manufacture	20	Non-Metallic Mineral Product Manufacturing
C09	Basic Metal Industries	21	Basic Metal Manufacturing
C10	Fabricated Metal Products, Machinery and Equipment	22	Structural, Sheet and Fabricated Metal Product Manufacturing
		23	Transport Equipment Manufacturing
		24	Machinery and Equipment Manufacturing

Table G.2: Translation Between the Energy Account Industry Classification (EAIC) And The 49 Industry Group Classification (IGC)

EAIC Code	EAIC Description	IGC Code	IGC Description
C11	Other Manufacturing Industries	25	Furniture and Other Manufacturing
C12	Construction	29	Construction
D01	Water Works and Supply	28	Water Supply
D02	Wholesale and Retail Trade - Non Food	30	Wholesale Trade
		31	Retail Trade
D03	Wholesale Trade - Food	30	Wholesale Trade
D04	Retail Trade - Food	31	Retail Trade
D05	Motels, Hotels, Guest Houses	32	Accommodation, Restaurants and Bars
D06	Communication	36	Communication Services
D07	Finance, Insurance, Real Estate and Business Services	37	Finance
		38	Insurance
		39	Services to Finance and Insurance
		40	Real Estate
		41	Ownership of Owner-Occupied Dwellings
		42	Equipment Hire and Investors in Other Property
		43	Business Services
D08	Central Government Administration	44	Central Government Administration, Defence, Public Order and Safety Services
D09	Central Government Defence Services	44	Central Government Administration, Defence, Public Order and Safety Services
D10	Local Government Administration	45	Local Government Administration Services and Civil Defence
D11	Education Services: Pre-School, Primary and Secondary	46	Education
D12	Education Services: Tertiary Education	46	Education
D13	Health and Welfare Services	47	Health and Community Services
D14	Other Social and Related Community Services	48	Cultural and Recreational Services
		49	Personal and Other Community Services
D15	Sanitary and Cleaning Services	45	Local Government Administration Services and Civil Defence
E01	Domestic Transport and Storage	33	Road Transport
		34	Water and Rail Transport
		35	Air Transport, Services to Transport and Storage

Table G.3: Fuel Demands by Industry Group Classification (IGC): Year Ended March 1996

Coal	Lignite	Crude Petroleum	Natural Gas	LPG	Petrol	Diesel	Fuel Oil	Aviation Fuels & Kerosene
0	0	0	0.017	0	5.029	9.032	0.014	0.070
0	0	0	0.004	0	1.197	2.149	0.003	0.017
0	0	0	0.004	0	1.200	2.156	0.003	0.017
0	0	0	0.003	0	0.909	1.632	0.003	0.013
0	0	0	0.466	0	0.631	4.029	0.374	0.009
0	0	0	0	0	0.635	1.564	0	0
0	0	0	0.723	0	0.008	4.525	0.580	0
0.454	0	0	0.012	0	0.171	1.333	0.179	0
0.284	0	0	0.007	0	0.107	0.832	0.112	0
2.273	0.318	0	1.184	0.412	0.403	0.099	0.138	0
5.784	0.808	0	4.455	0.045	0.001	1.524	0.457	0
0.537	0.075	0	2.602	0.504	1.434	0.925	0.715	0
0.187	0.026	0	0.905	0.175	0.498	0.321	0.248	0
0.557	0.078	0	0.962	0.047	0.140	0.504	0.383	0
0.310	0.043	0	0.936	0.043	0.008	0.149	0.677	0
0.572	0.080	0	2.649	0.150	0.006	0.083	1.310	0
0.251	0.035	0	1.160	0.066	0.002	0.036	0.573	0
0	0	152.267	0	0	0	0	0	0
0.279	0.039	0	86.372	0.193	0.116	2.467	0.566	0
4.272	0.597	0	1.134	0.645	0	0.346	0.094	0
13.862	0	0	7.955	0.392	0.007	0.160	2.191	0
0.017	0.002	0	0.136	0.078	0.048	0.454	0.044	0
0.036	0.005	0	0.292	0.168	0.103	0.972	0.094	0
0.061	0.009	0	0.503	0.289	0.177	1.674	0.163	0
0.092	0.013	0	0.167	0.012	0.104	0.016	0.002	0
5.290	0	0	51.118	0	0.068	0.134	0	0
0.233	0	0	0.006	0	0.088	0.683	0.092	0
0	0	0	0	0	0.023	0.051	0	0
0	0	0	0.111	0.594	1.946	7.201	0	0.192
0.789	0.043	0	0.374	0.331	9.764	0.779	0.028	0
0.923	0.050	0	1.043	0.366	11.228	0.810	0.030	0
0.033	0.002	0	0.934	0.355	0.704	0.159	0.541	0
0.009	0	0	0.194	0	1.083	2.199	0.318	3.579
0.013	0	0	0.295	0	1.647	3.345	0.484	5.443
0.056	0	0	1.274	0	7.126	14.473	2.092	23.551
0	0	0	0.038	0.018	0.827	0.562	0	0
0.008	0	0	0.056	0	0.150	0	0.045	0
0.008	0	0	0.058	0	0.153	0	0.046	0
0	0	0	0.002	0	0.006	0	0.002	0
0.020	0.001	0	0.146	0	0.388	0	0.117	0
0.056	0.003	0	0.415	0	1.104	0	0.333	0
0.002	0	0	0.012	0	0.032	0	0.010	0
0.010	0.001	0	0.074	0	0.198	0	0.060	0
0.530	0.029	0	0.299	0	0.643	1.902	2.194	1.918
0.034	0.002	0	0.332	0	0.921	0.425	0.014	0
1.240	0.067	0	0.518	0	0	0	0.144	0
3.156	0.170	0	0.976	0	0.835	0	0	0
0.051	0.003	0	0.036	0	0.636	0	0.056	0
0.029	0.002	0	0.020	0	0.359	0	0.032	0

Bibliography

[1] Amiel, Y., Creedy, J. and Hurn, S. (1999) Measuring attitudes towards inequality. *Scandinavian Journal of Economics*, 101, pp. 83-96.

[2] Atkinson, A. B. (1979) Horizontal equity and the distribution of the tax burden. In *The Economics of Taxation* (ed. by H.J. Aaron and M.J. Boskins). Washington, DC: The Brookings Institution.

[3] Attanasio, O. P. and Japelli, T. (1997) The life cycle hypothesis and consumption inequality. *Institute For Fiscal Studies Working Paper*, no. W97/17.

[4] Bahl, R., Bird, R. and Walker, M. B. (2003) The uneasy case against discriminatory excise taxation: the soft drink taxes in Ireland. *Public Finance Review*, 31, pp. 510-532.

[5] Baines, J. T. (1993) *New Zealand Energy Information Handbook*. Christchurch: Taylor Baines and Associates.

[6] Baker, P. and Brechling, V. (1992) The inpact of excise duty charges on retail prices in the UK. *Fiscal Studies*, 13, pp. 48-65.

[7] Bakker, A. and Creedy, J. (1999) Macroeconomic variables and income inequality in New Zealand: an exploration using conditional mixture distributions. *New Zealand Economic Papers*, 33, pp. 59-79.

[8] Banks, J. and Johnson, P. (1994) Equivalence scale relativities revisited. *Economic Journal*, 104, pp. 883-890.

243

[9] Barker, F. (2002) Consumption externalities and the role of government: the case of alcohol. *New Zealand Treasury Working Paper*, no. 02/25.

[10] Barthold, T. A. (1994) Issues in the design of environmental excise taxes. *Journal of Economic Perspectives*, 8, pp. 133-151.

[11] Barzel, Y. (1976) An alternative approach to the analysis of taxation. *Journal of Political Economy*, 84, pp. 1177-1199.

[12] Bell, M. (2003) Fiscal drag and the long term fiscal model. *New Zealand Treasury Internal Paper*.

[13] Blundell, R. and Preston, I. (1994) Income or consumption in the measurement of inequality and poverty. *Institute For Fiscal Studies Working Paper*, no. W94/12.

[14] Blundell, R. and Preston, I. (1997) Consumption inequality and economic uncertainty. *Institute For Fiscal Studies Working Paper*, no. W97/15.

[15] Brannlund, R. and Nordstrom, J. (2004) Carbon tax simulations using a household demand model. *European Economic Review*, 48, pp. 211-233.

[16] Brashares, E. and Aynsley, M. (1990) Income adequacy standards for New Zealand. *New Zealand Treasury Internal Paper*.

[17] Buhmann, B., Rainwater, L., Schmaus, G. and Smeeding, T. M. (1988) Equivalence scales, well-being, inequality, and poverty: sensitivity estimates across ten countries using the Luxembourg income study (LIS) database. *Review of Income and Wealth*, 34, pp. 115-142.

[18] Carraro, C., Galeotti, M. and Gallo, M. (1996) Environmental taxation and unemployment: some evidence on the double dividend hypothesis in Europe. *Journal of Public Economics*, 62, pp. 141-181.

[19] Cnossen, S. (2005) *Theory and Practice of Excise Taxation: Smoking, Gambling, Polluting and Drinking.* Oxford: Oxford University Press.

[20] Colman, G. and Remler, D. K. (2004) Vertical equity consequences of very high cigarette tax increases: if the poor are the ones smoking, how could cigarette tax increases be progressive? *National Bureau of Economic Research Working Paper*, no. 10906.

[21] Coulter, A. E., Cowell, F. A. and Jenkins, S. P. (1992) Equivalence scale relativities and the extent of inequality and poverty. *Economic Journal*, 102, pp. 1067-1082.

[22] Cowell, F. A. (1984) The structure of American income inequality. *Review of Income and Wealth*, 30, pp. 351-375.

[23] Cowell, F. A. and Mercader-Prats, M. (1999) Equivalence scales and inequality. In *Handbook on Income Inequality Measurement* (ed. by J. Silber), pp. 405-435. Boston: Kluwer.

[24] Creedy, J. (1985) *Dynamics of Income Distribution.* Oxford: Basil Blackwell.

[25] Creedy, J. (1997) *Statics and Dynamics of Income Distribution in New Zealand.* Wellington: Institute of Policy Studies.

[26] Creedy, J. (1998a) Measuring the welfare effects of price changes: a convenient parametric approach. *Australian Economic Papers*, 37, pp. 137-151.

[27] Creedy, J. (1998b) *Measuring Welfare Changes and Tax Burdens.* Cheltenham: Edward Elgar.

[28] Creedy, J. (1998c) Are consumption taxes regressive? *Australian Economic Review*, 31, pp. 107-116.

[29] Creedy, J. (2004a) The effects of an increase in petrol excise tax: the case of New Zealand households. *National Institute Economic Review*, 188, pp. 70-79.

[30] Creedy, J. (2004b) The excess burden of taxation. *Australian Economic Review*, 37, pp. 454-464.

[31] Creedy, J. and Cornwell, A. (1996) Carbon taxation, prices and inequality in Australia. *Fiscal Studies*, 17, pp. 21-38.

[32] Creedy, J. and Cornwell, A. (1997) Measuring the welfare effects of price changes using the LES, with an application to a carbon tax. *Empirical Economics*, 22, pp. 589-613.

[33] Creedy, J. and Gemmell, N. (2002) The built-in flexibility of income and consumption taxes: a survey. *Journal of Economic Surveys*, 44, pp. 509-532.

[34] Creedy, J. and Gemmell, N. (2003) The revenue responsiveness of income and consumption taxes in the UK. *The Manchester School*, 71, pp. 641-658.

[35] Creedy, J. and Gemmell, N. (2004) The built-in flexibility of income and consumption taxes in New Zealand. *Australian Economic Papers*, 43, pp. 459-474.

[36] Creedy, J. and Martin, C. (2000) Carbon taxation, fuel substitution and welfare in Australia. *Australian Economic Review*, 33, pp. 32-48.

[37] Creedy, J. and Scutella, R. (2004) The role of the unit of analysis in tax policy reform evaluations of inequality and social welfare. *Australian Journal of Labour Economics*, 7, pp. 89-108.

[38] Creedy, J. and Sleeman, C. (2005a) Carbon dioxide emissions reductions in New Zealand: a minimum disruption approach. *Australian Economic Papers*, 44, pp. 199-220.

[39] Creedy, J. and Sleeman, C. (2005b) Carbon taxation, prices and welfare in New Zealand. *Ecological Economics*, 57, pp. 333-345.

[40] Creedy, J. and Sleeman, C. (2005c) Excise Taxation in New Zealand. *New Zealand Economic Papers*, 39, pp. 1-35.

[41] Creedy, J. and Sleeman, C. (2005d) Adult equivalence scales: inequality and poverty. *New Zealand Economic Papers*, 39, pp. 51-83.

[42] Creedy, J. and Sleeman, C. (2006) Indirect taxation and progressivity: revenue and welfare changes. *FinanzArchiv*, 62, pp. 50-67.

[43] Cullen, M. and Hodgson, M. (2005) *Implementing the Carbon Tax: A Government Consultative Paper*. Wellington: Inland Revenue Department.

[44] Cutler, D. M. and Katz, L. (1992) Rising inequality? Changes in the distribution of income and consumption in the 1980s. *American Economic Review*, 82, pp. 546-551.

[45] Davies (2003) Efficiency implications of a petrol tax in the Auckland region: report to Auckland regional transport funding steering group. *New Zealand Institute of Economic Research Report*.

[46] Deaton, A. S. and Muellbauer, J. (1980) *Economics and Consumer Behaviour*. Cambridge: Cambridge University Press.

[47] Decoster, A. and Ooghe, E. (2002) Weighting with individuals, equivalent individuals or not weighting at all: does it matter empirically? *Catholic University of Leuven Centre for Economic Studies Discussion Paper*, no. DPS 02.15.

[48] Dixon, P., Parmenter, B. R., Sutton, J. and Vincent, D. P. (1982) *ORANI: A Multisectoral Model of the Australian Economy*. Amsterdam: North Holland Publishing Company.

[49] Dower, R. and Zimmerman, M. B. (1992) *The Climate for Carbon Taxes: Creating Economic Incentives to Protect the Environment*. Washington DC: World Resources Institute,

[50] Ebert, U. (1997) Social welfare when needs differ: an axiomatic approach. *Economica*, 64, pp. 233-244.

[51] Fortin, B. and Truchon, M. (1993) On reforming the welfare system: workfare meets the negative income tax. *Journal of Public Economics*, 51, pp. 119-151.

[52] Foster, J., Greer, J. and Thorbecke, E. (1984) A class of decomposable poverty measures. *Econometrica*, 52, pp. 761-762.

[53] Frisch, R. (1959) A complete scheme for computing all direct and cross demand elasticities in a model with many sectors. *Econometrica*, 27, pp. 177-196.

[54] Giorno, C., Richardson, P., Roseveare, D. and Van den Noord, P. (1995) Estimating potential output, output gaps and structural budget balances. *OECD Economics Department Working Papers*, no. 152.

[55] Glewwe, P. (1991) Household equivalence scales and the measurement of inequality: transfers from the poor to the rich could decrease inequality. *Journal of Public Economics*, 44, pp. 214-216.

[56] Holcombe, R. (2003) Excise taxation and interest group politics. In *Politics, Taxation and the Rule of Law* (ed. by D. P. Racheler and R. E. Wagner). Boston: Kluwer Academic Publishing.

[57] Jenkins, S. P. and Cowell, F. A. (1994) Parametric equivalence scales and scale relativities. *Economic Journal*, 104, pp. 891-900.

[58] Johnson, T. R. (1978) Additional evidence on the effects of alternative taxes on cigarette prices. *Journal of Political Economy*, 86, pp. 325-328.

[59] King, M. A. (1983) Welfare analysis of tax reforms using household data. *Journal of Public Economics*, 21, pp. 183-214.

[60] Labandeira, X. and Labeaga, J. M. (1999) Combining input-output analysis and micro-simulation to assess the effects of carbon taxation on Spanish households. *Fiscal Studies*, 20, pp. 305-320.

[61] McGee, R. W. (1998) The political economy of excise taxation: social ethical and legal issues. *Journal of Accounting, Ethics and Public Policy*, 1, pp. 558-571.

[62] McKitrick, R. (1997) Double dividend environmental taxation and Canadian carbon emissions control. *Canadian Public Policy*, 23, pp. 417-434.

[63] McLeod, R., Chatterjee, S., Jones, S., Patterson, D. and Sieper, T. (2001) *Final Report: 2001 Tax Review*. Wellington: New Zealand Treasury.

[64] Michelini, C. (1999) New Zealand household consumption equivalence scales from quasi-unit record data. *Massey University Department of Applied and International Economics Discussion Paper*, no. 99.02.

[65] Ministry for Environment (2005) *Review of Climate Change Policies*. Wellington.

[66] Ministry of Economic Development (2003) *New Zealand Energy Greenhouse Gas Emissions 1990-2002*. Wellington: Ministry of Economic Development.

[67] Muellbauer, J. (1974) Prices and inequality: the United Kingdom experience. *Economic Journal*, 84, pp. 32-55.

[68] Musgrave, R. A. and Thin, T. (1948) Income tax progression. *Journal of Political Economy*, 56, pp. 498-514.

[69] Nichele, V. and Robin, J.-M. (1995) Simulation of indirect tax reforms using pooled micro and macro French data. *Journal of Public Economics*, 56, pp. 225-244.

[70] Plotnick, R. (1981) A measure of horizontal inequity. *Review of Economics and Statistics*, 63, pp. 283-288.

[71] Powell, A. A. (1974) *Empirical Analytics of Demand Systems*. Lexington, Massachusetts: Lexington Books.

[72] Proops, J. L. R., Faber, M. and Wagenhals, G. (1993) *Reducing CO2 Emissions: A Comparative Input-Output Study for Germany and the UK*. Heidelberg: Springer-Verlag.

[73] Roberts, K. (1980) Price-independent welfare prescriptions. *Journal of Public Economics*, 18, pp. 277-297.

[74] Shorrocks, A. F. (2004) Inequality and welfare evaluation of heterogeneous income distributions. *Journal of Economic Inequality*, 2, pp. 193-218.

[75] Shughart, W. F. (ed.) (1997) *Taxing Choice: The Predatory Politics of Fiscal Discrimination*. The Independent Institute.

[76] Smith, S. (1998) environmental and public finance aspects of the taxation of energy. *Oxford Review of Economic Policy*, 14, pp. 64-83.

[77] Statistics New Zealand (2004) *New Zealand Energy Flow Account*. Wellington: Statistics New Zealand.

[78] Sumner, M. T. and Ward, R. (1981) Tax changes and cigarette prices. *Journal of Political Economy*, 89, pp. 1261-1265.

[79] Symons, S., Proops, J. and Gay, P. (1994) Carbon taxes, consumer demand and carbon dioxide emissions: a simulation analysis for the UK. *Fiscal Studies*, 15, pp. 19-43.

[80] Tulpule, A. and Powell, A. A. (1978) Estimates of household demand elasticities for the Orani model. *IMPACT Project Preliminary Working Paper*, OP-22.

[81] van de Ven, J. and Creedy, J. (2005) Taxation, Reranking and Equivalence Scales. *Bulletin of Economic Research*, 57, pp. 13-36

[82] van de Ven, J. (2003) Demand based equivalence scale estimates for Australia and the UK (Unpublished paper).

[83] van den Noord, P. (2000) The size and role of automatic fiscal stabilizers in the 1990s and beyond. *OECD Economics Department Working Paper*, no. 230.

[84] Whiteford, P. (1985) A family's needs: equivalence scales, poverty and social security. *Department of Social Security Research Paper*, no. 27. Canberra: Australia.

[85] Williams, R. A. (1978) The use of disaggregated cross-section data in explaining shifts in Australian consumer demand patterns over time. *Impact Project Research Paper*, no. SP-13.

[86] Young, L. (2002) Ad valorem indirect tax rates in New Zealand. *New Zealand Treasury Internal Paper*, no. 435217.

Index

Organization for Economic
  Cooperation and Development
  countries 120, 157, 183, 194
output, intermediate 73–4, 77
Overseas Travel 11, 37, 80, 126
Ownership of Owner-Occupied
  Dwellings 104

parametric equivalence scale 155
parametric scales 156
Pareto indifference or anonymity
  158, 160
partial equilibrium 4, 54
path dependency problem 205
petrol 2, 5, 7, 8, 9, 11, 187, 188, 189,
  190
  carbon tax, effects of 78, 89
  excise taxation, equity and
    efficiency 17, 19, 28, 29, 30,
    37, 42, 47, 51
  progressivity 140
  revenue elasticity of taxes 126,
    128
  see also petrol taxes
petrol taxes 2, 53–65
  inequality measures 58–63
    excise increase of 15 cents 64
    non-smoking households 61, 62
    smoking households 59, 60
  price changes 54–6
  welfare changes 56–8
petroleum and industrial chemical
  manufacturing 77, 99–100, 104,
  107, 109
plastics industry 77
Plotnick, R. 174
pollution externality 53
poverty 159, 160, 193, 195
  headcount measure 168
  income unit and income concept
    155, 156, 157, 183, 184
  line 168, 171, 173, 182
  P1 181
  profile 181
  see also poverty measures
poverty measures 167–73
  children 170
  income unit and income concept
    176

increasing alpha over high ranges
  172
increasing alpha over low ranges
  171
individual 169
P1 172
Powell, A.A. 20, 142, 148, 221
preference heterogeneity 139, 144,
  145, 154, 187, 193
  Almost Ideal Demand System 236
  simulation model 221
Preston, I. 161
price changes 5
  carbon tax 72–6
  petrol tax 54–6
price index of necessities 217
prices and taxes 78–80
principle of transfers 158, 159, 160,
  183, 194
progressivity 139–54, 192–3, 201
  Almost Ideal Demand System 235,
    236–7
  conditions for 146–7
  indirect tax system 149–53
    conflicting movements in tax
      and welfare measures 150
    disproportionality of tax system:
      adult couple, one child (non-
      smoking) 153
    disproportionality of tax system:
      single adult, no children
      (non-smoking) 153
    tax-disproportionality 152
    tax-regressivity and welfare-
      progressivity 151, 152
  and linear expenditure system
    229–31
  measurement 6
  single tax 148–9
  and tax revenue 141–2
  welfare changes with fixed
    parameters 142–3
  welfare changes with variable
    parameters 144–7
Proops, J.L.R. 70, 75, 91, 94, 96–9,
  105, 114
proportional consumption function
  125
proportional tax rate 199